KNOXVILLE !

By

Betsey Beeler Creekmore

EAST TENNESSEE HISTORICAL SOCIETY

First Edition
ISBN: 0-941199-08-8
Copyright © 1991 by Betsey B. Creekmore
All Rights Reserved
Published by the East Tennessee Historical Society
Knoxville, Tennessee

FAMOUS FIRSTS ASSOCIATED WITH KNOXVILLE

FIRST English fort in the Southwest (Fort Loudoun, 1756)

FIRST military draft in American history (John Sevier drafts men to stay home from the Battle of King's Mountain, 1780)

FIRST capital of a Federal Territory (Knoxville, 1791)

FIRST "planned city" in the west (Knoxville, 1791)

FIRST Territorial Legislature in America (Knoxville, 1794)

FIRST non-sectarian institution of higher learning (Blount College, now the University of Tennessee, chartered in 1794)

FIRST state created from a Federal Territory (Tennessee, 1796)

FIRST capital of the State of Tennessee (Knoxville, 1796-1811)

FIRST United States Senator to be tried for impeachment -- and the only one (William Blount, 1797)

FIRST college co-eds in America (Blount College, 1804)

FIRST man to perfect an entirely new alphabet or syllabary (Sequoyah's phonetic alphabet enables the Cherokee to have a written language, 1821)

FIRST, and only, city to withstand a Civil War siege (Knoxville, 1863)

FIRST Confederate state readmitted to the Union after the Civil War (Tennessee, 1866)

FIRST National Conservation Exposition (Knoxville, 1913)

FIRST national park given by the people to their government (Great Smoky Mountains National Park, 1926)

FIRST government-owned electrical system (Tennessee Valley Authority, 1933)

FIRST nuclear reactor placed in operation (Oak Ridge, 1943)

FIRST World's Fair in the southeastern United States (Knoxville, 1982)

FOREWORD

The people who founded, built and nurtured the City of Knoxville have carved for themselves an honorable and vital niche in American history.

Knoxville is a city of firsts: first capital of the state of Tennessee, first territorial legislature in America, first planned city in the west, and many more examples.

What intrigues me most is the number of people I have met who tell me they researched cities throughout the country and after doing so chose Knoxville as the city in which they wanted to live, work, and raise their families.

That speaks volumes about the people who have made Knoxville what it is today.

They were— and are— people who never have, and never will, set their sights on anything but the best.

Every month I go on a neighborhood walk in a different part of Knoxville. Having been born and raised in Knoxville, I enjoy it tremendously because when you talk to people in their neighborhoods and in their homes you find out what is really on their minds. Knoxvillians want their neighborhoods to be strong and their city to be looking to the future.

In 1991 we celebrate our 200th birthday, a marvelous opportunity to look at our past, assess our present, and advance confidently into the future. My personal thanks to Betsey Beeler Creekmore, who has made a great contribution to our Bicentennial with this book, *Knoxville!* It is an important addition to a landmark time in our history.

Victor H. Ashe, Mayor
City of Knoxville

TABLE OF CONTENTS

FAMOUS FIRSTS iii

FOREWORD iv

LIST OF ILLUSTRATIONS vi

CHAPTER 1   THE PEOPLE OF A DIFFERENT SPEECH 1

CHAPTER 2   WILLIAM BLOUNT'S TERRITORY 14

CHAPTER 3   KNOXVILLE, THE FIRST CAPITAL(S) 28

CHAPTER 4   JOHN SEVIER'S STATES 40

CHAPTER 5   HUGH LAWSON WHITE, A PRESIDENTIAL
                CANDIDATE 52

CHAPTER 6   ANTEBELLUM KNOXVILLE 65

CHAPTER 7   THE CITY THAT WITHSTOOD A CIVIL
                WAR SIEGE 71

CHAPTER 8   CONTROVERSIAL PARSON BROWNLOW 88

CHAPTER 9   INFLUENTIAL PEREZ DICKINSON 103

CHAPTER 10   AT THE TURN OF THE CENTURY,
                THE TYSONS 123

CHAPTER 11   THE GATEWAY TO THE GREAT SMOKIES 140

CHAPTER 12   THE GREAT LAKES OF THE SOUTH 154

CHAPTER 13   SPLITTING THE ATOM 166

CHAPTER 14   CHALLENGES AND CHANGES 173

CHAPTER 15   THIS WAY TO THE FAIR 182

CHAPTER 16   TWENTY-THREE FLAGS OVER KNOXVILLE 195

CHAPTER 17   THE AFTERSHOCK 206

CHAPTER 18   "THE PAST IS PROLOGUE . . ." 212

SELECTED BIBLIOGRAPHY 220

PHOTOGRAPHIC SOURCES 222

A NOTE FROM THE AUTHOR 223

INDEX   224

ILLUSTRATIONS
(Grouped between pages 122 and 123)

Prehistoric Indian mound
Portrait of Sequoyah
Knoxville's first house, built 1786
Residence of James Kennedy, Jr.
James White's house as the Kennedy kitchen
Uncovering the log house, 1906
James White's house on Woodlawn Pike
Reconstructing White's Fort, 1970
Governor William Blount
Blount Mansion complex
Major General Henry Knox
Silhouette of Charles and Margaret McClung
Statue of John Sevier
"Marble Springs"
First Presbyterian Church, cemetery
Hugh Lawson White
Old City Hall in 1862
Lamar House in 1877
General Longstreet's headquarters
Pencil portraits in the tower, 1863
1863 anchor and great iron chain
Removal of Governor Brownlow's portrait, 1987
James Mason
Knoxville Iron Company foundry, 1868
Dr. Thomas W. Humes
The Customs House
Perez Dickinson's Island Home
Knox County Courthouse plate, 1897
Knoxville flag pendant, 1897
Lawson McGhee
Bettie McGhee Tyson
Lawrence D. Tyson
Tyson House
Chilhowee Park bandstand
Cal Johnson Park
Elkmont summer cottage
Mrs. W. P. Davis
Colonel David Chapman
Sightseeing in the Smokies, 1934
1937 Knoxville souvenir plate
Fort Loudoun Dam, 1943
"Crackerbox houses" at Oak Ridge, 1944
The L&N Station
The Candy Factory
The Sunsphere and the Tennessee Amphitheatre
Technology & Lifestyle/Convention Center
Knoxville Museum of Art
Plaza Tower
Ice skating on Market Square
"Little Diamond"
Knoxville's first Dogwood Trail, 1955

CHAPTER ONE

 ## THE PEOPLE OF A DIFFERENT SPEECH

America's first territorial capital was established on the southwestern frontier in 1791 and named Knoxville, but the city's founding fathers were not the first settlers on its site. Even James White, who had built Knoxville's oldest house in 1786, was a latecomer.

Archeologists excavating along mid-East Tennessee's riverbanks, and sifting the soil of Indian village sites, have unearthed evidence of human presence stretching back through the ages to a time when the Archaic Indians roamed primeval forests, hunting bison, elk and bear with flint-tipped spears.

Permanent habitation began about 3,000 years ago with the Woodland Indians, who brought the bow and arrow into use, and were East Tennessee's first farmers. In the rich bottomlands beside the Little Tennessee River, they created an independent cradle of agriculture— one of the earliest on the North American continent. Long before maize was introduced from Central America in the second century A.D., they had domesticated such edible wild plants as sunflowers, squash, and lamb's quarter.

Within Knoxville's city limits, two of their large burial mounds are positive proof that this was once their dwelling place.

Around 1,000 A.D., the Woodland Indians were supplanted by a people known to anthropologists as the Early Mississippians. They were deeply religious and they dabbled in the arts, making decorative pottery, and painting recognizable pictures with red ocher on steep rock cliffs and the stone walls of caves. The Mississippian Indians, as the centuries passed, separated into several distinct tribes (including the Creeks, the Choctaw, and the Chickasaw) who continued to share a common language, Muskhogean.

By the time the first white explorer, Hernando de Soto, passed through this portion of the Tennessee Valley in 1540, East Tennessee had become the home of Indians who were quite distinct from the Mississippian groups then living in the rest of the South. They referred to themselves as the Ani-Yunwaya, or "Principal People", and they were closely related to the Iroquois whose language and customs were very similar. De Soto's guide-interpreters informed him that these Indians were the Tciloki, which meant "People of a Different Speech" in the Muskogee tongue, and the Spanish christened their area "Chelaque Province". Not averse to a name that set them apart from all their Indian neighbors, the Principal People began calling themselves the Chelaque, or Cherokee.

Historians are careful to speak of the Cherokee as a nation, rather than a tribe, for they lived in towns that were banded together in a form of representative national government. On the local level, they practiced a basic type of democracy in which each man (and some women) had an equal voice.

One of the principal Cherokee strongholds was a series of towns on the Little Tennessee River, some thirty miles southwest of present Downtown Knoxville, where they enjoyed a lifestyle that would have been the envy of early European colonists. Their houses were cleverly constructed, like enormous upside-down baskets, of posts driven upright into the ground at regular intervals and interlaced with pliant saplings; the walls were smoothly plastered with clay, outside and in. Cherokee men wore shirts and trousers of fringed deerskin, stitched together with bird-bone needles and strong sinews for thread. The women had similarly-sewn dresses, and everyone wore comfortable deerskin moccasins. Robes made from the pelts of bears or foxes doubled as warm winter overcoats, and as blankets for the houses' shelf-like beds.

Wild game was plentiful, and Cherokee braves were masters of the bow and arrow; they also excelled at fishing, trapping, and snaring birds. Wild grapes, berries, and nuts were available in quantity, and in the same rich bottomlands where plant-cultivation was first introduced by the Woodland Indians, every Cherokee home had a garden in which corn, beans, pumpkins, and squash were grown. In addition, each town had fields that were jointly owned by all inhabitants. Both men and women were required to work at planting and harvesting the community garden, for the Cherokee held firmly to their tribal rule that "he who will not work shall not eat".

The Cherokee loved to travel, paddling up and down the region's rivers in long dugout canoes made of hollowed logs. They roamed their own East Tennessee territory on foot, and went into the common at the towns on the Little Tennessee, and led northward to Virginia.

Until after the Revolutionary War, the Cherokee's homeland was part of a British colony, North Carolina, that extended in theory from the Atlantic Ocean to the Mississippi River; however, the western half of this domain lay beyond towering mountains covered with impenetrable forests. Even on clearly marked Indian trails, it was far easier to go around the mountains than to go across, and the first white explorers did just that. As early as 1673, the towns on the Little Tennessee were visited by English traders from Virginia, who had followed the Warriors Path.

Eighteenth century explorers found the Cherokee towns fascinating, and were much impressed by the intelligence and dignity of the people. When one of these admirers, Sir Alexander Cuming, invited seven Cherokee chieftains to accompany him to England in 1730, the chiefs accepted with alacrity, taking horse-drawn carriages and sailing ships in stride. This was travel in the grand manner! A hundred years earlier, Pocahontas had been received in England with the same mixture of courtesy and curiosity that now greeted the chieftains. They were elaborately entertained, and the climax of the visit was their formal presentation to King George II.

When the travellers returned from that memorable voyage, the waiting Cherokee were gratified to hear of the honors heaped upon their leaders. Thereafter, they regarded the British as their special friends, referring to England's sovereign as "Great-King-Over-the-Water".

During the French and Indian War, the Cherokee Nation signed a treaty of mutual aid with the English, who agreed to build and garrison a fort at the mouth of the Little Tennessee River for the protection of the Indian towns. In 1756, red-coated British troops arrived from South Carolina and selected a site, not far from the Cherokee's capital city of Chota, for the promised fort. This first English outpost in the then southwest copied European fortifications of the day by being diamond shaped, with a projecting bastion at each corner; its earthen outer walls were topped by a palisade of sharply pointed logs, and surrounded by a wide dry moat. It was named in honor of John Campbell, the fourth Earl of Loudoun, who was commander-in-chief of all British forces in North America at the time.

The Cherokee were vastly entertained by the bustle of construction as Fort Loudoun took shape; they greatly admired the officers' riding horses, and the packhorses that carried tools and cannon to the site.

When the British presented them with several horses, the princely gift was received with great rejoicing, and a group of braves promptly rode north along the Warriors Path to join their allies in a short campaign against the French. The warriors acquitted themselves well, but several of the precious steeds were battle casualties. On the way home through southwest Virginia, the braves who had lost their mounts selected replacements from among a herd of horses they found grazing unprotected. Probably they thought the animals were wild. Certainly they could not have known that horse stealing was a capital crime in the British colonies— Furious settlers overtook the unsuspecting Cherokee, reclaimed the stolen horses, and killed the braves who had been riding them.

Returning to Chota, the war party reported their loss of face at the hands of the English in Virginia. There had been other points of disagreement between the Cherokee and their British allies, and when the story of the horses had been told in the council house of every town, the braves gathered at Chota in war-paint and turkey-feather headbands, ready for war with the British.

Except for the small garrison at Fort Loudoun, there were no British in East Tennessee; therefore, the war party attacked the fort that had been built to protect their towns, and placed it under siege. After months of dwindling rations, the English officers sent a message to Chief Oconostota at Chota, offering to surrender the fort if he would spare the soldiers' lives, and exchange them for Indian prisoners held in South Carolina. When the Chief agreed to these terms, the British flag was hauled down from Fort Loudoun's flagpole for the last time, and the half-starved garrison marched out to surrender.

To their infinite relief, Oconostota kept his promise. Declaring them prisoners of war, he furnished a group of guides to escort them back to South Carolina. At the end of the first day's march, they halted for the night in a small clearing, and the guides disappeared one by one into the gathering dusk. At daybreak, a large band of painted savages attacked from all sides, killing most of the huddled prisoners on the spot.

The Cherokee were remarkably inconsistent in dealing with their prisoners of war. Sometimes they made slaves of the conquered foes; on other occasions, they treated them as honored guests. At the time of Fort Loudoun's surrender, one of the British officers had the good fortune to be claimed as a personal prisoner by Chief Attakullakulla, the youngest of the chieftains who had visited England more than twenty years before. He was taken to the Chief's home, and welcomed as a member of the family. After some weeks had elapsed, the Chief announced that he was going hunting, and that he wanted no companion except his prisoner, the white captain. During the hunting trip, Attakullakulla permitted his captive to escape, after carefully pointing out to him the trail back to South Carolina.

Meanwhile, in 1748, intrepid Stephen Holston had followed the river that bears his name from its Virginia source to its confluence with the French Broad, and beyond; he was the first to travel the full length of the Tennessee River to the Ohio and the Mississippi, and to discover the inland waterway that links the Great Smoky Mountains with the Gulf of Mexico. Holston's river opened a new route from Virginia to upper East Tennessee, and settlement spread out from it along the Watauga River and the Nolichucky.

The Cherokee, who claimed East Tennessee as their traditional hunting grounds, strongly protested against the influx of settlers. In 1777, North Carolina's Revolutionary-wartime government acknowledged their rights and set the boundary of the Indian Territory just north of the future site of Greeneville.

This agreement was ignored at the end of the Revolutionary War, when the impoverished new State of North Carolina paid its soldiers not in money, but in "warrants" good for tracts of state-owned land beyond the mountains. Then a new source of revenue was desperately needed, so North Carolina's legislature decreed in 1783 that only the mountainous area southwest of the French Broad River, and south of the Tennessee River, was reserved to the Cherokee. They announced that all the rest of the state's western territory was for sale— cheap— to homesteaders or investors.

As soon as this "Land Grab Act" was passed, prospective buyers flocked to East Tennessee in search of desirable property. But, early in 1784, North Carolina suddenly ceded the entire area beyond the mountains to the United States government, in settlement of Revolutionary War debts.

There was rejoicing in upper East Tennessee, where the settlers were delighted to be free of North Carolina's dominance. Congress had recently enacted the Jeffersonian Ordinances that encouraged the formation of new states in the West, so they hastened to organize the "State of Franklin". They elected John Sevier its governor, selected Jonesborough as its first capital, adopted a state constitution, and applied for admission to the Federal Union.

Revolutionary War debts.

There was rejoicing in upper East Tennessee, where the settlers were delighted to be free of North Carolina's dominance. Congress had recently enacted the Jeffersonian Ordinances that encouraged the formation of new states in the West, so they hastened to organize the "State of Franklin". They elected John Sevier its governor, selected Jonesborough as its first capital, adopted a state constitution, and applied for admission to the Federal Union.

North Carolina's vacillating legislators were having second thoughts, and in November of 1784, they repealed the Act of Cession. Officials of the State of Franklin chose to ignore this action, and for a time, East Tennessee had two governments, issuing contradictory orders.

In June, 1785, Franklin's governor John Sevier met with a number of Cherokee chieftains at Dumplin Creek, and negotiated a treaty that permitted white settlement as far southwest as the watershed between the Little River and the Little Tennessee. This good news travelled fast, and settlers rushed to take up residence on the land they had purchased from the State of North Carolina, or had acquired in payment for their wartime services.

Before the first forest-clearings could be made, the Cherokee had repudiated the Treaty of Dumplin Creek, declaring that the chiefs who signed it had done so without the consent of the people. Furthermore, the Cherokee Nation had gone over the heads of the disputing states by demanding, and getting, a meeting with representatives of the United States government. In November, 1785, the resulting Treaty of Hopewell confirmed the earlier Indian boundary north of Greeneville.

There was right on both sides of the bitter land-dispute that followed this pronouncement. Incoming settlers held valid deeds from the State of North Carolina, to which East Tennessee once again belonged. They had paid for their property in hard-earned cash, or had obtained it at the risk of life and limb by fighting for freedom against the British. They had severed all ties with their former homes, and had brought with them everything they owned. They could not leave, because they literally had no place to go.

On the other hand, by the terms of their agreement with the United States government, the Cherokee were justified in viewing all homesteaders south of the Indian Boundary Line as trespassers to be driven out. They systematically destroyed the settlers' crops, slaughtered their livestock, and raided their isolated cabins. No white traveller was safe from ambush.

This was the situation in 1790, when North Carolina conveyed her western lands to the federal government— again. This time, the ceded area was immediately organized as the Territory of the United States South of the River Ohio; the official title was shortened in everyday use to "Southwest Territory", counter-companion to the name of the Northwest Territory that had been established three years earlier. William Blount of North Carolina was appointed governor.

The British had always believed that the best way to obtain land for their colonists was to purchase it from its rightful Indian owners, and the newly independent United States government continued to rely upon this treaty-purchase method of settling Indian land disputes. Accordingly, with his constituents' lives and property at stake, Governor Blount summoned the Cherokee chieftains to a treaty meeting at the frontier outpost of White's Fort.

James White was one of the many settlers whose property had been deeded to them by the State of North Carolina before the federal government gave mid-East Tennessee back to the Indians.

In 1783, when the state set a bargain price on public lands beyond the mountains, he had visited and purchased the future site of Knoxville. He returned in 1786, and built a two-story log house beside First Creek, a short distance from the Tennessee River; the following year, he turned his house into a fort by adding outbuildings and a protective palisade of sharpened stakes. White's Fort was the logical site for the all-important treaty meeting because it was close (but not *too* close) to the Indian towns on the Little Tennessee, and because it offered a modicum of protection for the governor's party should the Cherokee turn hostile.

William Blount had attended the Hopewell Treaty Meeting, and he was well aware of the Cherokee's love for pomp and ceremony. He therefore erected an elaborate bunting-draped pavilion at the mouth of First Creek where he would receive the chieftains, and he appointed a Master of Ceremonies, Trooper James Armstrong, whose former military service in European capitals qualified him as an expert on courtly etiquette and protocol. Blount insisted that the members of his official party wear their showiest and best attire, to impress the Indians with the wealth and power of the United States, and as the ultimate compliment to his guests, he dressed his own interpreter in Cherokee costume.

In the event, the Cherokee chiefs beat the governor at his own game. They, too, were wearing every bit of finery they possessed, and they were accompanied to the meeting by *twelve hundred* braves who viewed the proceedings, like spectators in an amphitheater, from the steeply sloping sides of the First Creek valley! Many of the chieftains' ornaments had been gifts to them at earlier treaty meetings, but one sachem eclipsed all the others by draping himself with yards of silver lace, and carrying a crimson parasol.

The Cherokee thoroughly enjoyed the alternate parlaying and feasting that continued for several days. On July 2, 1791, the ceremonial pipe of peace was smoked, and the Treaty of Holston was signed by forty-one chiefs and a jubilant Governor Blount who had succeeded in purchasing the Cherokee's rights to much of the East Tennessee Valley.

The area governed by William Blount was not the first to be designated a federal territory, but it was the first for which an on-site government was authorized. Believing that the Treaty of Holston had secured to his constituents the peaceful possession of their lands, Blount decided to build America's first territorial capital on the site of his successful meeting with the Cherokee, and to name the city "Knoxville" in honor of Major General Henry Knox who, as Secretary of War in President Washington's cabinet, would be responsible for its defense "against all enemies, foreign and domestic".

The Cherokee, however, were immediately dissatisfied with the treaty. They claimed that they had misunderstood the amount of money to be paid them, and demanded five times as much as the treaty called for. Once again, their democratic form of government stood them in good stead: they claimed that the chiefs had signed the treaty without the consent of the people, and they threatened to revoke the entire agreement if the extra payment was not forthcoming. Federal officials in Philadelphia had had no experience with the Cherokee in treaty making and breaking. Anxious to ensure peace on the frontier, they met the Indians' demands.

Despite this concession, Governor Blount began to receive reports of serious Indian harassment. Settlers' cattle were stolen; barns and dwellings were burned; men who went on solitary hunting trips disappeared to be seen no more. Blount was unable to convince Secretary Knox that these attacks were unprovoked. He was informed that the costly Treaty of Holston must be honored by *both* parties, and he was forbidden to use the militia to strike back against the Cherokee. Then, as now, the regular army was composed of professional soldiers; but each state and federal territory had its own militia, made up of voluntary enlistees who were called into temporary service in emergencies. President Washington had appointed John Sevier the commanding brigadier general of militia for the Southwest Territory's Washington District, which included all of East Tennessee, and Governor Blount was the unfortunate middle man between intractable Henry Knox and belligerent John Sevier, whose experience with Indians had taught him that they despised weakness above all things.

Secretary Knox was astounded in 1792, when he was informed that the Cherokee of the Lower Towns (near present day Chattanooga) had formally declared war on the United States! Belatedly, a large blockhouse fort was built for the protection of the territorial capital, and garrisoned with a detachment of regular army troops.

The fort served its purpose in 1793, by preventing an attack on Knoxville. After the Cherokee formed an alliance with the fierce Creek Indians, chiefs John Watts and Doublehead joined forces to capture the Territory's capital. Before dawn on the morning of September 25, the large war party was moving toward Knoxville from the west when the chiefs heard the distant boom of the sunrise cannon at the Blockhouse. Unwilling to face artillery fire, they abandoned the assault on Knoxville. However, they were determined to make a raid on white settlers somewhere, for the war party would have lost face had it returned to the Cherokee towns without fighting. They turned aside, then, to nearby Cavett's Station (in the Walker Springs area). Like most of the "stations" on the frontier, it was a farmhouse sturdily built of squared logs, with slits in the walls through which rifles could be fired. There were only thirteen people in the station, but the first attack by the Indians was repulsed by the Cavetts' vigorous rifle fire. The Indians then suggested, through one of their number who spoke a little English, that if the people in the station would surrender and come outside, their lives would be spared and they would be exchanged for an equal number of Indian prisoners. This trick worked as well at Cavett's Station as it had at Fort Loudoun. The Cavetts (men, women and children) emerged only to be set upon by the Creeks; they were murdered and horribly mutilated. Before leaving, the Indians set fire to the empty station.

In reprisal, General John Sevier led the militia in an attack on two Cherokee towns. His men first captured the small village of Estanaula in a night foray, going on the next morning to larger and more important Etowah. Etowah's Chief King Fisher was killed in the battle for the town, and after his death, the inhabitants abandoned their homes and fled into the forest. Sevier burned Etowah to the ground, and had its ashes scattered.

From this time on, the Cherokee seemed inclined to honor the treaties they continued to make with the white men. In each treaty they gave up more of their lands in return for gifts and payments until 1835, when they ceded to the United States government all their remaining territory.

The federal government might not have been so anxious to purchase the last tract of Cherokee land if gold had not been discovered in the mountains of North Georgia in 1831. Gold fever swept the neighboring states, and pressure was put on the national government to force the Cherokee out of the whole mountainous area so that miners could search for the precious metal without fear of Indian attacks. (A branch of the U.S. Mint operated from 1838 to 1861 in a town whose name, Dahlonega, was the Cherokee word for "Gold.")

By this time, it had become the policy of the federal authorities to remove all Indian tribes and nations from the area east of the Mississippi, and to concentrate them in what was then called Indian Territory but is now the State of Oklahoma. The treaty in which a small number of Cherokee chiefs agreed to the sale of their last lands required the entire nation to leave the mountains within two years and relocate in the Indian Territory.

The Cherokee at once rejected the treaty, saying as usual that the chiefs had signed it against the people's wishes, and they refused to move. They appealed directly to the federal government as they had done before when treaties did not suit them. This time, however, President Andrew Jackson (who knew the Cherokee of old) listened to their complaints about the treaty and told them that they would have to abide by it. After the two years' grace period had expired, General Winfield Scott was ordered by President Martin Van Buren to remove the Cherokee by force. Scott's soldiers rounded up the people they found in the villages, most of whom were women, children, old men, and the sick. The missing able-bodied men had fled into the Great Smoky Mountains, where they had hidden themselves so well that the General despaired of finding them.

Finally, after one of the searching soldiers had been killed by Indians in the Smokies, General Scott offered a face-saving compromise. If the Cherokee responsible for the soldier's murder would surrender to him, Scott would allow the other hidden braves to remain in the mountains instead of moving to Indian Territory. Chief Tsali and his two sons voluntarily gave themselves up for trial and execution, to secure the freedom of their people. (Whether Tsali and his sons actually killed the soldier, none of the Cherokee would ever say.)

Although it was by then late autumn, General Scott proceeded to "escort" the Cherokee to Oklahoma. This forced march at bayonet point lasted through the worst of winter weather, and it was the weakest members of the Cherokee Nation who were forced to make it. Those who survived the hardship of the "Trail of Tears" were heartsick to find themselves in a flat land with no cool green forests or sparkling streams. By twos and threes many ran away and straggled back, carrying young children and the sick, to join the men still hiding in the mountains they so fondly remembered.

The descendants of those invincible people have never left the Great Smokies. They live on the Qualla Reservation at Cherokee, North Carolina, and they are known officially as the Eastern Band of the Cherokee Nation.

It was while the Cherokee were still attending treaty meetings in Tennessee that a member of their race accomplished a feat unequalled in recorded history. His statue stands in the Hall of Fame at the National Capitol in Washington, representing the State of Oklahoma, but Sequoyah was born in a Cherokee town on the Little Tennessee River, and spent all but the last few years of his life in East Tennessee.

No one would have chosen that handicapped child of a single-parent home as the Cherokee most likely to succeed. Sequoyah was the son of a white trader and a Cherokee mother, with whom he lived. He was lame from birth, but he hunted and fished with other boys in spite of his clubfoot. As a young man, he became a skilled silversmith whose bracelets, amulets, and necklaces were highly prized by the Cherokee chieftains; wishing to mark these pieces as his work, he asked one of the well-educated chiefs to write his name for him in English letters. He then copied this signature carefully, engraving "Sequoia" on his silver jewelry as part of the pattern of decoration.

Most of the Cherokee thought that the greatest achievement of white men was their ability to write down what happened, in such a way that their words could be understood by others. When this skill was discussed and praised by his fellows, Sequoyah always declared that he saw nothing remarkable about it; he was fond of saying that he himself could probably figure out a way to write down the Cherokee language. At the age of forty, he actually began the project, and his ultimate success was all the more amazing because he knew no other language than Cherokee, and had no idea how an alphabet was supposed to work. At first, he planned to have one "letter" for each Cherokee word, but he soon realized that so many symbols would be difficult to memorize and remember. It then occurred to him that all words were composed of sounds, in varying combinations. Beginning all over, he invented an alphabet of eighty-five characters, each representing a different sound of human speech.

By 1821, Sequoyah had finished his phonetic alphabet, or syllabary. The main advantages of this method of writing were its simplicity, and the ease with which it could be learned. There were of course no schools for Cherokee children, so he undertook the teaching of his alphabet himself. He taught it first to his five-year-old daughter, and then to his friends (who naturally could not admit they were unable to master what a small child had learned). Children and adults enjoyed playing Sequoyah's new game, and many of the intelligent Cherokee learned to spell in a single day.

Now that their language could be written down, the National Council of the Cherokee decided to publish a newspaper. In 1825, they purchased a printing press and, with the aid of white missionaries, produced the *Cherokee Phoenix*, a weekly paper with side-by-side columns printed in English and Cherokee. Its appearance brought Sequoyah's astonishing invention to the attention of the world at large. In 1828, he was invited to Washington, where he appeared before a joint session of the United States Congress and received a gift of five hundred dollars in recognition of his contribution to his people. Not to be outdone, the Cherokee Nation presented him with a gold medal.

Sequoyah was convinced that any Indian dialect could become a written language through the use of his alphabet. He therefore left his home for the newly established Indian Territory in Oklahoma where, before his death, his syllabary had opened the door to literacy for all the tribes and nations gathered there. It is eminently fitting that North America's tallest native tree bears the name "Sequoia" in honor of the most illustrious Native American.

A century after the Cherokee unwillingly joined Sequoyah in Oklahoma, the Tennessee Valley Authority built a series of dams on the Tennessee River and its upper tributaries. The rising waters of TVA lakes covered the entrances to many decorated caves in steep rock cliffs beside the rivers, and inundated the sites of many Indian towns. The University of Tennessee's Department of Anthropology raced against time to examine the caves and excavate the townsites, in order to recover and catalogue the relics and artifacts found therein. The University's McClung Museum houses an outstanding collection of these Indian artifacts, including intricately patterned baskets, "effigy" ceramic pots, and ceremonial pipes of carved stone. A Cherokee dugout canoe, hollowed out by burning and chipping from a single mammoth log, is an astounding 32½ feet long, 25 inches wide, and 10 inches deep.

A dam on the Tennessee River's mainstream was named for nearby Fort Loudoun, preserved in outline as an historic site. Fort Loudoun Lake extended all the way upstream to Downtown Knoxville, linking the first English outpost in the southwest with the site of the Southwest Territory's capital. Both the outpost-fort and the capital city owed their existence to the People of a Different Speech.

THE PRESENCE OF THE PAST

Knoxville has experienced many periods of growth and change in the two centuries since its founding, and each passing era has left some visible imprint on the city of today. One sight summarizes the lengthy preamble to this on-going story:

A prehistoric Indian burial mound overlooks Fort Loudoun Lake from the centerstrip of Cherokee Boulevard, in Sequoyah Hills.

CHAPTER TWO

WILLIAM BLOUNT'S TERRITORY

In 1790, President George Washington was looking for just the right man to serve as governor of the newly created Territory of the United States South of the River Ohio. The job was difficult to fill, because it was two-fold: its holder would, under the aegis of the State Department, govern North Carolina's ceded sector that extended from the crest of the Great Smoky Mountains to the Mississippi River; but he would also, under the direction of the War Department, supervise all Indian affairs south of the Ohio River and east of the Mississippi. Seeking someone who combined administrative ability with a first-hand knowledge of Indians, the President was pleased to find a candidate with exactly those qualifications in William Blount of North Carolina.

When he accepted the appointment, William Blount had never set foot upon the territory he was to govern, and was unknown to most of its inhabitants, yet he was definitely the man for the job. At forty-three, he had already served a long apprenticeship in public affairs. He had joined the Continental Army, and for two years had held the difficult and thankless post of paymaster for the North Carolina militia as well as for the Continental troops within the state. He had served in the North Carolina Legislature, as speaker of the lower house, and on the national level, he had been a member of the Continental Congress. Then, to climax his career, he had inscribed his name upon the page of history by signing the United States Constitution for his native state. He had fulfilled the President's second requirement by holding a watching-brief for the State of North Carolina at the significant Hopewell treaty-meeting between the Cherokee Nation and the United States government. In 1790, William Blount was already a figure of national prominence. He brought to his new position not only the experience gained in public service, but also a dignity that was needed and wanted in the frontier area.

Even his early training had been the right kind for his new job.

He was born in Bertie County, North Carolina, in 1749. His father, Jacob Blount, a prosperous farmer who had many commercial interests in addition to his large land holdings, insisted that each of his sons become acquainted with every facet of the family business. William Blount learned how to farm profitably, as well as how to manage foundries, mills, and stores. Best of all, he learned to manage men.

With his father and his brothers, he formed a sort of family holding company that engaged in a wide variety of enterprises. Jacob Blount understood farming best, so he managed all the farms. John Gray was the practical businessman, and he supervised all the stores and factories. Thomas was the family linguist and cosmopolitan, so he lived abroad to oversee the family's shipping interests and handle import-export trade. William was the family diplomat, and so he turned to politics, where his influence helped the family business, and where the family business aided him financially and furthered his ambitions. A much younger half-brother, whose name was spelled Willie but pronounced "Wylie", would be assigned to William as a secretarial assistant and political apprentice.

Although he had never crossed the mountains into the area ceded to the federal government by North Carolina, William Blount owned large tracts of land there. It would have been rather surprising if he hadn't. In lieu of payment for service in the Revolutionary War, North Carolina had given her militiamen land warrants entitling the holders to parcels of state-owned land beyond the Smokies. Since very few of the ex-soldiers wanted to move west, great quantities of the warrants were for sale, and they were bought by almost every well-to-do citizen as a speculation. The buyers usually turned over their warrants to a land agent, whose business it was to locate the tracts called for, and file the correct claims with the proper authorities.

Considering land to be the basic "good investment", the Blount family bought land warrants right and left. They also acquired land under North Carolina's "Land Grab Act" of 1783, which permitted speculators to buy as much as they wished for the equivalent of $5.00 per hundred acres. As the owner of much of its acreage, William Blount had a proprietary interest in the development of the Southwest Territory.

At the time of his appointment, Blount was considered a man of wealth, but like other so-called "rich men" of his day, he made most of his investments on credit, and seldom saw any hard cash. In 1790, he had to delay his departure for the west to put his financial affairs in some semblance of order. He collected various accounts due him (not without difficulty, for his business associates were as short of funds as he was) and sold some of his slaves, in order to pay off his most pressing debts in North Carolina. He still needed money to outfit himself and his body servant for his first appearance in the Southwest Territory, but as usual, he had no cash in hand. As governor, he would receive a handsome salary in future, so he borrowed against his expectations for clothes, horses, luggage, and spending money.

After providing himself with a wardrobe befitting the dignity of his new position (no fringed buckskin for William Blount!) he set out across the mountains in 1791 to take over the reins of government of the Territory. He went first to Rocky Mount, the comfortable log home of William Cobb near the Watauga Settlement, where he visited for several weeks and transacted such business as was brought to him. People who met him for the first time were much impressed by his appearance. He was a handsome man, with a full face and regular features; he had great dignity, and was as formal in his attire as in his manner. He wore his hair powdered and clubbed; he dressed in rich fabrics, well cut and ornamented with touches of gold lace; his shoes were silver-buckled. Always the diplomat, he was courteous but noncommittal, approving but not enthusiastic, deliberate but not dilatory— in short, the very man to set a standard of deportment for a frontier area. His dress and manner were in sharp contrast to those of the leaders in the Territory he had come to govern, but so great was his charm and magnetism that, instead of mistrusting him as a stranger to their problems, they respected him as a man of substance and worldly wisdom. So, from the very first, Governor Blount found friends and admirers in the west.

Most of the people who sought him out at Rocky Mount had come to rail against the Indians. White settlers who had taken up North Carolina land warrants, or who had bought "Land Grab" property, lived in constant danger from the Cherokee whose rights to all the area south of Greeneville had been confirmed in the Treaty of Hopewell, by the United States government. His constituents flatly informed him that concluding a new treaty with the Cherokee must take precedence over all other business. Therefore, as the first important official act of his administration, he held a treaty meeting with the Cherokee chieftains at White's Fort.

His previous experience at the Hopewell Meeting guided him in preparing for it. When the meeting day arrived, the Governor donned his finest uniform trimmed with gold lace, and received the chiefs of the Cherokee Nation with the same gracious formality he would have shown to the emissaries of any foreign power. When the forty-one chieftains signed the Treaty of Holston, the Blount administration was off to an auspicious start.

Having (so he thought) settled the Indian land dispute once and for all, the Governor set about establishing a permanent government for the Territory. The first step was to choose a location for the capital, and since White's Fort had been the locale of the successful treaty meeting, it was selected as the site where a new city would be built, and named "Knoxville" in honor of Major General Henry Knox.

Knox, a former Boston bookseller whose hobby was the study of ordnance and military tactics, had put his theoretical knowledge to practical use in the Revolutionary War as commander of General George Washington's artillery. Now as Secretary of War in President Washington's cabinet, he was Blount's immediate superior in all matters relating to Indian affairs. Knox had made no secret of his feeling that the settlers had been at fault in past disputes with the Indians, and by naming the territorial capital for him, the Governor hoped to interest him in the welfare of its citizens. (Blount's strategy didn't work. Secretary Knox fully approved the Treaty of Holston, and subsequently acceded to the Cherokee's demands for five times the amount of money it specified. He continued to insist that there would be no Indian harassment without provocation from the settlers, and not until the Cherokee of the Lower Towns formally declared war on the United States in 1792 were army troops dispatched to Knoxville to aid the militia in defending the Southwest Territory's capital.)

With another diplomatic maneuver, William Blount was more successful. His wife, the former Mary Grainger of Wilmington, North Carolina, had travelled with him to New York and Philadelphia for the sessions of the Continental Congress and the Constitutional Convention, and had enjoyed every moment of the social life to which her husband's prominence entitled her. Mary was of course pleased and proud when William was appointed governor of the Southwest Territory, but she was horrified to learn that he had every intention of moving his household to the western wilderness. She had no desire to be a "pioneer woman" and she flatly refused to bring up her children in a log cabin! When William went west to take up the reins of government and begin his new career, Mary remained at home with their three girls and two boys.

As soon as he settled upon Knoxville as the capital city, Governor

Blount ordered a log house built to serve as his headquarters during the construction of his permanent residence. He then returned to North Carolina, where he undoubtedly explained to Mary that his position as governor called for a standard of living equal to that of the eastern seaboard. He had in mind, he must have said, a spacious, many-windowed frame dwelling, plus a separate office for transacting official business in private. He had already approved the plans for these structures, and ordered the building materials, but he was at a loss when it came to selecting suitable furnishings, or planning a garden. Of necessity, there would be a great deal of official entertaining, and he had no idea what equipment would be needed for the kitchen...

The upshot was that the three little girls were left behind with relatives in North Carolina, while Mary and the boys went west with William.

The Blounts' first stop in the Southwest Territory was at the home of Colonel James King, near Bristol, where frontier families gathered to welcome the Governor's lady with two days of games and feasting. Governor Blount had invested rather heavily in King's Iron Works, one of the Territory's indispensable industries, and his investment had made possible the installation of a large iron-smelting furnace. The new smelter was charged with ore and charcoal, and a raised platform was built beside it. While the spectators applauded, Mary gracefully ascended the platform and, with a beribboned bottle of rum, christened the furnace "The Barbara" in honor of the Governor's mother.

Reassured by these ceremonies that the amenities of life could be maintained even on this far frontier, Mary visited with the Cobbs at comfortable Rocky Mount while William went on to Knoxville to check on the progress of their home.

A less stubborn man than William Blount would have admitted that building a house comparable to those on the eastern seacoast was impossible in new-born Knoxville, where there was not so much as a saw pit, much less a foundry or a glass works. Furthermore, the sole supply route was a wagon road to Abingdon, Virginia, that consisted of two parallel wheel ruts liberally sprinkled with boulders.

In a sense, the structure was prefabricated, since all its component parts were manufactured elsewhere and assembled on the site. The problem of transporting these materials had been solved by letting rivers take the place of roads. Lengths of dressed lumber were floated down the French Broad River from North Carolina; nails and hardware came down the Holston by flatboat from the iron works in which the

Governor owned an interest. Flatboats were unloaded, and lumber brought ashore, on the bank of the Tennessee River, just below the building site. Window glass would have arrived in slivers had it come from Abingdon in a jolting wagon, so the carefully wrapped panes were brought by packhorse. For its time and place, Governor Blount's new house was indeed a mansion!

When word reached Mary that the mansion was in the final stages of completion, she exchanged the niceties of Rocky Mount for the inconveniences of William's log headquarters in Knoxville. It was important that she be on the spot to supervise the equipping of the kitchen, and to direct the placement of the flower beds and herb plots in the garden. Orders went off to North Carolina for seeds, plants, and cuttings, but before they arrived, the Blounts' sixth child was born. This little daughter was named Barbara, and for many years, the slope on which her log birthplace stood was known as "Barbara Hill."

A man who had gone to such trouble to build an imposing house would obviously not put up with makeshift furnishings. As soon as the site of the capital was selected, Governor Blount had ordered the wagon road from Knoxville to Abingdon widened and improved. It connected with a road from Salisbury, North Carolina, and by that circuitous route came handsome beds (curtained, or field-canopied), chests, dressing tables, and looking-glasses. Most of the first floor was taken up by a combination living/dining room, with fireside chairs as well as dining chairs, buffets, and corner cupboards. Its most important piece was a long banquet table with removable sections that were pushed back against the wall when only the family was present.

The house faced Hill Street on a corner lot, and an entrance from State Street served the Governor's office that was the Southwest Territory's actual seat of government. This small one-room building was the first in the nation to be used exclusively as a territorial capitol. It was customary at the time to offer every visitor a glass of wine before settling down to business, and the Governor's favorite Madeira was kept in a shallow cooling-cellar just outside the office door.

To minimize the danger of fire, and to keep cooking odors out of the family living quarters, the more pretentious 18th century southern homes banished their kitchens to small separate buildings. Blount Mansion's kitchen boasted not only a mammoth fireplace, but an oven built into the chimney breast at waist height. Food had to be carried outside, and through the back door of the main house into the dining room; it was kept hot in transit on covered platters whose hollow bases were filled with boiling water.

It was soon apparent that the dual-purpose room was not only inconvenient, but too informal for official entertaining. In 1794, a small wing was added, and the house acquired a "company" entrance between the newly built drawing room and the original large room that could now be reserved for dining; with the table moved to one side, it could be used for dancing or for evening receptions. The drawing room was fashionably furnished with armchairs, a sofa, and a tea table from which Mary Blount dispensed refreshments to afternoon callers. Music was provided by a box-spinet that had travelled by wagon with its legs removed.

Unique on the frontier were the Mansion's elegant finishing touches. Since his family owned ships engaged in international trade, luxury-loving William Blount was able to summon up oriental bowls and Persian carpets, Delft vases to hold summer garden flowers or winter "everlastings", and opalescent English Queensware china— to say nothing of mold-blown glass decanters from New Jersey.

There were a number of visiting dignitaries to be entertained, along with a steady stream of envoys from the national government in Philadelphia, and even the humblest settlers felt free to bring their problems directly to the Governor. As administrator of Indian affairs, he made many friends among the Choctaw, the Chickasaw, and the Natchez. Members of these tribes came frequently to visit the distinguished Governor at his mansion, which they called "the house with many glass eyes". Mary Blount got on famously with her husband's dignified Indian guests. The chiefs admired her very much, and felt complimented when she named the new baby, born in 1794, Eliza Indiana.

During the war with the Cherokee of the Lower Towns, Knoxville's citizens expected an Indian attack to occur at any moment, and apprehension was at its height when a friendly Chickasaw named John Morris arrived to visit the Governor. On his way to Blount Mansion, Morris was attacked and killed by two settlers who mistook him for a Cherokee. This incident might have touched off a full-scale war between Indians and whites had not Governor Blount reacted with courtesy and diplomacy. He at once posted a $100 reward for the apprehension of the killer of John Morris. Then he ordered (and paid for) an elaborate funeral for his friend, at which he walked immediately behind the casket as chief mourner, and the Indians *still* liked William Blount.

In 1794, there were enough white settlers in the Territory to have a legislative body, and to take a census with a view toward petitioning the federal government for statehood. The Governor proclaimed a date for the election of representatives from the various counties, and America's first territorial legislature convened in Knoxville in 1794. The representatives were leaders in their own communities, most of them pioneers who had arrived in North Carolina's western district before it became a federal territory. It would have been understandable for such men to dislike the prosperous and polished Governor from across the mountains, but once again Blount proved himself a master of diplomacy. He announced (and stuck to it) that he had no intention of interfering with the legislators, who were perfectly capable of enacting proper laws for the Territory. So the legislators, as well as the Indians, liked the Governor, and they proved it by chartering a college in the capital city, and naming it in his honor.

A most unusual feature of that charter is the following admonition:

> *And the trustees shall take effectual care that students of all denominations may and shall be admitted to the equal advantages of a liberal education, and to the emoluments and honours of the college, and that they shall receive alike fair, generous, and equal treatment during their residence.*

This one sentence made Blount College the first in America whose non-denominational status was guaranteed by the legislative act granting its charter.

In 1796, the Territory having a population according to census of more than enough people to entitle it to statehood, Governor Blount called a convention in Knoxville to frame a constitution for the new state. The resulting document was patterned after the constitutions of North Carolina and Pennsylvania; like them, it protected the rights and liberties of individuals. Thomas Jefferson called it "the least imperfect and most republican" system of government adopted by any American state. Once again, Blount's previous training proved helpful. Having been a member of the United States Constitutional Convention, he knew how to secure the delegates' agreement to such a document.

With great reluctance, the Congress of the United States admitted Tennessee to the Union on June 1, 1796. The bitterly contested presidential campaign between John Adams and Thomas Jefferson was in progress. It was well known in the national capital that William Blount and John Sevier, the two most influential men in the new state, would favor Jefferson; therefore, the Adams faction opposed the state's admission to prevent the Jefferson side from gaining votes. William Blount incurred the enmity of John Adams when Tennessee, by a narrow margin, became the sixteenth state in time to cast three votes in the electoral college for Thomas Jefferson. (A compromise had secured admission by allowing only three electoral votes instead of the customary four).

Even before statehood became official, John Sevier had been elected Tennessee's first governor; William Blount was chosen (with William Cocke) to represent the new state in the United States Senate. Tennessee's proud citizens deemed it fitting and proper that the polished Blount should have the honor of going to Philadelphia, where he would be such a credit to his constituents.

The Blounts set out joyfully for the nation's capital, where they were welcomed to the inner circle of Philadelphia society. There were dinner parties and receptions, plays and balls, and Mary was positively radiant in such a rarefied atmosphere. From the Senate gallery, she saw the inauguration of President John Adams and Vice President Thomas Jefferson.

Even William Blount's old friends found nothing in his appearance or his manner to indicate that he was facing a financial crisis. International disputes over the control of the Mississippi River had so depressed the value of western land that, even on paper, he was less than wealthy. His patient creditors began to press for settlement of their claims, but he was unable to raise cash to satisfy them. In desperation, he evaded bankruptcy by the stratagem of deeding to his half-brother and secretary (Willie Blount) much of his land, all of his slaves, and even his household belongings. On the heels of this financial ruin came an even worse disaster.

At this time Louisiana, which had originally belonged to France, was owned by Spain. It was generally believed that the Spanish holdings, including the important port of New Orleans at the mouth of the Mississippi, were about to be ceded to the French Republic, and that the French would close the river to American shipping. Spain was at war with Great Britain, whose leaders were also interested in acquiring Louisiana, and many Americans felt that it would be to the advantage of the United States to have the mouth of the Mississippi under the control of England, whose stated policy would be to encourage trade with the upstream settlements. There was a movement afoot among the owners of land in Western Tennessee to support England in her war against Spain, although this was in violation of the United States' position of neutrality.

No doubt President John Adams rejoiced in secret over a letter given to him shortly after his political foe, the new senator from

Tennessee, arrived in Philadelphia. The missive, which purported to be from William Blount, contained an outline of the western landowners' plot to aid the British. It had somehow fallen into the hands of David Henley, the U.S. Army's agent in Knoxville, who immediately forwarded it to his superiors in the War Department.

This letter was sent by President Adams to the Senate on July 3, 1797. On that day, Senator Blount became bored with debates on consular salaries and taxes on parchment, and went out for a walk. On the steps of the Senate chamber he met the President's secretary, Samuel Malcom, carrying a document. When the Senator stopped Malcom and asked what news he was bringing to the Senate, the embarrassed secretary stammered that the message was confidential and hurried inside. Blount continued his walk.

As he reentered the Senate chamber, every head turned in his direction. There was a motion to reread something that the clerk of the Senate had just finished reading aloud. To his horror, he listened to a letter addressed to James Carey and signed "William Blount". Vice President Thomas Jefferson, who was presiding, asked whether he had written the letter. The stunned Senator replied that he had written letters to James Carey, but that he could not identify this one. He requested time to prepare a proper answer, and walked with dignity from the room.

In the confused days that followed, sentiment against Blount was running high. He asked for an opportunity to testify before the Senate, but the request was denied. His personal effects and papers were seized by the senatorial committee investigating his case. On July 8, after a cursory hearing at which he was not permitted to speak, William Blount was expelled from the United States Senate. He was released under bond, to appear at a later date to be tried for impeachment, but he had had enough. Bond or no bond, he was going home.

Word of the events in Philadelphia, of course, preceded him, and he must have had serious doubts as to his reception in Tennessee's capital. He need not have worried. As he approached the city, ex-governor (and now, ex-senator) Blount was met by a large group of citizens who conducted him home in triumph to his mansion.

As the time approached for Blount's trial on the impeachment charges, James Mathers, the Sergeant-at-Arms of the United States Senate, was sent to Knoxville to arrest the former senator and bring him back to Philadelphia. Mr. Mathers found himself in a peculiar position upon his arrival in the capital of Tennessee, for he was greeted by William Blount and everyone else as though he had come upon a purely social visit. Pleasant entertainments were planned for him by the state officials, and he was for several days a guest at Blount Mansion. Feeling that the time had come to return to Philadelphia with his prisoner,

Mathers asked the United States Marshall to appoint a posse to act as
escort. His request was met with courteous indifference. Appealing
publicly for a posse, he found not a single man willing to be a member
of it. Realizing that he would not be able to force the former Senator
to return to Philadelphia, the Sergeant-at-Arms announced his intention
of leaving alone. It developed that the posse so unwilling to escort
William Blount out of Tennessee had no such reluctance with regard to
James Mathers. A large group of citizens accompanied Mathers several
miles on his way, assuring him firmly the while that William Blount
could never be taken from Tennessee as a prisoner. Having impressed
this point upon the Sergeant-at-Arms, the posse then bade him a most
polite farewell.

The truth of the matter was that the people of Tennessee *liked*
William Blount, and had confidence in him. As historian J.G.M.
Ramsey wrote: "Whatever foundation there may have been for the
impeachment of William Blount, and whatever truth there may have
been in the charges preferred against him, there was no one in
Tennessee who viewed his conduct as criminal, unpatriotic, or unfriendly
to the true interests of the State or the West, and all refused to sanction
the proceedings against him."

This attitude on the part of his neighbors is confirmed by what
happened next. While the federal charges were still pending against
him, William Blount was signally honored by the citizens of his own
state. James White, who represented Knox County in the State Senate,
resigned in 1797 and William Blount was immediately elected to the
vacated seat. At a called meeting on December 3, the Senate of
Tennessee unanimously named Senator Blount of Knox County as its
speaker. So, at the very time William Blount was being tried for
impeachment from the United States Senate, he was serving as Speaker
of the Senate of the State of Tennessee!

When the impeachment proceedings finally began in the House of
Representatives, they were of short duration. The articles of
impeachment charged that Blount had conspired to set on foot a
military hostile expedition against the territory of the King of Spain in
the Floridas and Louisiana, for the purpose of wresting them from
Spain and conquering them for the English king. As soon as the
attorneys for Blount were allowed to speak, they pointed out to the
august body that, the Senate having expelled William Blount, he was no
longer a member of the United States Congress and was therefore not
subject to its deliberations or punitive judgments. They also argued that
under the Constitution of the United States, senators are not subject to
impeachment. No trial was held. Instead, the impeachment charges
were dismissed on grounds of lack of jurisdiction. William Blount thus
achieved the dubious distinction of being the only United States Senator

ever arraigned for impeachment, for in his case a precedent was set.

It was not until 1835 that any explanation or vindication of his conduct was written, and even then it was not for the eyes of the public. In that year, Willie Blount wrote a full account of the affair for the information of the Blount children. It was unnecessary in Knoxville to defend William Blount. Like the Indians and the legislators, the people still liked him.

For two years after the impeachment trial, the Blounts lived in Knoxville and were the center of a circle of devoted and admiring friends. William Blount was Speaker of the State Senate, and kept open house at Blount Mansion for a constant stream of visitors, but he was experiencing recurrent attacks of the fever and chills that characterized malaria. So precarious was his health that his friend, Dr. Fournier, lived with the Blounts in order to keep a close watch over his condition. On the surface, life at the mansion was as serene and prosperous as ever, but there were renewed financial difficulties. In spite of his calamitous record as a land speculator, William Blount was still convinced that land itself was the only safe investment, and he was buying more acreage in Middle Tennessee (where many of his former holdings had been seized for delinquent taxes) in an attempt to recoup his losses. But western land values continued to decline: the boom in real property was over along with the general business inflation, based on credit alone, that had made the Blount family appear wealthy.

In 1800, usually healthy Knoxville was struck by an epidemic of typhoid fever that left hardly a household unscathed. Mary Blount's mother, who was visiting at Blount Mansion, was the first member of the family to be stricken; the next was Mary. When one of his sons sickened, William Blount watched at the bedside for several days and nights; then he too came down with fever. He recovered sufficiently to sit up, and to feel that he needed no further nursing, but a sudden relapse brought the end quickly to a man who, at fifty-three, had had more than a fair share of triumph *and* disaster.

Mary Blount survived her husband by only two years. She had shared the heights and depths of William Blount's career, but she left her own mark on his Territory. The members of America's first Territorial Legislature complimented her when they created Blount County, by giving the name "Maryville" to its county seat; a later legislature of the State of Tennessee named Grainger County for her; and she established a tradition of hospitality in Knoxville that continues to this day. After Mary died of jaundice in 1802, Willie Blount took over the education of the children and called upon John Gray Blount in North Carolina for help in realizing as much as possible from their brother's depleted estate.

Even his family did not fully appreciate the affection and loyalty reposed in the Governor of the Southwest Territory, who is regarded with respect in Tennessee to this day. A plain marble slab covers his tomb in the churchyard of the First Presbyterian Church, engraved simply: *William Blount, died March 21, 1800, aged 53 years.* John Gray had written from North Carolina to Willie in Knoxville:

"As that is a new country the face of which will be in a few years totally changed I hope you will procure to be engraved on some lasting stone his name, age, etc., which will for a time point out the place of his interment."

THE PRESENCE OF THE PAST

A far more appropriate memorial to William and Mary Blount stands three blocks away, at the corner of State Street and Hill Avenue.

Blount Mansion, where much of Knoxville's earliest history took place, became the city's first house museum in 1930, and is the area's only Registered National Historic Landmark. This treasure barely escaped destruction in 1925. Until the end of the 19th century, the Mansion had been the cherished home of the prominent Boyd family; but as successive owners turned it into rental property, it first became a shop, and then a slum. It was on the point of being torn down for a parking garage when Miss Mary Boyce Temple rallied historically-minded Knoxvillians to purchase and restore it.

The buff-painted house that seemed so spacious and imposing in 1792 is small by comparison with nearby downtown buildings, but its dignity is undiminished. It is filled with elegant furnishings, all made prior to the date of Governor Blount's death in 1800, and the free-standing kitchen is equipped with 18th century labor-saving devices. Together, the two buildings reflect the affluent and hospitable lifestyle of the first family in the first territorial capital.

The typical 18th century garden, designed by Colonial Williamsburg's landscape architect, Donald Parker, has been maintained by the Knoxville Garden Club since 1934. Native wildflowers compete for attention with medicinal herbs, and with flower varieties that would have been available to Mary Blount; a fig tree flourishes beside the kitchen chimney. Here stands Governor Blount's one-room office, the first building in the nation to be constructed as a territorial capitol. It is also called "the cradle of Tennessee history", and displayed here is David Henley's massive standing desk, on which the Constitution of Tennessee was signed in 1796.

Craighead-Jackson House, on the Mansion grounds, contains woodwork handcarved by Knoxville's first architect, Thomas Hope. Here, too, is the desk owned by Tennessee's first governor, John Sevier, who presented it to Dr. J. G. M. Ramsey. On it, Knoxville's early history was written down for posterity in the *Annals of Tennessee.*

CHAPTER THREE

KNOXVILLE, THE FIRST CAPITAL(S)

Rivers were the interstate highways of the 18th century, and America's first territorial capital was ideally situated where a river from Virginia merged with one from North Carolina to form the major inland waterway that crossed and recrossed the Southwest Territory. This was the first "planned city" in the west, with a name selected, a pattern of streets laid out, a drawing for lots held, and a newspaper in operation before the second house was built within its limits. The first house was already five years old.

It was in 1785 that James White, a quiet, staunch Presbyterian from Iredell County, North Carolina, brought his family and household goods to what would soon be east Knox County. White had been here before. Two years earlier, he had crossed the mountains in company with several prospective settlers, including Francis Alexander Ramsey. They had found the spot where the rivers join, and had followed the mainstream of the Tennessee River as far west as an area they christened Grassy Valley. Convinced that this beautiful country was the very place to live in peaceful solitude, James White had purchased a large tract of land.

Surprising though it seems, the French Broad River rises on the North Carolina side of the Great Smokies, and the exploring party had followed its steep and rocky course through the mountains. It was fortunate for Mrs. White and the children that there was an alternate (although much longer) route to the western foothills. As soon as preparations for the move could be completed, the Whites set out on the wagon road from Salisbury, North Carolina, to Abingdon, Virginia. They halted nearby until the State of Franklin's treaty with the Cherokee was signed at Dumplin Creek, and then came south— first by wagon road, and when the road ran out, by wagon trace— to the Forks of the River.

After spending the winter in a hastily constructed cabin on the north bank of the French Broad (at Riverdale), James White moved downstream to the portion of his property that would become the site of Knoxville. He found a large creek flowing into the winding Tennessee River, and followed it up to a wooded hillside where a sizable spring bubbled from a rock outcrop. There he began felling trees to build his house.

When the tree-trunks had been stripped of branches and sawed to the proper length, they were squared with a broad-axe to remove the bark and the inner sapwood layer that harbored insects; all four sides were then levelled and planed with a foot adze, so that the logs would lie flat, one above another, as the walls were raised. This was not to be a cramped log cabin, but a comfortable house thirty feet long and twenty feet wide, with shuttered windows and a sleeping loft, plus an ell that backed up to the hillside and enclosed the valuable spring.

By sowing turnip seed on the patch of cleared land where the trees had stood, the Whites obtained an almost immediate crop of greens from the turnip tops, and a later root crop that would keep through the winter. With wild game and fish so plentiful, the family fared well from the first. James White had chosen wisely. His land was fertile, his water supply assured, his way of life admirably suited to his new homeland.

The plot on which he built his house and planted his turnips was directly across the river from the Indian Territory, and the Cherokee towns on the Little Tennessee were less than thirty miles away. He was not one to tempt Providence by failing to take sensible precautions, so the following spring, he turned his house into a small rectangular fort by adding an outbuilding at each corner and surrounding the sides with a palisade of sharpened saplings.

(A similar stockade was constructed five miles north of White's Fort, by John Adair. As recompense for his service as entry-taker for Sullivan County, Adair had received a 640-acre North Carolina land grant that covered all of present-day Smithwood and Fountain City. In 1789, Fort Adair became the supply depot for the Cumberland guards who guided and protected families headed for Middle Tennessee on the perilous overland route that had been marked in 1779. In that year, Colonel Evan Shelby literally launched an expedition against the "scorpions' nest" of renegade Indians and white outlaws who had taken over five Cherokee towns near Muscle Shoals. His 500 militiamen from North Carolina and Virginia felled trees and hollowed them into dugout canoes, in which they floated down the Holston and Tennessee rivers. After surprising and scattering the early-day terrorists, Shelby's men returned on foot, blazing a trail northeastward from the Emory river to the Holston. This wilderness trace still exists, as Emory Road.)

Suddenly, in 1790, White's Fort was part of the federal territory created from North Carolina's ceded lands. William Blount, the newly appointed territorial governor, was also to be supervisor of Indian affairs for the entire area west of the mountains and south of the Ohio River, and his double duties required him to conclude a treaty with the

Cherokee that would define, once and for all, the boundaries of the lands relinquished by the Indians and open to settlement. Blount selected White's Fort for his momentous meeting with the Cherokee Chieftains, at which James White's property was at last legally acquired from them.

To capitalize upon the success of the Treaty of Holston, Governor Blount decided to build a capital for the Territory at the same location. His chosen townsite was a high, defensible plateau bounded on the south by the broad Tennessee River, on the east and west by the valleys of large creeks, and on the north by a deep ravine— the identical area now called Downtown Knoxville. The bottom of the northern ravine was then covered by a small natural lake, called the "Flag Pond" for the wild iris that grew along its banks. Surrounded by the wide river, the two swift creeks, and the spreading Flag Pond, the plateau rose like a castle ringed by a protective moat.

The plateau belonged to James White, and in fact, his fort was on its eastern edge. He agreed to sell the land for the capital city, reserving certain portions of it for his own use, and he took an active interest in establishing the new town.

In 1788, a young man named Charles McClung had travelled south from Pennsylvania to White's Fort where he found much to admire, including particularly James White's eldest daughter Margaret, whom he married in 1790. He was familiar with large eastern cities, and had had some practical experience of surveying, so he was commissioned by his father-in-law to plan the new capital of the Southwest Territory. After surveying the terrain, he was to divide the land into parcels that would be assigned to purchasers by a public lottery.

Carving a town out of a primeval forest was a challenging and back-breaking task, but in a remarkably short time, McClung had laid out a grid pattern of ten streets enclosing sixteen square blocks; he divided these blocks into sixty-four half-acre lots. The town covered only one corner of the plateau, leaving plenty of space for future expansion. It was bordered on the south by the river, and on the east by First Creek; the northern boundary was the present Church Avenue, and the cleared area ended on the west at Walnut Street. A lottery to determine the ownership of the town's sixty-four parcels was held on October 3, 1791— and this date is Knoxville's official birthday.

In 1791, a newspaper was a status symbol for a city, and William Blount was determined that his territorial capital should have one. He induced George Roulstone, a printer in Fayetteville, North Carolina, to move his press to the other side of the mountains, but Roulstone arrived in the Territory while Knoxville's streets were still being cut through the forest. He set up shop temporarily at Rogersville where, on November 5, 1791, the first issue of the *Knoxville Gazette* printed the revised results of the town lottery. (After the original drawing, considerable trading took place among the lot-holders; when it was over, William Blount had managed to acquire the corner property he wanted, on a hill overlooking the river.)

James White did not agree with the Governor that a newspaper would be Knoxville's most important asset: he was convinced that a church was absolutely essential to the town's well being. He had retained eight of the sixty-four town lots, and he gave two of them for the meeting house and cemetery of the Presbyterian church being organized by the Reverend Samuel Carrick, in which he himself was a founding elder. Considering the character of Knoxville's original settler, it was surely no accident that the property he gave for church purposes was the very plot he had first cleared in 1786, and planted to turnips.

A building boom began in 1792, as the owners of town lots hastened to improve upon their investments. Trees cleared away from streets and city blocks provided on-site building materials, and with the exception of William Blount's mansion, Knoxville's earliest buildings were all of squared-log construction. One of the first to be completed was John Chisholm's tavern that overlooked the river from a lot adjoining the garden of Blount Mansion, and offered convenient housing to a number of the Governor's guests.

By October of 1792, Roulstone and his press were established in Knoxville, and the *Gazette* was advertising J. Chisholm's Tavern, Nathaniel and Samuel Cowan's stores in Knoxville and Jonesborough, and Charles McClung's "goods for sale or trade".

By far the largest log structure was the two-story blockhouse-fort built by the U.S. Army, after the Cherokee declaration of war against the United States, for the protection of the Territory's capital. (The Old Knox County Courthouse now occupies its site.) The garrison arrived in time to take a leading part in the Independence Day celebrations on July 4, 1793. The *Gazette* proudly reported that at two o'clock in the afternoon, Captain Rickard's company paraded through the streets and fired the fifteen-gun federal salute. At four o'clock, all the citizens of the town partook of a sumptuous banquet that ended with the drinking of no fewer than fifteen toasts. After nightfall, Captain Rickard's men "fired a 'feu de joie' which, from the darkness of the evening and the judicious manner in which the company was disposed, produced a most pleasing effect; after which there was a display of fireworks, from an elegant colonnade in front of Mr. Rickard's marquee."

The Blockhouse grounds were surrounded by a palisade of pointed logs, within which Knoxville's women and children were to take shelter whenever a warning shot from one of the fort's cannon alerted the town that an Indian attack was imminent. Families availed themselves of this protection only once, on the evening of September 24, 1793, when army scouts reported that a large war-party of Cherokee and Creeks was moving relentlessly toward the town. Even then, the dreaded dawn assault failed to materialize. That was the day when more than a thousand Indian warriors massacred the thirteen defenders of tiny Cavett's Station. In retaliation, General John Sevier's territorial militiamen burned two Indian towns, and Knoxville's citizens began to breathe easier as months went by without further incident.

The large room on the second floor of the Blockhouse was made available for public gatherings, and America's first territorial legislature held its sessions there in 1794. Delegates took time off from their deliberations to watch the garrison drill, and uniformed officers mingled with the representatives at many social events.

According to Abishai Thomas, who came that year to visit William Blount, Knoxville was already larger than the Blounts' home town of Washington, North Carolina. "Here are frame Houses and Brick Chimnies," he recorded with surprise, and went on to enumerate "ten stores and seven taverns, besides tippling houses." There was a Court House, but citizens pointed out to him with pride that their law-abiding town had no jail.

A special census showed in 1795 that the Southwest Territory had more than enough residents to qualify for statehood, and while waiting for the application to be approved by Congress, Governor Blount called a convention to draft a constitution for the new state. Excitement ran high. Everyone was aware that history was being made in Knoxville on January 11, 1796, when fifty-five delegates gathered in the large office of U.S. Army Agent David Henley (at the corner of Gay and Church Streets) which had been rented as a meeting place for the Constitutional Convention. On the following morning, the delegates "Resolved, that economy is an admirable trait in any government and that, in fixing the salaries of the officers thereof, the situation and resources of the country should be attended to." They then proceeded to reduce their own pay from the $2.50 set by the act providing for the assembly to $1.50 *per diem*!

Five delegates from each of the Territory's eleven counties had been elected to the Constitutional Convention, but it was immediately apparent that a smaller group would be needed for the actual writing. Accordingly, a committee consisting of two members from each county was appointed to draft the document, with William Blount and Charles McClung representing Knox County. Local tradition has always held that the twenty-two committee members entrusted the task to five of their number, including McClung and Blount. The select sub-committee is said to have retired to the office of William Blount, where they hammered out the Constitution that was discussed, amended, and finally adopted by the entire convention.

An official seal should be ready and waiting for the use of Tennessee's first governor, so Charles McClung agreed to design one. "Agriculture and Commerce" had been chosen as the motto of the 16th state, and McClung illustrated it on the original Great Seal of the State of Tennessee by grouping a plow, a corn shock, and a tobacco plant above a river flatboat. Since statehood had not yet been granted, the seal bore the date on which the state constitution was signed: FEBRUARY 6, 1796.

The Constitution specified Knoxville as the capital of Tennessee until 1802, at which time the location of the capital should be voted on again. (Actually, with the exception of one day's session at Kingston in 1807, Knoxville remained Tennessee's capital until 1811, when the legislature set the next year's meeting at Nashville. The capital returned to Knoxville in 1817-1818, but the state's seat of government was destined to be located in Middle Tennessee for reasons of geographical convenience— first in Murfreesboro and later in Nashville, which was not designated Tennessee's permanent capital until 1843.)

Tennessee was admitted to the Federal Union on June 1, 1796. Only five years had elapsed since the streets of the nation's first territorial capital were cut through a trackless forest, and William Blount was certainly entitled to congratulate himself upon his city's progress. He had provided local autonomy by creating Knox County on June 11, 1792; its governing body was the County Court. There was a Sheriff to maintain law and order, and a Registrar of Deeds to record land grants and property transfers. Knoxville had attracted settlers from all walks of life, including doctors, lawyers, pedagogues, and gentlemen farmers. Blacksmiths, tanners, wheelwrights, and cabinet makers were plying their trades, and there were also skilled jewelers and tailors. There were a number of white "hewers of wood and drawers of water", and nearly 100 free blacks; the slaves counted by the 1795 census represented 20% of Knox County's total population. Taverns had multiplied, to serve the visitors who came on government business, or to shop for luxuries unavailable at outlying trading posts. In Knoxville, it was possible to buy not only salt and coarse brown sugar, but white loaf-sugar, chocolate, pepper, allspice, tea and coffee. Bibles and spelling books were available, and so were world histories, hymnals, medical texts, and the latest works of Addison and Steele. Shop shelves were crowded with a miscellaneous assortment of dress goods, hair oil, window glass, hunting knives, and china plates. In payment, merchants accepted "Cash, Deer and Bear Skins, Furs, Hemp, Bees-wax, ...Tallow, Flax, etc. etc." To supply the growing number of stores, the wagon road to Greeneville, Jonesborough, and Abingdon had been widened and improved; a new road to Virginia, via Rutledge and Kingsport, was in the planning stages. Furthermore, the town's amenities already included a church, a college, a newspaper, and a military post.

On April 30, 1797, Knoxville welcomed internationally famous visitors for the first time when Louis Philippe, the Duc d'Orleans, arrived with his two younger brothers. These members of the royal family of France were then in exile in the United States, and spent their time travelling about the country. They were entertained with all possible ceremony at Blount Mansion, and found accommodations for themselves and their retinue at Chisholm Tavern. Years later, when Louis Phillipe had ascended the throne of France as the Citizen King, he startled an American tourist from Tennessee by remarking: "Tennessee— Ah, yes! Tell me, do they still sleep three in a bed in Knoxville?"

Immediately after it was chartered by the Territorial Legislature in 1794, Blount College opened in the home of its president, the Reverend Dr. Samuel Carrick, on the Holston River at present day Boyd's Bridge. James White was a trustee of the college, and he sold two of his six remaining lots to the college, for a campus. Funds were raised by public subscription to erect a two-story frame building at the corner of Gay and Clinch streets, where the Tennessee Theatre now stands, and the college moved to Gay Street in 1797. Following the custom of eastern colleges in the 18th century, qualified students could be admitted at the age of twelve; they were instructed by a faculty of two, including the president. The price of tuition was $8 for the five-month session, and board cost an additional $25. From those fees, Blount College was entirely self-supporting!

History was made in 1804, when Blount College admitted America's first coeds: Barbara Blount, Polly McClung, Jenny Armstrong, Mattie Kain and Kittie Kain.

Who were those five pioneers in higher education for women? Barbara Blount was born in Knoxville in 1792, and was orphaned at the age of ten by the deaths of William Blount in 1800 and Mary Grainger Blount in 1802. She made her home with her sister Mary Louisa (Mrs. Pleasant M. Miller) while attending the college named for her father, and she was married in 1815 to General Edmund Pendleton Gaines, a hero of the War of 1812. Polly McClung was also born in Knoxville in 1792. Her parents were Charles McClung, who planned the Territorial Capital, and his wife Margaret, the daughter of Knoxville's first settler, James White. In 1811, Polly was married at "Statesview" to Thomas Lanier Williams, the first chancery judge for 18 East Tennessee counties. Mattie and Kittie Kain were the daughters of John and Mary (McMullen) Kain whose large plantation home "Trafalgar" was east of the city on the Holston River. Mattie was married there in 1808 to Robert King, who began a family tradition of steamboat ownership. Kittie married Enoch Parsons, a city alderman, in 1813. Jane Crozier

(Jenny) Armstrong was the daughter of "Trooper" James Armstrong, the master of ceremonies at the Holston Treaty-Meeting; her mother was Susan Wells. Jenny is the only one of the five coeds whose likeness has been preserved. A portrait, painted after her marriage to a prosperous merchant, William Park, (and presented by her descendants to the University of Tennessee) shows a serious young woman with a long face, deep set dark eyes, and black hair closely covered by a white lace cap.

Two of the four homes in which these coeds lived were designed and built by Knoxville's first professional architect, Thomas Hope. By the time the capital of the Southwest Territory had become the capital of Tennessee, log houses were considered beneath the dignity of Knoxville's prominent citizens. After all, this was a place where "proper" building materials were readily available. The red clay soil was perfect for brickmaking, and the tall straight forest trees were ideal for beams and lintels, floors and stairs, as well as for fine furniture. River sand and crushed limestone, in varying proportions, were the essential elements of window glass, as well as of mortar and plaster. There was no dearth of skilled artisans and day laborers, but only a lack of design; and this lack was remedied in large part by Thomas Hope's arrival.

In his early youth, Hope had proved himself a gifted woodcarver and cabinet maker in his native County Kent. He had later trained in London as an architect and had come from England to Charleston, South Carolina, to design and construct a large house for Ralph Izard. He then moved with his family to Knoxville, where his first important commission was the building of a plantation home for Francis Alexander Ramsey near the Forks of the River, six miles east of the city.

Ramsey was one of the group of explorers who visited the area in 1783, and he had been especially impressed with the fertility of the soil in the triangle between the Holston and the French Broad rivers. There, he purchased a 500-acre tract, and named the property "Swan Pond" for its small lake that was a nesting place for waterfowl. He did not return to take up residence until 1792, after Knoxville had been designated the territorial capital, at which time his family moved into a log house overlooking the little lake. No doubt well-read Francis Ramsey had learned of a new scientific theory that blamed "stagnant water" for the "miasmas" that were then believed to cause fevers. He had the Swan Pond drained before his permanent home was built.

Possibly Thomas Hope was homesick, in the raw and empty countryside between the rivers, for the compact stone houses of civilized, tidy England. Probably, he was influenced by the abundance and variety of building materials ready to his hand. For whatever reason, he chose to design for Francis Ramsey a Gothic-style "gentleman's residence", ornamenting its walls of rough-cut pink marble with a belt course, window-tops, and quoins of blue limestone. In the fashion of the times, he carved elaborate cornices of wood, and painted them to resemble marble, although the real marble for the outer walls was quarried less than a mile away. Since the house was made of fire-retardant stone, he gave it the convenience of an attached kitchen adjacent to the dining room; in one wall of the kitchen wing he placed a tiny window, where a light was kept burning to guide "benighted" travellers to this hospitable haven. During the construction period, while he and his family were living in a log cabin near the building site, Hope further demonstrated his talents by making an elegant tall secretary-bookcase for the parlor, and a massive "beaufet" for the dining room.

Francis Ramsey's stone house, the first in Knox County, was a great curiosity. It was also a splendid testimonial to the skills of Thomas Hope, who was thenceforth in great demand among Knoxville's prosperous citizens. In 1804, Charles McClung secured his services to design and build a new house west of town, near Ten Mile Creek.

In 1792, at the behest of the first Knox County Court, McClung had agreed to construct a good wagon-road westward from the county seat at Knoxville to the county line at Kingston by way of Campbell's Station. This was a toll-road, called (then and now) the Kingston Pike. It began on the town plateau, and the first few miles were easy: it was only necessary to widen an existing bridle path. For the rest of the distance, the dirt road was hacked out through the dense forest that covered steep hills and rocky valleys, by man-power and mule-power. McClung was proud of his fine turnpike and he chose a site overlooking it for the house he named "Statesview": it turned its back on the panorama of the Great Smokies, behind whose crest lay North Carolina, and faced toward Tennessee's westernmost settlements on the Cumberland Plateau.

Several years in the Knoxville area had left their impress on Thomas Hope, and he was developing a style less reminiscent of England and more suited to East Tennessee's climate. He designed Statesview as a spacious rectangle with a large wing at one side and a kitchen at the back, and built it of rose-red brick burned on the spot from the rich clay soil. It seemed far more at home in its surroundings than had Swan Pond.

Hope built other brick houses and trimmed them with real stone instead of painted wood. He laid the bricks in a unique double herringbone design for "Trafalgar," the vanished home of John Kain which stood on the site of the Southern Railway's John Sevier Yards. He also executed several commissions for fine cabinet work in Knoxville: a staircase, mantel, and wainscoting at Chisholm Tavern were carved by his hand. In addition, he made the furniture for the large office of David Henley (for whom Henley Street and Bridge are named,) including the mammoth standing-desk on which the Constitution of Tennessee was signed.

Obviously, the vast majority of Knoxville's early residences were not planned by Thomas Hope. Most of them were built by well-trained slaves and artisans, from plans found in some book of architectural drawings; but Hope's influence was present in the simple and uncluttered style, combining red brick with white stone, that became a tradition in the area.

After the Blockhouse was constructed for the defense of Knoxville, James White had been able to remove the protective stockade around his fort. His house, once the last outpost on the frontier, was soon engulfed by Tennessee's bustling capital city. Early in the 19th century, Knoxville's first settler moved out of town, in search of peace and quiet, to riverside property he owned east of First Creek where he duplicated his original house. He sold the former fort to his friend, James Kennedy, Jr., who built a large and fashionable brick residence trimmed with stone, facing State Street between Clinch and Union avenues.

"Adaptive use" is by no means a new concept. James Kennedy felt that Knoxville's oldest house, which had been in existence for five years before the city's founding, should not be wantonly destroyed, and he preserved it in a most ingenious way. Disguised with weatherboarding, James White's log house became the kitchen wing that linked the Kennedy mansion with its servant's quarters.

The first detailed account of Tennessee's beginnings was written in 1853 by Dr. J.G.M Ramsey, who was born in the log house on his father's Swan Pond property in 1797. Because of the author's first-hand knowledge of persons and events in the area, Ramsey's *Annals of Tennessee* is acknowledged as the definitive work on Knoxville's early history. He concludes his chapter on the state's first capital with these words:

> *[Knoxville] became the seat of government of the state of Tennessee, and so continued to be for many years after. The scepter has departed from her, but time, and change, and progress cannot deprive her of her ancient honors, nor make her less venerable for the proud associations that cluster round her early history. Here Chieftains of the Cherokee nation met Governor Blount in council, smoked the pipe of peace, and formed the Treaty of Holston; — here the pious White pitched his tent in the wilderness, lived his life in patriarchal simplicity and unostentatious usefulness; ....Here too was born the infant Hercules — since become a giant — Tennessee. Tennessee looks back to Knoxville, and recognizes her as the home of her youth, and the fond centre of her hallowed recollections.*

THE PRESENCE OF THE PAST

First Presbyterian Church still occupies the original plot of ground cleared by Knoxville's earliest settler in 1786, and given by him for church purposes. This churchyard on State Street, between Church and Clinch avenues, was the town's first cemetery, and it is eminently appropriate that James White, who gave the land, and William Blount, who envisioned the city, are both buried here.

Nine of the ten streets laid out by Charles McClung in 1791 for America's first territorial capital exist today in Downtown Knoxville. Some of their names have changed several times in the interim, but the original north/south streets are presently called Walnut, Market, Gay, State and Central (which until recent years was bordered by vanished First Creek.) Those running east and west are now known as Church, Cumberland, Main, and Hill avenues. Missing is (river) Front Street, which was erased in the 1960's by Neyland Drive.

After Knoxville became Tennessee's first capital, prosperous John Chisholm updated his 1792 log hostelry with weatherboarding, and "improved" its interior with woodwork and a staircase carved by Thomas Hope. In spite of strenuous public protest, historic Chisholm Tavern was demolished in 1962 for Neyland Drive's construction. Preservationists managed to save at least a portion of the past by incorporating the handcarved mantel and wainscoting of the Tavern's principal room, and its handsome staircase, in nearby Craighead-Jackson House (built in 1818) which was then undergoing restoration as the Visitors' Center for Blount Mansion.

In 1793, Nicholas Gibbs built a capacious log house not far from Fort Adair, on the Emory Road. (A great-grandson, William Gibbs McAdoo, married President Woodrow Wilson's daughter, Eleanor, while he was serving as Secretary of the Treasury in her father's cabinet.) Present day descendants of Nicholas Gibbs have formed a support group to preserve his restored house— the oldest in Knox County that has been continually occupied as a private residence.

Tennessee marble was first employed as a building material in 1796, when Thomas Hope used it for the exterior walls of Francis Alexander Ramsey's fine new home. Ramsey House, on Thorngrove Pike, is reached from Asheville Highway by the John Sevier Highway. Few people were aware of the house's existence until Mrs. Thomas Berry (Ellen McClung) set out to rescue it from oblivion. Under her leadership, a Knox County Chapter of the Association for the Preservation of Tennessee Antiquities was formed to purchase it in 1952, and its painstaking restoration is ongoing. The result is a period museum, surrounded by extensive grounds and filled with the fine furniture and household equipment required to maintain a high standard of living in an isolated frontier area.

Statesview (on Peters Road near Kingston Pike) has changed hands many times since its building was begun by Thomas Hope in 1804, but is still a privately owned residence. The house was partially destroyed by fire in 1820, but was at once rebuilt— presumably in its original form. After the death of Charles McClung in 1835, it was purchased by the editor of the *Knoxville Register*, Frederick S. Heiskell, an early advocate of soil conservation who maintained that Knoxville's steep hillsides were ideally suited to fruit-growing. He planted apple, pear, and peach orchards on the grounds, and rechristened the property "Fruit Hill". (The trees outlasted the name.)

The house built by James White in 1786 served for a century as the kitchen wing of a State Street mansion, and has since survived *two* moves to remain a local landmark. Before the Kennedy house (to which it was attached) was razed in 1906, the historic addition was bought by Isaiah Ford, a Knoxville printer who became interested in history as a child, when he shook the hand of President Abraham Lincoln. Determined to preserve the physical evidence of his city's founding, he removed the weatherboarding from the log house, and carefully numbered its timbers as they were lifted down. He then reassembled the structure south of the river on Woodlawn Pike, where it was the home of the Ford family for more than fifty years. James White's house was then purchased by the City Association of Women's Clubs, and moved in 1970 to a lot on East Hill Avenue near the James White Memorial Auditorium/Coliseum. By adding old log cabins and a new stockade of sharpened stakes, the ladies recreated James White's Fort across the First Creek valley from its original location. As a museum containing frontier furnishings and essential tools, Knoxville's first house stands as a monument to pioneer life, and to historic preservation by adaptive use!

CHAPTER FOUR

 ## JOHN SEVIER'S STATES

In the Hall of Fame at the National Capitol in Washington, not far from the statue of Sequoyah, Tennessee is represented by a man known to his contemporaries as "The Scourge of the Cherokee." This was the same man who served as governor of two states (although one was refused admission to the federal union), and was elected to the U.S. Congress from two states, (one of which had previously tried him for high treason.) His name was John Sevier.

He was born in the Shenandoah Valley of Virginia in 1745, and entered military service as a captain of the King's troops in his native state. In 1772, he visited the new settlements on the Holston and Watauga rivers, and liked what he saw there; he returned the next year with his wife Sarah, his parents, and his brother, to settle near the present site of Bristol. By 1775, he had moved his growing family to the Watauga Settlement; a few years later, he built a log house called "Plum Grove" on the Nolichucky River; afterwards, his frontier friends and neighbors nicknamed him "Nolichucky Jack."

All this area in the western foothills of the Unaka Mountains was part of England's Colony of North Carolina, but His Britannic Majesty's representatives on the far away eastern seacoast preferred to ignore the existence of any British subjects who dressed like Indians in shirts and trousers of fringed buckskin, and wore coonskin caps. The self-reliant frontiersmen looked upon any shortage as a challenge to be met, so when they found themselves in need of a government, they organized one of their own in 1772.

John Sevier's political career began with his election as one of the five commissioners of the Watauga Association that had been formed by the settlers to maintain law and order, and to provide for their mutual defense against the Indians.

The Cherokee regarded East Tennessee as their private hunting grounds, and they reacted against the encroaching whites by raiding isolated farms, setting up ambushes beside narrow trails, and making savage attempts to destroy established settlements. On one occasion, Chief Old Abraham led an attack on the Watauga Settlement. As the Indians approached the fort where the settlers had taken refuge, they surprised and almost surrounded a young white girl outside the stockade. As soon as Catherine Sherrill realized her danger, she sprinted for the gate of the fort. She was unusually tall, and sufficiently fleet of foot to outrun the pursuing Indians, but her path to the gate was blocked by other Cherokee. *"Over here!"*— turning swiftly to the right, she jumped up and caught the hand of Captain John Sevier who hauled her up and over the high wooden palisade to safety. A few years later, after the death of Sarah Hawkins Sevier, Catherine Sherrill married her rescuer. The second Mrs. John Sevier was an erect and smiling woman with brilliant blue eyes and raven-black hair; her husband called her "Bonny Kate."

In reprisal against such attacks as Old Abraham's, John Sevier made several victorious forays against the Cherokee, copying their own fighting methods, and imitating their spine-chilling warwhoop. Experience taught him that the Cherokee despised cowardice, and held in contempt an enemy who ran from them. It became his lifelong policy to let Indians strictly alone, unless and until they first attacked; then he was ruthless in exacting retribution.

When the Revolutionary War began in 1775, the Watauga Association was reorganized as the "Washington District"— the first governmental entity to be named for George Washington. Sevier was a member of the District's Committee of Public Safety, and was one of its delegates to a North Carolina convention at which he helped to form the constitution of the very state from which he would later try to carve a new state. After North Carolina's wartime government appointed him colonel of the Washington militia, Sevier led his neighbors in several brief campaigns against the British and the Tories in the western Carolinas.

In 1780, word reached him that Colonel Patrick Ferguson, the British commander in North Carolina, planned to cross the mountains and seize the frontier settlements. John Sevier and Isaac Shelby were the two colonels of militia in the overmountain area. They borrowed $13,000 from the fees collected by North Carolina's entry-taker for the district, John Adair, to supply and pay an expeditionary force, and called a muster for September 25, at Sycamore Shoals on the Watauga River. At this time, the entire fighting strength of the western district was less than a thousand men, but when the appointed day dawned, every able-bodied settler appeared at Sycamore Shoals. Shelby and Sevier could not leave the frontier families defenseless during their absence, so they conducted the first military draft in United States history on the spot. They conscripted half the men to stay at home! With a force of only 480 volunteers, they then started east to head off Ferguson's army. These first volunteers from the future Volunteer State were joined en route by Virginia troops under Colonel William Campbell, and by eastern North Carolinians under Colonel Charles McDowell.

According to C. Stedman, who wrote a history of the American Revolution from the British point of view,

> *The enemy was composed of the wild and fierce inhabitants of settlements beyond the Alleghenies, who had assembled from different places...The men were well mounted on horseback, and each carried his own provisions in a wallet, [so they] were not encumbered by wagons.*

This was a force whose mobility was incomprehensible to old-world military strategists, but it was from new-world natives that the overmountain men had learned to travel light in order to travel fast.

As the frontiersmen moved east across the mountains, Colonel Ferguson retreated before them with his well-trained troops. Finally he found a spot he considered advantageous, and took up his position atop an eminence he named "King's Mountain." To his horror, his pursuers did not line up in proper battle formation. Instead, they raised a blood-curdling Indian warwhoop and charged the mountain from all sides, simultaneously. The desperate and chaotic fighting lasted only an hour, but it turned the tide of the Revolutionary War in the South: Ferguson was killed, and the baffled British troops surrendered unconditionally.

After the Revolution was over, North Carolina relinquished to the federal government all her lands west of the mountains in exchange for cancellation of the state's war-incurred debt. The legislature passed this act of cession in 1784, and once again, the overmountain settlers organized a government of their own.

The recently enacted Jeffersonian Ordinances had established the procedure for admitting new states to the federal union. Although the Washington District's population fell short of the required five thousand inhabitants, the residents decided to set up the government of their future state immediately, and live under it while waiting to qualify for statehood. "Franklin" was the name ultimately chosen by these rugged individualists for their independent government— not only to honor a patriot they much admired, but because the old-English meaning of the word was "a free man."

John Sevier was elected governor of the State of Franklin, and its officials included several future Knox Countians. James White became speaker of the Senate and John Manefee (who later built a fortified station in the Powell vicinity) was speaker of the House of Representatives. Francis Ramsey, then living at Limestone, was clerk of the Superior Court *and* secretary of the constitutional convention that met at Jonesborough in 1785.

Meanwhile, North Carolina's General Assembly had repealed the act of cession, on grounds that the state had not been adequately compensated for its own wartime expenses, and had reclaimed the Washington District. The legislators attempted to conciliate the angry westerners by authorizing a court system for the District, and by promoting John Sevier to brigadier general of its militia— an appointment ignored by the Commander-in-chief of Franklin's militia.

The town of Greeneville, which had been named the State of Franklin's permanent capital, was actually in Indian Territory: it was just south of the boundary line established by treaty in 1777. Many ardent Franklinites owned property even farther south, and at their urging, Governor Sevier called a treaty meeting with the Cherokee chieftains at Dumplin Creek. Only one faction of the Cherokee Nation was represented, but the chiefs who attended the meeting acceded to Sevier's demand that white settlement be permitted to within a few miles of their towns on the Little Tennessee. Under the implacable gaze of the man they hated and feared above all others, the chiefs signed the treaty of Dumplin Creek— knowing full well that it would be rescinded by the Cherokee's democratic process.

After the Dumplin agreement had been nullified by the United States government at the Hopewell treaty-meeting, and the Indian boundary line replaced north of Greeneville, a special session of the North Carolina General Assembly was called to do something about the situation in the west. The legislature published a proclamation declaring that North Carolina desired to furnish proper civil government and adequate representation to her counties beyond the mountains, and promising pardon for all insurgents who would swear allegiance to their sovereign state. Many residents sheepishly returned to North Carolina's fold, but many others persisted in their efforts to establish an independent state. Consequently, East Tennessee had two sets of conflicting laws, and two court systems attempting to enforce them.

In neighboring Georgia, the state militia had been powerless to control the widespread burning and pillaging of outlying settlements by the savage Creek Indians. Governor George Matthews appealed to the man known throughout the South as the Scourge of the Cherokee, asking for an expeditionary force under his command. Matthews offered two inducements: each of Sevier's volunteers would receive a sizable land grant in the Bend of Tennessee area; and (which was of far greater importance to Sevier) the State of Georgia would actively support Franklin's acceptance into the federal union. The expedition was a success, but in spite of Georgia's sponsorship, Franklin's application for statehood was denied.

During the entire life-span of the State of Franklin, Spain not only owned both Florida and Louisiana, but claimed the lands on both sides of the Mississippi River including all of future Tennessee west of the Hiwassee and Clinch rivers. Don Estevan Miro, the Governor of New Orleans, was a man of great charm and political acumen. By promising a profitable market for their productions, and protection from the Indians, he tried to persuade the settlers in states along the Mississippi to sever their ties with the United States and become citizens of Spain. He so impressed Middle Tennessee's leaders that, in early 1788, they chose the misspelled name Mero District for the area on the Cumberland Plateau comprising Davidson, Sumner, and Tennessee counties. John Sevier then made one last desperate attempt to save his faltering state. He began corresponding secretly with officials at New Orleans, who had offered the State of Franklin the status of a Spanish province.

It was at this point that Governor Samuel Johnston of North Carolina issued an order to the sheriff of Washington County, commanding him to apprehend "John Sevier, who styles himself captain-general of the State of Franklin, [and] has been guilty of high treason, in levying troops to oppose the laws and government of the State...and...order him to be committed to the public gaol."

Some days later, Sevier was arrested, manacled, and taken under armed guard to Morganton, North Carolina, where a court was convened to try him for high treason. Two of his sons, James and John, went to Morganton with a few friends, arriving singly and unnoticed among the crowds that had gathered to witness the trial. As court was adjourning in the evening, these friends created a mock disturbance in which court officers and spectators became embroiled. In the confusion,

John Sevier and his sons rode out of Morganton and across the mountains, beyond pursuit. Back at the courthouse, Sevier's co-commander at the Battle of King's Mountain, Colonel Charles McDowell, was making bond for his release.

In November, 1788, North Carolina's General Assembly passed an act granting pardon to all who had taken part in the Franklin "revolt" *except John Sevier*, who was specifically barred from any office of profit, honor, or trust, anywhere in the State. Sevier's arrest had convinced even the die-hard Greene Countians that statehood for Franklin was a lost cause, but they found a way of showing their abiding loyalty to its erstwhile governor: blatantly ignoring the legislative interdict, they elected John Sevier to represent Greene County in the Senate of North Carolina. He had already arrived in Fayetteville when the legislature convened there on November 2, 1789, but "on account of disabilities" he tactfully waited a few days before presenting himself to the Senate. This delay allowed time for the General Assembly to repeal the clause barring him from public office, and to reinstate him as brigadier general for the western counties.

Taking his seat in the Senate of North Carolina, he voted (of course) for the second cession of the portion of the state he represented. It is entirely possible that North Carolina had found her western counties too hot to handle, and was glad to be rid of them. Be that as it may, this time the legislators were not "Indian givers."

As a state senator, Sevier was a member of the North Carolina convention that ratified the Constitution of the United States— at long last. North Carolina was then divided into four congressional districts, and in 1790, John Sevier was elected to the U.S. House of Representatives from the western district of the very state that had tried him for high treason.

While attending Congress in Philadelphia, he sat for a portrait-miniature painted by Charles Willson Peale. It depicts a middle-aged man with a lengthy nose, abundant graying hair, and bright blue eyes, in the dress uniform of a militia officer with the two stars of a brigadier general on one epaulet.

Sevier's seat in Congress was abolished when his district became a federal territory, but he kept his cherished military rank: President Washington appointed him brigadier general for the Southwest Territory's Washington District.

The federal government wasted no time in placing North Carolina's ceded lands under the jurisdiction of the State Department, and authorizing an on-site government for this area so far removed from the national capital. The Territory's citizens were pleased with their new governor, William Blount, who had represented North Carolina at the Hopewell treaty-meeting, and had vehemently protested the inclusion of mid-East Tennessee in the Indian Territory.

Blount further endeared himself to the people by appointing Brigadier General Sevier to serve as one of the United States Commissioners at the Holston treaty-meeting. This was more than a shrewd political move on Blount's part, since John Sevier's presence at the meeting would virtually guarantee the safety of the Governor and his party: The Cherokee chiefs had a healthy fear of the man who had fought— and outfought— them many times.

After the Cherokee declaration of war against the United States in 1792, General Sevier spent most of his time at Knoxville, the southern tip of settlement in East Tennessee, which lay directly in the path of the Cherokee and their fierce Creek allies. The U.S. Army's Blockhouse was solely for the defense of the Territory's capital, so it was up to Sevier and his militia to protect the settlers in outlying areas. He began by identifying the largest and sturdiest fort or station in each sector, and assigning a detachment of militia to guard it. He then notified all the families on widely scattered farms that, at the first hint of trouble, their women and children should take shelter at the nearest fort, and remain there until he sent word that the danger was past. He established his own headquarters south of the river at Ish's Station, the outpost closest to the Cherokee towns on the Little Tennessee.

When scouts reported that a thousand Cherokee and Creek warriors were approaching Knoxville, it was peaceable James White who rounded up the men of the vicinity to help defend the town. Every able-bodied settler answered the call to arms, including the Reverend Samuel Carrick whose beloved wife had just died at their home beside the Holston River. (That night, courageous neighbor women floated Elizabeth Carrick's body downstream in a dugout canoe, and buried her by starlight in the churchyard at Lebanon-in-the-Forks.)

Before dawn on September 25, 1793, White deployed his forty riflemen along the Indians' route, a mile northwest of the Blockhouse where the Army garrison would be making a last stand, and waited to ambush the war party that never came. The sun was high in the sky when black smoke from the funeral pyre at Cavett's Station appeared on the western horizon. To avenge the massacred Cavett family, John Sevier led one last expedition against the Indian towns. After Etowah was burned, and its ashes scattered, the Cherokee War was over in East Tennessee.

Unfortunately, some of the Cherokee's Creek allies stayed on in the Knoxville area to pillage and burn. Several times the militia was called out to protect the settlers "forting" at Manefee's Station to the north of town, at Wells' Station to the west, and elsewhere. George Mann became Knox County's last victim of an Indian massacre on May 25, 1795, when he surprised a raiding party at his barn (near Tazewell Pike). As the Creeks then crept toward the nearby cabin, Indian file, Mrs. Mann saved her children's lives by wounding the first and second savages in line with a single rifle bullet, fired through a crack in the door. Carrying their wounded leaders, the marauders fled.

Great changes were in the making for Knoxville, and for John Sevier. He was not a delegate to the convention held in January, 1796, to draft a constitution for Tennessee, but he obviously conferred with Governor Blount beforehand. Blount was following the example of the Lost State of Franklin when he organized a complete government months before statehood became official. (This procedure, since known as the "Tennessee Plan," has been copied by several petitioning territories, including Alaska.)

The outcome of the gubernatorial election was never in doubt. The voters had always meant for John Sevier to be the governor of their state when it entered the Union, and they were only sorry it was not called Franklin. They liked a name that meant "a free man" better than one borrowed from the Cherokee's "river of the big bend."

After Tennessee became a state on June 1, 1796, the Governor was required by law to live in the capital; however, his family did not arrive in Knoxville until the following year. John Sevier's two wives had presented him with seventeen children, and even though the eldest were no longer living at home, the move from Plum Grove was a major undertaking. Governor Sevier liked farm life, and did not agree with most residents of the capital city that log houses were passé. He purchased a plantation south of the river, not far from his former militia headquarters near the Indian towns, and christened it "Marble Springs." There he built a log house very similar to Plum Grove, and surrounded it with outbuildings: a spring-house where crocks of milk and butter were immersed in cool flowing water; a corn-crib for storing ears still in their shucks; a smoke-house in which fresh-killed meat was cured by long smoking over a fire of green hickory wood; a barn with a hay-loft above its stalls; and a weaving-house where a flat-bed loom produced linsey-woolsey, that well-nigh indestructible pioneer material with a warp of strong linen threads and a weft of wool. The main house contained only one very large room with an overhead sleeping loft, and a lean-to kitchen. Compared with sophisticated Ramsey House, which was built in the same area in the same year, Marble Springs was primitive in the extreme; however, it represented comfort and convenience in rural Tennessee at the end of the 18th century.

Much as he liked plantation living, Sevier found Marble Springs too inconvenient for a governor's residence. By the time Bonny Kate and the children joined him in Knoxville, he had rented a commodious town house from Charles McClung. This two-story frame dwelling (which stood on the southwest corner of Cumberland and Central avenues until the 1920's) had a long one-story wing at the rear, so there was room not only for family living quarters but for the state offices.

(Very little office space was needed by the State of Tennessee at a time when there was not much business to transact, and almost no money to administer. Although Knoxville remained the seat of government for fifteen years, the State never owned a capitol building here.)

Tennessee's first "first lady" made no attempt to copy the Blounts' lavish lifestyle, but she was equally hospitable— in a way that was less intimidating to the average Tennessean: no relative, friend, King's Mountain veteran, or political petitioner left her home without "partaking of refreshment." To return the invitations of capital city "society," she frequently entertained at tea, and did so with considerable formality.

Three times in succession, the voters elected John Sevier to a two-year term as governor, but since the state constitution limited a governor's successive terms to three, someone else had to take over the office in 1801. The Seviers retired to Marble Springs while Archibald Roane, a Knoxville lawyer, served as Tennessee's second governor until 1803. Then there was no legal reason why John Sevier should not be governor again, for another three terms if he and the people saw fit. Everyone agreed that this would be a good idea— except Archibald Roane, who announced his candidacy for a second term.

Roane's supporters felt that the only way to overcome Sevier's enormous personal popularity was to discredit him with the voters, and they tried the same smear-tactics that had ousted William Blount from the United States Senate. But when Roane's advisors publicly accused Sevier of dishonest dealings in the public lands, they overlooked one salient fact: The people of Tennessee never believed that William Blount was guilty of conspiracy. Nor did they believe that John Sevier was guilty of fraud. This was the same man they had elected to the North Carolina Senate in the face of charges of high treason, and they elected John Sevier to a fourth gubernatorial term by a very large majority.

Yet bitter and acrimonious things had been said on both sides, and the campaign left its scars. Andrew Jackson, who was then Superior Court Judge for East Tennessee, had supported Roane and had supplied the evidence on which the land-fraud charges were based. Shortly after Sevier's inauguration, while Jackson was holding court in Knoxville, the two men met on the street. Sevier violently denounced Jackson to his face for his part in the campaign, and the fiery Jackson replied in the same vein. As James Phelan's *History of Tennessee* reports,

> *Jackson's anger flamed out at [a] reference to his wife, and he made desperate efforts to reach Sevier, but was restrained. Jackson, seeing his antagonist with a drawn cutlass, and having only a cane himself, prudently yielded to the remonstrances of the bystanders. The next day, he sent a challenge [to a duel]. Sevier returned a mocking reply, accepting for any time and place "not within the State of Tennessee." Jackson insisted on the meeting taking place in the neighborhood of Knoxville, since the insult had been passed here. Sevier declined. "I have some respect," said he, "for the laws of the State over which I have the honor to preside, although you, a judge, appear to have none."*

Eventually, an uneasy peace was patched up between Tennessee's two most popular men, who were much alike in appearance, temperament, and talents.

As everyone had expected, Sevier served another three consecutive terms as governor. Alongside the handsome houses being built by Knoxville's affluent citizens, the makeshift residence-cum-capitol was looking very shabby, so the Governor purchased two lots at the corner of Cumberland and Walnut streets, and laid the foundations for a large V-shaped brick mansion. Shortly thereafter, when Walnut Street was being widened and extended, surveyors found the foundations directly in their path. They moved the street over several feet, to give the Governor house room, but on the other side of Cumberland, they returned it to its intended location. This created a "dog-leg" that caused Walnut Street to be called "Crooked Street" for many years, and is the reason for the jog that is still there today.

In 1809, it was time to change governors again. William Blount was still remembered with respect in Tennessee, and the voters chose his half-brother, Willie Blount, to be the state's third governor.

John Sevier then repeated an earlier phase of his career, but with a difference. He had gone from Governor of the State of Franklin to State Senator of North Carolina, and he now progressed from Governor to State Senator in Tennessee. Recurrence continued in 1811, when he was elected to the U.S. House of Representatives for the second time, from a second state. He was reelected in 1813, and during both his terms, the veteran of the Revolutionary War served on the Military Affairs Committee that concerned itself with a second war against the British.

Andrew Jackson, who became a national military hero during the War of 1812, had already won a hard-fought war against the Creek Indians before he and his Tennessee volunteers won a famous victory over the British at the Battle of New Orleans. The treaty of peace that officially ended the Creek War was signed in 1815. John Sevier's reputation as the greatest Indian fighter of all time had preceded him to Washington, and President James Monroe called on him to run and mark the boundary line stipulated in the treaty. Sevier set out for Alabama in late summer, accompanied by a detachment of U.S. Army troops. Shortly after his departure, he was elected to a third congressional term, but this news never reached him.

On September 24, 1815, John Sevier died suddenly of a fever, at the Indian town of Tuckabatchie. His soldiers buried him near Fort Decatur, Alabama, and erected a cairn of stones above the spot on the banks of a slow-moving stream. For more than seventy years, Tennessee's first governor lay in an isolated grave in another state.

Not that John Sevier was forgotten— he had become a legend in Tennessee, and the story of how he rescued Bonny Kate was repeated to the children at every fireside.

Belatedly, in 1889, the legislature of Tennessee appropriated funds to remove the body of the State's first governor from its distant grave, and re-inter it in the State's first capital. A special train, crowded with state and local dignitaries, quickly made the trip from Knoxville to Alabama, and returned at a funereal pace with the flag-draped casket. Perhaps to atone for the long delay, John Sevier's interment ceremonies on the Courthouse grounds were by far the most elaborate that anyone in the audience had ever seen.

THE PRESENCE OF THE PAST

In time for the Centennial Celebration of one state he had governed, a tall plain shaft of Tennessee marble was erected on the northeast corner of the Old Knox County Courthouse lawn to mark the final resting place of John Sevier. His Bonny Kate had died in 1836 at the home of her son, Dr. Samuel Sevier, in Russellville, Alabama, and Bonny Kate Chapter of the DAR was instrumental in having her remains brought to Knoxville in 1922, for re-burial beside her husband. Then, in 1946, a monument to Sarah Hawkins Sevier was erected by *her* descendants, on the opposite side of John Sevier's grave.

The Seviers never moved into the handsome V-shaped house that stands on Cumberland Avenue, beside the jog in Walnut Street: It was sold unfinished, and remained the home of the prominent Park family for more than a hundred years. The beautifully restored and maintained Sevier-Park House is now the headquarters of the Knoxville Academy of Medicine.

Marble Springs Plantation, on Neubert Springs Road, is appropriately reached by John Sevier Highway from either the Chapman or the Alcoa Highway. Now the property of the State of Tennessee, it has been restored and opened to the public as a State Historic Shrine. This is the one early home in the Knoxville area that typifies the isolation, and the self-sufficiency, of Tennessee's pioneer families.

CHAPTER FIVE

HUGH LAWSON WHITE, A PRESIDENTIAL CANDIDATE

It is a common fallacy to think of a man well known in history as having moved through the stirring events of his life and times alone—to say, for example, "In 1786, *James White* built the first house on the future site of Knoxville." We may be able to visualize that house in a forest clearing, but we are not apt to people it with Mrs. White and seven children, three boys and four girls!

The Whites' eldest son was "bookish." At thirteen, he was certainly old enough to take part in raising the log house beside First Creek; it could have been his hand that scattered seed over the nearby turnip patch. But even while he was helping to set up the stockade of sharpened stakes that turned his family home into a fort, Hugh Lawson White was probably pressing his parents for further education.

No doubt the Whites considered it providential that one of the earliest settlers in their vicinity was the Reverend Doctor Samuel Carrick, a Presbyterian minister with an excellent education and a willingness to impart his knowledge. At fifteen, Hugh was sent to live with the Carricks at their home five miles east of White's Fort, where Dr. Carrick established the first church in this part of Tennessee, Lebanon-in-the-Forks. Dr. Carrick was often called upon to preach in far-flung settlements. In his absence, Archibald Roane (a recent graduate of Dartmouth College) took over the task of tutoring Hugh in Latin, Greek, ancient and medieval history, natural and moral philosophy, mathematics, physics, and astronomy, with lighter excursions into English literature. Needless to say, Dr. Carrick placed strong emphasis on Holy Writ.

All three of the persons involved in that classical curriculum were important to Knoxville's future, and to Tennessee's. Dr. Carrick organized the First Presbyterian Church in Knoxville, preached the opening sermon for America's first Territorial Legislature, and was the first president of Blount College (now the University of Tennessee).

Archibald Roane, a very able lawyer and a district judge in Knoxville, became Tennessee's second governor. As for Hugh Lawson White, that is a considerably longer story.

At eighteen, he was an interested observer at the Holston treaty-meeting, and shared the excitement when White's Fort was chosen as the site of the Southwest Territory's capital. At twenty, he went to work for his father's friend and business associate, William Blount: for a year, as the Governor's private secretary, he wrote out the official correspondence of the Territory in small, neat script.

Like every other able-bodied male citizen, he belonged to the territorial militia, and he was called to duty at the time of John Sevier's last campaign against the Cherokee. He served as Sevier's aide, and was by the General's side during the attack on Etowah. When Sevier later reported that the great Cherokee chief, King Fisher, was killed in the battle for the town, he refrained from saying who had fired the fatal shot. The bullet came from the gun of Hugh Lawson White, who was horrified and sickened by King Fisher's death at his hands. For the rest of his life, he never mentioned his part in the battle, and he never allowed the Etowah campaign to be discussed in his presence.

Upon reaching his majority, Hugh went north in search of still more education. After a year in Philadelphia, spent studying the practical applications of higher mathematics, he went to Lancaster, Pennsylvania, for a year of intensive reading in the law. Feeling qualified at last to make his way in the world, he returned to Tennessee's first capital in 1796 to practice law, serve as a judge of the Superior Court, and be elected to the State Senate. In 1809, Tennessee's judicial system was revised and a State Supreme Court was created; Hugh Lawson White was appointed one of its first justices.

Knoxville was by now an up and coming town. There were two roads (that would later be known as US 11 E and US 11 W) leading to the northeast, and Charles McClung's turnpike had been extended west beyond Kingston to Nashville. The river was of great importance, but it was a one-way thoroughfare where all the heavily laden rafts and flatboats moved downstream with the current, never to be seen again. (When they reached their final destination, they would be sold along with their cargoes, and broken up for firewood.) Since land travel was so much improved, many stores and taverns had left the crowded waterfront for the top of the plateau, while "manufactories" were springing up alongside First and Second creeks.

Knoxville's first industry had been the mill erected by James White to grind his own and his neighbors' corn into meal. It was a tub-mill, of a type in use throughout most of recorded history: water channeled across the angled blades of a horizontal waterwheel turned a vertical driveshaft connected to the grindstone. The mechanism of such a mill could be made entirely of wood, and a large rock already rounded and flattened by nature could be shaped into a millstone without too much difficulty. A dam had been constructed across First Creek to provide a constant flow of water through the mill-flume, and it had backed the creek up to and beyond the Flag Pond in the ravine at the north end of the plateau.

James White's gristmill worked so well that other water-powered industries were soon in operation along both large creeks. Cotton and flax were staple crops in East Tennessee's early years, and every farm had a small flock of sheep. There were therefore spinning-mills producing linen, wool, and cotton thread, and a press for extracting linseed oil. In addition, the town could boast a foundry, a papermill, and an ironstone-pottery.

Up to this time, Knoxville had struggled along with a frontier economy based in large part upon a barter system, in which "cash" meant coin. As stores burgeoned and industries multiplied, it became obvious that a bank was needed to furnish credit, issue convenient paper money, and serve as a safe repository for heavy, bulky coins.

No one was more aware of this situation than Mr. Justice White, and in 1811 he embarked upon a new career for which his education had uniquely qualified him. In that year, the Bank of the State of Tennessee was established, and he was elected its president even though he was serving on the State Supreme Court. He managed to fill both positions until 1814, when he resigned from the court in order to devote his full energies to the bank that was of primary importance to his city. As soon as the Bank of Tennessee opened on the northwest corner of Gay and Main streets, it began to issue paper money in the form of bank-notes which, unlike the notes of Nashville and Virginia banks, continued to be accepted everywhere at face value. In spite of the banking scandals and financial crises that subsequently rocked the state and the nation, White's conservatively managed institution remained financially sound, and was always able to redeem its notes in specie, on demand.

After the deaths of Governor and Mrs. Blount, Willie Blount had moved to Montgomery County in order to develop his own and his brother's land holdings. He was serving as Tennessee's third governor when the state capital was relocated at Nashville in 1812, and angry Knoxvillians blamed him for the change, insisting that he was anxious to increase the value of his Middle Tennessee investments. "Wily is as W[y]lie does", was how they put it.

Governor William Blount had appointed three commissioners— John Adair, Paul Cunningham, and George McNutt— to oversee the lottery that established Knoxville in 1791. These three town-commissioners were retained in office in 1795, when the Territorial Legislature passed an act providing local government for the Territory's capital, and they were reappointed in 1797 when Tennessee's legislature reconfirmed Knoxville's status as the state capital. Even after Knoxville ceased to be Tennessee's capital, the town's commissioners continued to be appointed by the legislature. As time passed, new appointees were less vigilant in the performance of their duties.

After the establishment of Knox County in 1792, the County Court considered itself the governing body for the entire area within the county's boundaries, including the county seat. In 1814, the Court was so dissatisfied with the town commissioners' work that it appointed the first grand jury to examine and report upon some obvious eyesores. The jury, whose grandiose title was "The Grand Inquest for the Body of the County," returned an indictment that declared the abandoned U.S. Army blockhouse a "public nuisance", and the County Court sent a copy of the report to Congressman John Sevier with the request that he ask the federal government to remove the building.

Knoxvillians took umbrage. It was all very well for Knox County to maintain a courthouse and a jail on Main Street, and to be responsible for pike roads and ferries, but the County Court had no business trying to take over Knoxville. A town with almost a thousand inhabitants had special needs that could only be met by a municipal government whose officials were elected by its own citizens. In response to a strongly-worded petition, the City of Knoxville was incorporated by the state legislature in 1815, and Thomas Emmerson, a prominent lawyer, was chosen by his duly elected fellow aldermen as the city's first mayor.

A few doors up the street from the Bank of Tennessee, Thomas Humes began constructing a dual-purpose Renaissance style building at the corner of Gay and Cumberland. It would have contained a street-floor mercantile establishment, with family living quarters above, had its owner not died suddenly in 1816. The three-story, fifteen room brick building became the city's newest and finest hotel in 1817, just in time to welcome the state legislators when Tennessee's capital returned to Knoxville for a one-year stay.

By this time, farms and towns were dotting Middle Tennessee, and even West Tennessee (which was not finally acquired from the Indians until 1818) was beginning to build up. People in the western portions of the state were saying that Tennessee now extended in reality from the Great Smokies to the mighty Mississippi, and that the state capital ought to be halfway in between.

In the days when the state had neither buildings nor full-time employees, no expense was involved in moving the capital, and only the innkeepers in the chosen city profited from the legislature's presence. There was, however, considerable distinction attached to being the capital city, and Knoxvillians bitterly resented the legislators' decision to meet in Murfreesboro in 1818. A committee consulted the man who had come to be known as Hugh Lawson White, the Just. If he said "Keep the capital" they were prepared to put up a fight for it.

White said exactly the opposite. He pointed out that it would indeed be fairer if the capital were equally accessible from all sections of the state, and he reminded his fellow citizens that Knoxville was no longer the last outpost of civilization; the frontier had moved west, years ago. Their city had clearly demonstrated that it did not have to be the capital of Tennessee in order to thrive and prosper: while the legislature was convening elsewhere, Knoxville had become the hub of finance, trade, and industry for a wide area while maintaining the reputation of a cultural center. Within the last two years, three important "refinements" had been added. Frederick S. Heiskell's erudite *Knoxville Register* was a newspaper to be proud of, and the new Hampden-Sydney Academy not only offered a splendid classical curriculum for boys, but also housed a fine subscription library. (Its 48 members included one lady, the widowed Mrs. Thomas Humes.)

So with Hugh White's blessing, but with an occasional backward glance, the capital of Tennessee moved permanently to the state's mid-section. (As late as 1840, there was a strong movement in East Tennessee to bring the capital "back where it belonged.")

Hugh White was Knoxville's most respected citizen, but another member of his family was enjoying well-earned admiration. When James White moved to his second home, east of First Creek, he gave a nearby tract of land to his daughter Melinda. Her husband, Colonel John Williams, was to have a most distinguished career: after serving under Andrew Jackson in the Creek War and the War of 1812, he was

U.S. Minister to Guatemala under President John Quincy Adams, and represented Tennessee in the U.S. Senate from 1815 to 1823. When Colonel Williams returned from the wars, Melinda was waiting for him in a brand-new home. She had designed a large and handsome house for her plantation property, and had taken her servants to the site to build it; she supervised every step of its construction, from the firing of the first bricks to the installation of the last doorknob. The crowning surprise for John Williams was a small private law office for him, in the front yard. Melinda's house was so pleasing to look upon and so comfortable to live in that her sister Mary (Mrs. John Overton) copied it almost exactly in Nashville, at "Travellers Rest."

In 1820, Melinda's brother began to talk of retiring from the bank— his health, he said, was poor, and he was getting on in years— but a man of Hugh White's capabilities could not possibly be permitted to retire at forty-seven. He was still president of the bank in 1821, when President James Monroe appointed him a Claims-Commissioner during the transfer of Florida's ownership from Spain to the United States. With two other judges, he presided over a Court of Claims where monetary disputes arising out of the treaty provisions were heard and settled. The legally and financially astute White was a splendid choice for the Claims Commission, and he enjoyed his challenging duties.

In Knoxville, the mayor and aldermen had been taking their responsibilities very seriously, voting in 1817 to spend the munificent sum of $340 on street improvements. All the streets were surfaced with hard-packed clay that turned to sticky red mire in rainy weather, and stepping stones were required at every corner. Improving them meant leveling out the deep and permanent wheel-ruts dug by heavy-loaded wagons. A few years later, the city fathers levied an *ad valorem* tax: all the money collected from property owners along a street was spent on keeping that particular street in repair.

In 1822, they purchased a fine hand-pumper fire engine that consisted of a water-reservoir on wheels with an eight-foot-long brass nozzle, but no hose. In case of fire, the water tank was kept filled by a bucket brigade. The aldermen then organized all male residents between the ages of fifteen and fifty into a volunteer fire company, and passed an ordinance requiring every household to own *two* leather fire buckets. They reasoned that, in fighting a fire on Gay Street, men would have to form a line and hand full water-buckets uphill from First Creek, while women and children formed a second line to pass the empty buckets back down hill.

Claims Commissioner White had completed his work in Florida (but was *still* president of the bank) when he was elected to the United States Senate in 1825. He replaced Andrew Jackson, with whom he had become well acquainted during the years when they both were lawyers and judges in Knoxville.

The trip to Washington was long and arduous, and after two years of hurrying back and forth in an attempt to juggle two demanding jobs, Senator White resigned as president of the Bank of Tennessee in 1827, and flatly refused to reconsider his decision. The bank's directors obviously considered him irreplaceable, for after publishing a lengthy resolution praising his probity and financial acumen, they liquidated the bank!

Knoxvillians saw a steamboat for the first time in 1828, when the wood-burning sidewheeler *Atlas* steamed majestically upstream, trailing a white plume from her smokestack, and saluted the wildly cheering crowds on shore with a boom from the small cannon on her afterdeck. Her captain was host to local dignitaries on a cruise to the Forks of the River, and was himself the guest of honor at an elaborate reception.

The *Atlas* had conclusively shown that it was possible for traffic on the Tennessee River to move upstream as well as down. A group of local investors promptly commissioned a steamboat from a Cincinnati shipyard, and the long-delayed arrival of the *Knoxville* in 1831 was greeted with great rejoicing. Muscle Shoals was still a barrier on the waterway to the sea, but the legislature appropriated funds for dredging a continuous channel, with a minimum depth of a full twenty-four inches "at extreme low water," from Knoxville to the Alabama line. By 1835, the upper Tennessee River was passable for rafts and flatboats all year long, and for steamboats whenever the water was deepened by heavy rain (which usually meant from November to June).

Senator White, who was spending much of his time in Washington, saw economic growth in Knoxville each time he came home, and he was pleased to note an increase in cultural advantages. Professional actors had first performed in the city in 1823, when Samuel Drake's well-known travelling troupe converted a Gay Street building into a temporary theatre and presented a comedy called "The Honeymoon," followed by an afterpiece entitled "The Hunters of the Alps, or, Unexpected Happiness." This premier production was well received, and Drake's actors spread the word that they had found a good theatre-town; by the 1830's Knoxville had become a regular stop for several theatrical touring companies.

Scholarly Hugh White was delighted when the Knoxville Female Academy opened in 1827. In its fine brick building on Main Street (at the present site of Church Street United Methodist Church), young ladies were introduced to literature, history, geography, and the arts as represented by vocal and piano music, watercolor painting, and fine embroidery. He heartily endorsed the Knoxville Lyceum which began offering a monthly series of improving lectures, plus debates on timely topics, in 1831.

As a traveller, he welcomed the advent of the stagecoaches that provided public transportation not only to the eastern cities, and to Nashville by the new and vastly better Walton Road, but to Kentucky (via Jacksboro Pike and Cumberland Gap) and, through Maryville, all the way to the seacoast at Savannah, Georgia. The first stage of the Knoxville-to-Nashville route followed Kingston Pike— past hilltop East Tennessee College, Drury P. Armstrong's riverside "Crescent Bend," and Charles McClung's "Statesview"— to Campbell's Station where Samuel Martin operated two stores, a race-track, and an inn. Business was so brisk that, in 1835, he built a large brick annex onto David Campbell's original log station.

In 1835, Andrew Jackson's second term as President of the United States was half over. He was determined to have his policies carried on, and he demanded that the Democratic Party nominate Martin Van Buren to succeed him. This high-handed attitude was unpopular in the South, where people believed that no President should remain in office for more than two terms, and that no incumbent should attempt to influence the voters who were choosing the next chief executive. Nowhere were those beliefs more firmly entrenched than in Andrew Jackson's home state, and the General Assembly of Tennessee proved it by formally nominating for President of the United States— Senator Hugh Lawson White!

Andrew Jackson and James K. Polk, the leaders of the Democratic Party in Tennessee, had been White's close political friends and allies for many years and confidently expected him to decline the "favorite son" nomination. But White held the same views as did the legislators. He accepted the mandate of the General Assembly, and ran for President as an independent candidate, with the endorsement of the newly formed Whig Party. He had little chance of actually being elected, and he knew it. The Democrats had dutifully nominated Van Buren, and Jackson's influence in his behalf would be felt throughout the country, while the name of Hugh Lawson White was virtually unknown outside his own state. His purpose in campaigning was to stand up for a principle he held dear. He and his principle were both approved by the people of his state, for in spite of bitter opposition from the leading Democrats in strongly Democratic Tennessee, Presidential candidate White carried the state by a margin of ten thousand votes. In 1836 in Tennessee, a ten thousand vote majority was astounding.

White had not resigned his seat when he ran for President, and after his predictable defeat by Martin Van Buren, he gladly returned to the Senate. His colleagues, who had always admired him for his scrupulous honesty and his reasoned judgement, now admired him all the more as a man who had the courage of his convictions.

Although he was away in Washington, Senator White was well aware that 1838 was a sorrowful year for Tennessee. The forcible expulsion of the Cherokee from their homeland must have brought back haunting memories of Chief King Fisher's death and the burning of the town of Etowah, but the news that the steamboat *Knoxville* was involved in the exodus was surely a surprise. The first locally owned steamboat had not been a profitable venture for its Knoxville investors. Under new ownership, she was renamed the *Indian Chief* in 1838, and plied the Tennessee River below Muscle Shoals, conveying groups of Cherokee to the west.

Spring rains were exceptionally heavy in the Knoxville area in 1838, and the creeks and rivers were already full to overflowing when a torrential downpour created flash floods on First and Second creeks. A towering wall of water swept through each narrow valley, washing out all the dams and inundating mills and factories; in the aftermath of the flood, the Flag Pond in the northern ravine drained away to a shadow of its former self. This natural disaster that wiped out all the dams might have been the end of industry in Knoxville, but instead it was a blessing in disguise. The factories were soon back in operation, with a difference. Dams were no longer needed, since their power was now provided not by waterwheels, but by new-fangled steam engines.

Hugh White had always been a man of principle, and his firmly held convictions did not change as he grew older. It was over a matter of principle that he and the Tennessee General Assembly reached the parting of the ways in 1839. The legislators contended that Tennessee's United States Senators, who were not elected by popular ballot but were chosen by the General Assembly, represented the state's law-making body rather than the citizens of the state. Having so said, they undertook to instruct Tennessee's senior Senator how to vote on national issues. Now, this was a point of principle on which former Tennessee Supreme Court Justice White's stand was unequivocal. Government in the United States, he informed the legislators, was by and with the consent of the governed. He was representing the people of Tennessee, *only*. To make his position unmistakably clear to the people he had always represented to the best of his ability, he resigned from the United States Senate and published a full explanation of his action.

On January 11, 1840, Hugh Lawson White finally attained the retirement he had looked forward to for twenty years. It came too late, for he had hardly arrived in Knoxville when he died on April 10.

"The Honorable Hugh L. White: 'He has ever been faithful in confided trusts.'" That toast, offered at a testimonial dinner in his honor at Nashville while he was a candidate for President, sums up in one short sentence his exemplary career on the bench, in banking, and in public office. It says nothing of the sensitive and scholarly man whose private life was scarred by a tragedy that was all too typical of his times.

While he was a student living in the home of Dr. Samuel Carrick, he met his future wife Elizabeth, the intelligent and extremely attractive daughter of his mentor. They were married in 1798, and became the parents of twelve children, two of whom died in infancy. Their eldest son was a brilliant young lawyer, married and the father of two children, when his health began to fail at twenty-seven; there was no cure for Carrick White's malady, "galloping consumption." One by one, their other children contracted that most dreaded of diseases, for which there was neither treatment nor hope. Eight young Whites died of tuberculosis within a short six years.

In 1831, Elizabeth developed the tell-tale symptoms. When Hugh received an urgent summons to the Senate, she urged him to go, and to take her with him. She had accompanied him to Washington several times, and knew how strenuous the journey would be; this time, she packed a small trunk with the clothes in which she wished to be buried. It was on the return trip to Knoxville that the need for them arose. The Whites were travelling in a comfortable carriage, followed by a wagon with their baggage. They halted for the night at Natural Bridge, Virginia, and Elizabeth died there. After a coffin had been hastily procured, and servants had unpacked the little trunk, it is said that Hugh himself drove the baggage wagon that brought Elizabeth's body home.

Senator White, bereft of his wife and all but two of his twelve children, returned to Washington a desperately lonely man. Within the year, he married Mrs. Ann Peyton, a charming widow whose select boarding house was a home away from home for many famous members of the Congress and the Cabinet. She encouraged him to run for President, and willingly gave up her Washington residence to retire with him to Knoxville. Hugh's old friends had hardly welcomed the distinguished couple before Ann was receiving calls of condolence.

Although he was a man of strict morality and uncompromising rectitude, Hugh White was not a church-goer. He had neither attended the Presbyterian church in which he was born and educated, nor the Methodist church to which he had donated its first site in Knoxville. Funeral services were held at his home that overlooked the city from Flint Hill, and in keeping with the custom of the day, they were attended by men only; mourners who could not crowd inside the house waited outside on the lawn to take their places in the procession to the cemetery. Immediately behind the hearse, Hugh White's favorite horse, Rienzi, was led riderless. Then walked the dignitaries of church and government, bench and bar; the faculty and students of East Tennessee College, of which he was a trustee; the teachers and pupils of Hampden-Sydney Academy; and his friends and admirers from all walks of life.

Hugh Lawson White was travelling back in time as the cortege crossed the wooden bridge above First Creek and climbed slowly to the graveyard beside the small First Presbyterian Church— back to the original plot of ground he had helped his father clear before a capital city was imagined, and before there was any thought of a State of Tennessee that would support his candidacy for President of the United States.

THE PRESENCE OF THE PAST

James White constructed a sturdy log house here in 1786, but it was May Lawson White who built Knoxville's first home. She was greatly loved and admired by her family, and her descendants continue to call their daughters "Lawson" in her honor. Exactly a hundred years after the Whites' arrival, Knoxville's public library was established as a memorial to her great granddaughter, Lawson McGhee, who was the granddaughter of Hugh Lawson White.

Still standing— but just barely— at 2325 Dandridge Avenue is the house built by Melinda White Williams in 1815 to surprise her husband, John. (Their 20th century descendant, Thomas Lanier Williams, changed his first name to emphasize his heritage. As Tennessee Williams, he became a famous playwright.) The Williams house was purchased by the State of Tennessee in 1881, and was the meticulously maintained Colored Branch of the Tennessee School for the Deaf for more than eighty years. Now empty and in disrepair, it is still state property.

The Renaissance style building that graces the corner of Gay Street and Cumberland Avenue was built by 1816, became a hotel in 1817, and has been known since the 1850's as the Lamar House. A strange thing happened to it in 1848, when Gay Street was regraded in preparation for paving: the Cumberland Avenue corner was lowered some twelve feet, and the three-story building became four floors tall! The hotel's former basement rose to street level, and the original entrance, elevated high above the sidewalk, acquired an ornamental iron balcony that was perfect for political speech-making. Five Presidents of the United States— Andrew Jackson, James K. Polk, Andrew Johnson, Ulysses S. Grant, and Rutherford B. Hayes— visited the hotel in its palmy days, and it was commandeered for an officers' hospital during the Siege of Knoxville in 1863. The Bijou Theatre was added onto the rear of the historic building in 1909. After a long period of neglect, the Lamar House/Bijou became a Knoxville/Knox County Bicentennial Project in 1976; the Bijou Theatre has since been restored by Knoxville Heritage, Inc., as a community center for the performing arts.

The Armstong-Lockett House at 2728 Kingston Pike was called "Crescent Bend" when it was built by Drury P. Armstrong in 1832. It has been the property of the Toms Foundation since the 1970's, and serves as an elegant showcase for the fine collection of 18th century furniture and silver amassed by William Perry Toms. The dining room walls are decorated with the handpainted scenic wallpaper that was ordered from Paris in 1833 by Colonel Joseph Scott, for his house (now Stevens Mortuary) on Oglewood Avenue, near North Broadway. When Colonel Scott's house became a church in 1946, Ellen McClung Berry rescued the colorful paper. It was removed with its canvas backing, restored, and later rehung at Crescent Bend, which was opening as a house museum.

Robert Houston, the first sheriff of Knox County, owned a large tract of land east of Knoxville which he christened "Cold Spring Farm." According to tradition, he built the spacious red brick house at 2639

Martin Luther King Avenue, some years before his death in 1834. Since it was enlarged and modernized at the turn of the 20th century, this early residence has been Mount Rest Home "for destitute elderly ladies."

The substantial brick residence at the corner of Kingston Pike and Campbell's Station Road was erected in 1835, as a "modern addition" to the log station built by David Campbell in 1787. The historic inn went out of business after stagecoach travel was made obsolete by passenger trains, and its large brick annex became the home of the Russell family. In November of 1863, the Battle of Campbell's Station was waged along nearby Turkey Creek.

CHAPTER SIX

 ## ANTEBELLUM KNOXVILLE

Memory, like the sundial, marks only shining hours. Trapped in the nightmare that was Knoxville during the War Between the States, people looked back upon the two preceding decades as "the happy times."

An elaborate celebration of Knoxville's Semi-centennial was held on February 10, 1842. It began with a lengthy and fulsome oration by the Episcopal minister, Thomas W. Humes, and concluded with a sumptuous "temperance" banquet at which a total of 53 toasts were drunk in clear spring water. (It was not the fault of the event's organizers that the city's 50th birthday party was held in the wrong year. They relied on a letter from Hugh Dunlap, the sole survivor of the original lot holders, who mistakenly recalled that the town lottery had taken place in February of 1792 instead of in October, 1791.)

In the 1840's, education was of paramount importance. Blount College had changed its name in 1807 to East Tennessee College, and had moved in 1828 to a dignified square brick building with a tall tower, on top of "Barbara Hill." The college was searching for a new president in 1834, and the trustees brought off a coup by luring Joseph Estabrook away from the Knoxville Female Academy: the girls' school had far outshone its all-male counterpart, Hampden-Sydney Academy, while he was serving as its principal. Estabrook, a graduate of Dartmouth, saw no reason why East Tennessee College should not offer a course of study comparable to that of the best eastern institutions of higher learning. To that end, he revised the curriculum, brought in a faculty of well-educated and dedicated teachers, and insisted on quality performance from the students. He also embarked upon an ambitious building program, and by 1837, handsome brick dormitories stood on either side of the original "Old College." Estabrook's achievements did not go unnoticed. The college, having attained larger scope, was promoted to university status by the legislature in 1840, and the campus became known as University Hill, or simply as "The Hill."

Regarding these achievements as a challenge, the Knoxville Female Academy amended its charter in 1846; as the East Tennessee Female Institute, it began conferring upon its graduates the degree of "Mistress of Polite Literature."

When the state legislature established a school for the blind at Nashville in 1843, representatives from East Tennessee succeeded in securing a similar school for deaf mutes in Knoxville. In 1848, its few pupils moved from a rented house to an elegant Greek Revival building, on a knoll diagonally across the Second Creek valley from the hilltop quadrangle of the University, and by 1861, Knoxville's Deaf and Dumb Asylum was among the nation's largest and finest schools for the hearing handicapped. (The word "asylum" had no unpleasant connotations; it was used in its original sense, "a safe and sheltered refuge.")

At the outbreak of the Mexican War, President James K. Polk's call for 2,000 men from his home state of Tennessee was answered by an astonishing 30,000 volunteers. In 1846, the Knoxville Dragoons marched proudly off to war, attired in bright blue swallow-tail coats and white-plumed kepis held in place by chin-straps; two other volunteer companies left Knoxville in the following year. People long remembered the splendid uniforms of the local units, and the stirring music of the Knoxville Military Brass Band; but at the time, they almost forgot the faraway war in the excitement of getting ready for important company.

The railroad was coming at last! In 1848, the East Tennessee & Georgia Railway began laying 145 miles of track that would give Knoxville access to a main line between Savannah and Atlanta, and it was no coincidence that Dr. J.G.M. Ramsey was in charge of selling the state-issued railroad bonds. Twenty years earlier, he had first suggested the feasibility of a rail connection to the sea. Charles McClung's ten-street Territorial Capital had grown to cover the "high defensible plateau" selected as its site by William Blount, and the low-lying level ravine at the north end of town would be the perfect place to put the railroad tracks.

In west Knox County, the line was to follow the river, by-passing Campbell's Station, and a new town called Concord sprang up beside the right-of-way to be the shipping point for marble from the nearby quarries. The small depot at the Erin community was named Bearden Station for Marcus deLafayette Bearden, an investor in railroads and former steamboat captain who, with his cousin Gideon Morgan Hazen, owned a steam-assisted paper factory beside Third Creek, on Papermill Road. (His son, Marcus D. Bearden, would become Knoxville's mayor in 1868-69.)

By this time, regular steamboat passenger service was available from the docks at the foot of Gay Street, which had attracted three-fourths of all the city's business establishments. Main Street was next in importance, and in 1851, the Board of Aldermen decreed that those two streets should be paved with river rock and given new sidewalks eleven feet wide. (The width of all other sidewalks would remain four and a half feet.)

Obviously neither of those fine paved streets should any longer be lined with the curb markets that had been supplying Knoxville households with farm-fresh vegetables and live poultry, but two civic- (and profit-) minded citizens solved the produce problem in 1853. William G. Swan and Joseph A. Mabry, Jr. jointly presented to the city a square block on Prince (now Market) Street, on condition that a suitable market house be built there; a reversionary clause in the deed of gift required the square to be returned to the donors' heirs should it ever cease to be used as a public market place. The delighted aldermen at once began construction of a long, one-story brick building filled with market stalls that opened in the center of the square on January 30, 1854.

Citizens took pride in the fact that Knoxville was beginning to be known as "the city of churches." Since 1820, the block of Prince Street just south of the new Market Square had been occupied by the sanctuary and the cemetery of Second Presbyterian Church. In 1818, doctrinal disputes (plus a disagreement over pew rental) had caused a rift among the city's Presbyterians. The original congregation had long since outgrown the small brick meeting house begun in 1812, and a handsome new First Presbyterian Church was finally going up on the land donated by James White. (As the Civil War approached, these two churches were divided anew: First Presbyterian was referred to as "a hotbed of secessionism" by members of Second Presbyterian, who tended to support the Union cause.)

Little "White's Chapel," Knoxville's earliest Methodist church, was built in 1816 on land donated by Hugh Lawson White. In 1834, its enlarging membership moved into the fine new Church Street Methodist Church, located between Prince and Walnut streets. Although Baptist congregations had existed in Knox County since the late 1700's, no church was organized within the city until 1843. Its founders chose a site on Gay Street for the First Baptist Church. In 1845, the cornerstone of St. John's Episcopal Church was laid at the corner of Cumberland and Walnut, across from the Park family's V-shaped home begun by John Sevier; the church had been founded one year earlier, by the Reverend Thomas W. Humes. There were very few Roman Catholic families in Knoxville, but in 1852, Mass was celebrated for the first time in a tiny brick mission chapel, on Summit Hill.

Only the Presbyterian churches had downtown graveyards, and in 1850, the members of other denominations welcomed the opening of a new cemetery outside the city limits toward the north. (Several meetings of plot-purchasers were held before a name could be agreed upon. Finally, a lady quoted from the "Elegy in a Country Churchyard," and suggested the name Gray Cemetery in honor of the popular poem's author, Thomas Gray.)

Ever since Territorial days, public lighting had been limited on Knoxville's dark streets to the bobbing lanterns of night watchmen, who called out the time and weather while keeping an eye peeled for suspicious loiterers and signs of fire, but William Churchwell and William G. Swan convinced the aldermen that a city with a Market Square and a railroad to the sea should shine by night as well as by day. The gas-works they built in 1855 beside the river, at the foot of Locust Street, was a huge brick oven in which coal roasted at high temperature released a flammable mixture of hydrogen, methane, and carbon dioxide. After such impurities as ammonia and tar had been removed by filtering it through water, the illuminating-gas was piped to public lamp posts along Main and Gay Streets, and into the homes and stores of private subscribers. The gas-jets on the street corners were lit one by one at dusk, and extinguished at dawn, by a city-employed lamplighter who carried a long ladder; below the glass-shaded mantle on each lamp post was a metal crossbar to support the ladder's siderails.

Everything seemed to be in readiness as the ET&G tracks approached the city, until someone remarked that the muddy swamp at the edge of the railroad ravine would hardly be a salubrious sight for visitors arriving by train. In a final flurry of preparation, the vestigial Flag Pond was declared a health hazard, and filled in with a two foot layer of tamped clay.

On June 22, 1855, the distant clangor of a bell and the hooting of a steam-whistle blended with the joyous music of the Military Brass Band. The crowd shrank back as the flag-decorated engine bore down like a juggernaut on wheels, and surged forward when the cars filled with dignitaries ground to a halt beside the platform at the depot.

On that day, civic pride was boosted even higher by the announcement that Knoxville was to have *another* railroad, and that track-laying for the East Tennessee & Virginia would begin immediately from both its terminals, Knoxville and Bristol. On May 14, 1858, the last spike was driven at Greeneville, and, as the meeting place of the ET&G and the ET&V, Knoxville was the mid-point of a continuous rail connection between the Northeast and the Deep South. In the future, this would not be an unmixed blessing, but the only immediate concern was that flying sparks from the shuttling switch-engines might start a rash of fires in wooden buildings near the tracks. Therefore, the aldermen purchased two additional brass fire engines for the outlandish sum of $1,200 each, and to ensure a reliable and convenient water-supply for the new hand-pumpers, ordered huge underground cisterns dug at two Gay Street corners.

In 1860, Knoxville was a prosperous and self-satisfied little city of some 5,300 souls, sandwiched between the busy steamboat docks and the bustling railroad depot. That year's census listed Knox County's total population as 22,813, and of that number, 2,370 were slaves.

THE PRESENCE OF THE PAST

It was the response of 30,000 men to President Polk's call for 2,000 Mexican War volunteers that clinched for Tennessee the undisputed title of the Volunteer State. To emphasize this fact, the Color Guard at the University of Tennessee proudly wears the uniform of the Knoxville Dragoons who volunteered in 1846.

Before leaving for the Mexican War, Major Robert Reynolds had begun building a stately hilltop residence with a panoramic view of the Great Smoky Mountains. Construction continued during his absence, and his sisters passed on to carpenters and bricklayers the detailed instructions contained in his many letters home. The house perched high above Kingston Pike on Bearden Hill was visible for miles around, and before Major Reynolds saw it for the first time, it had become a Knoxville showplace; it was General Longstreet's headquarters at the beginning of the battle for Knoxville in 1863. Through the years, its successive owners have fended off encroaching business development, and the white-columned antebellum home remains a private residence.

After serving as Asylum Hospital during the Civil War, the classic-revival building on property donated by Calvin Morgan reopened as the Tennessee School for the Deaf; during the 1880's it acquired several undistinguished brick annexes to handle its escalating enrollment. The main building, with an unsupported spiral staircase rising three stories to the roof, became Knoxville's City Hall in the 1920's; the satellite structures were briefly used by Boyd Junior High School, but were soon required for municipal office space. All the buildings were then painted white, in an attempt to disguise their architectural dissimilarity. When Knoxville's government moved to the City/County Building in 1980, painstaking restoration brought back the 1848 appearance of Old City Hall, which now houses supplementary offices for TVA.

Middlebrook Pike originally led to the country home designed and built in the 1840's by Gideon Morgan Hazen, the co-owner of a papermill nearby on Third Creek. "Middlebrook" remained a residence until the 1980's. Since then it has been a museum house open on special occasions; it is supported by an endowment provided by its last private owner.

Old Gray Cemetery, with an entrance on North Broadway marked by a stone gatehouse, was surrounded by meadows when it was established in 1850 but is now in center-city. Two United States senators, William G. Brownlow and Lawrence D. Tyson, are among the many notable Knoxvillians buried here.

CHAPTER SEVEN

THE CITY THAT WITHSTOOD A CIVIL WAR SIEGE

With the approach of the Civil War, the people of Knoxville and Knox County held conflicting views, for unusual reasons. They were Southerners, but they lived in an area atypical of the South. East Tennessee's hilly terrain did not lend itself to a plantation economy, and there were more slaves in the towns than on the farms; elsewhere, the reverse was true.

Many Knox Countians, notably those of German or Dutch descent, objected to slavery on moral or religious grounds, but there very few outright abolitionists. In fact— although this statement sounds like an oxymoron— almost all of the county's leading anti-secessionists were slaveholders. It was little more than sixty years since Tennessee was born, right here in their county seat, and these men had been weaned on stories of how John Sevier and William Blount struggled for the state's admission to the federal union. To their way of thinking, the preservation of that union, rather than the perpetuation of slavery, was the issue now at stake. As for slavery, they were convinced that it could be easily (and fairly) abolished at any time, if the federal government would simply buy the slaves from their rightful owners, and set them free. These "Unionist" sentiments were shared by a vast majority of East Tennesseans, from Bristol to Chattanooga.

On the other hand, most residents within the city of Knoxville (including a great many who did *not* own slaves) were firm believers in the principle of states' rights; and as such, they were outspoken advocates of secession. They contended that the sovereign state of Tennessee had voluntarily joined the federal union, and was at liberty to withdraw from it at any time.

Tennessee left the Union as the result of an election held on June 8, 1861, to determine whether or not the state should declare its independence and join the Confederacy: East Tennessee's Unionists were outvoted by the secessionists of Middle and West Tennessee. A majority of Knoxville voters cast their ballots for secession; in the rest of Knox County, the vote was overwhelmingly in favor of remaining in the union.

One month before the state-wide election, representatives of all the East Tennessee counties had attended a convention in Knoxville, and had strongly opposed secession and Confederate statehood for Tennessee. After the election, the East Tennessee convention met again at Greeneville on June 17, for the purpose of seceding from the Confederate State of Tennessee. A committee was appointed to appear before the state legislature "...asking its consent that the counties comprising East Tennessee...may form and erect a separate state." By a predictable two-to-one vote, the legislature declined this request.

A somewhat similar situation had existed in the western portion of Virginia, where the adamant Union sentiment of the people resulted in the formation of the state of West Virginia. The difference was that West Virginia had federal territory on three sides, while East Tennessee was surrounded entirely by Confederate states, except for a short section of Kentucky border. Had East Tennesseans been permitted to form an independent government, it is unlikely that a state so situated could have long survived. In the end, it was more advantageous to the Union cause to have East Tennessee in the Confederacy, a small but vigorous island of sympathy and support, but two years would go by before Union strategists took advantage of this unique situation.

However, the Confederate authorities immediately recognized East Tennessee as a danger spot, and General Felix Zollicoffer was sent to Knoxville with an occupying force on July 26. He was surprised and pleased by the cordial welcome he received from the city's civil authorities, and he set up headquarters on a hill east of First Creek, in a house belonging to wealthy Joseph A. Mabry, Jr., one of the donors of Market Square. Mabry was a fervent Southern sympathizer, and he promptly offered to outfit Knoxville's first volunteer Confederate infantry with uniforms of gray cashmere. At least one regiment of Confederate infantry, and two of cavalry, were recruited in the Knoxville area; but in the meantime, Knox County Unionists were streaming into Kentucky to join the United States Army.

The East Tennessee Edition of Goodspeed's *History of Tennessee* would say in 1886:

> *...unlike the volunteer from the Northern states, the Union soldier from Tennessee was not tempted to enlist by a munificent state*

bounty, nor impelled by the force of public opinion, but on the contrary, to do so, he was forced to escape from an enemy's watchful guard at night, and leaving his home and all he held dear to the mercy of a hostile foe, make his way across the bleak and cheerless mountains to the Union camps in Kentucky.

General Zollicoffer, who had worked in Knoxville as a journeyman printer some years earlier, was finding the city a hotbed of dissension. There were well-respected Knoxvillians on both sides, and it was fortunate for all concerned that the Confederate commanding officer was a man who knew and understood the people and their conflicting loyalties. Jefferson Davis, the President of the Confederate States of America, had ordered all citizens of East Tennessee to take an oath of allegiance to the Confederacy or leave the country by October of 1861. Some Unionists left; many took the oath without the slightest intention of being bound by it; and others categorically refused either to swear allegiance or to leave. After Union sympathizers burned five strategic East Tennessee bridges in November, the Confederate government abandoned its policy of trying to win over the powerful opposition in the Knoxville area. The city was placed under martial law, and the County Jail was filled with prominent Unionists accused of having had a hand in burning the bridges.

Government spokesmen on both sides of the conflict had confidently predicted that the war would be of short duration, and Knoxvillians were discouraged and dismayed as weeks stretched into months, and months lengthened into years of struggle. Imported foodstuffs disappeared very early from stores throughout the South, and in Knoxville, stocks of coffee, tea, and spices were exhausted before the end of 1861. Salt became so scarce that it was necessary to establish a Confederate Salt Agency to control its distribution; in Knoxville, the price rose from two cents to thirty cents a pound, if and when available.

After the Confederate government moved from Montgomery, Alabama, to Richmond, Virginia, the most direct route between the capital and the Gulf States led through East Tennessee; the two railroads that met in Knoxville centered the "lifeline of the Confederacy." Passengers changed trains here, and freight shipments were transferred from one rail line to the other. The number of CSA troops in the city increased sharply, and Unionists were careful not to express their sentiments in the presence of the swaggering Rebel soldiers. Military authorities took over the buildings of East Tennessee

University and the Knox County Court House, and hospitals were
opened by Dr. Francis A. Ramsey, Jr. and Dr. Richard O. Currey in two
houses and the Deaf and Dumb Asylum. Some of the patients died, and
obliging Joseph Mabry sold two acres of land for a Confederate Military
Cemetery.

The two doctors treated their patients as best they could with what
few medicines were still available, but they relied on volunteers to
furnish food and nursing care. There was no such thing as a dietitian
or a registered nurse in 1861. Supposedly, women were born knowing
how to tend the sick, just as they were presumed to have an instinct for
motherhood and a natural ability for cooking and sewing. Consequently,
the women of Knoxville took food prepared in their home kitchens to
the converted houses and the Asylum; they made bandages, and stitched
articles of clothing; and they went themselves to the military hospitals
to take care of the patients.

Some women *do* have a talent for nursing and one of them,
beautiful Sue Boyd, was known as Knoxville's "Angel of the Hospitals."
Judge Thomas Speed wrote of her: "At one time, she speaks cheering
words; at another time her voice is heard in marvelous song. With her
own hands she bandages wounds; and she holds a cup of water to pallid
lips." Later, as Mrs. Alvin Barton, she would be a featured soprano
soloist at the Philharmonic Society and Staub's Opera House; in 1861,
she was nineteen years old, and she lived with her parents, Judge and
Mrs. Samuel B. Boyd, at historic Blount Mansion which must have been
a lively and a tuneful place: The Boyds had fourteen children, and every
member of the family was musical!

In 1862, Blount Mansion welcomed another in its long series of
famous visitors. The *Knoxville Register* printed a short article entitled
"Belle Boyd," that read:

> *This fair and fearless Virginia heroine, whose daring defense of her*
> *father's house when Charleston, Virginia, was first invaded by the*
> *Yankees, and whose invaluable services in conveying information to*
> *our lines in spite of the espionage of the craven foe, have won for her*
> *from the Northern press the title of the most courageous and*
> *dangerous of rebel female spies, is now sojourning in this city, at the*
> *residence of her cousin, Samuel B. Boyd, Esq. She was serenaded*
> *last night by the Florida Brass Band, and on being called for by the*
> *crowd, appeared at the window and made the following laconic and*
> *graceful response: "Gentlemen, like General Johnston, I can fight but*
> *I cannot make speeches. You have my heartfelt thanks for your*

compliment."

In June of 1863, the Union high command finally realized the necessity of severing the connection between Virginia and the Deep South, and Colonel William P. Sanders was sent down from Kentucky to demolish the railroad link between the ET&G and the ET&V. Striking first at Lenoir City where he captured a small Confederate force, he turned toward Knoxville; his men rendered the rail line useless as they moved along it, by tearing up gaps in the tracks one mile apart.

(A detachment of foragers, sent out to requisition food from farms along the Kingston Pike, arrived at the white-columned residence of Dr. Harvey Baker, a dedicated physician and an equally dedicated Southern sympathizer. Warned of their approach, Dr. Baker gathered his family in an upstairs room, locked the door, and blocked it with heavy furniture. The raiders broke into the house and searched it, but were unable to force their way into the barricaded room. Dr. Baker was killed by a pistol shot fired through the bedroom door.)

General Simon B. Buckner, who was then in command at Knoxville, had taken the main body of his troops to Virginia. Informed of Colonel Sanders' approach, the two remaining Confederate companies hastily prepared to hold the city with eight cannon, and called on hospital convalescents and civilian volunteers for help. Their cannon battery on Summit Hill opened fire on the Union troops as they came in along the railroad tracks; in response, Union field artillery shelled the battery, killing its commander, Colonel Pleasant McClung. Then, making no attempt to occupy the city, Colonel Sanders moved off in the direction of Strawberry Plains, destroying the railroad as he went.

Three months later, Union General Ambrose Burnside arrived in Knoxville with a force of 10,000 men, comprising four infantry divisions and a troop of cavalry. In the face of such numbers, the Confederates beat a strategic retreat, and the Union forces were deployed in all sections of the city.

Now the shoe was on the other foot! Knoxville's Union sympathizers proudly brought out their hidden American flags, and gave General Burnside a rousing welcome, while the more rabid Confederates suddenly decided it was time to move south.

(Knoxville's first professionally-trained dentist, Dr. John Fouché, was a Unionist. Since 1860, he had occupied a street floor office with living quarters above in a building erected at the southwest corner of Gay and Clinch streets by William G. Swan and Columbus Powell, for whom Powell's Station was named. General Burnside established his headquarters in John Crozier's home, diagonally across the intersection, on the future site of the Farragut Hotel. Family tradition holds that on the following day, Dr. Fouché bought the property facing Union headquarters at a bargain price, but was required to make payment in Confederate bonds.)

The Confederate troops had hardly marched out of Knoxville before General Braxton Bragg at Chattanooga was ordering General James Longstreet to retake the city. Not until Knoxville was back in Southern hands could the indispensable railroads be rebuilt, and the direct route to Richmond reestablished.

General Burnside was well aware of the railroads' importance, and was sure a counter-offensive could not be long in coming. When he received word from General Grant's staff that Knoxville must be held at all costs, he ordered the city fortified.

General Orlando M. Poe, who commanded the U.S. Army Engineers responsible for the city's defenses, was a brilliant strategist. He saw immediately what William Blount had realized long before: The surrounding terrain provided natural protection for the town on top of the plateau. There was already water on three sides, and when he was told that the ravine containing the railroad tracks had once held a sizable pond, Poe ordered his men to dam up First and Second creeks. Just as he expected, the two creeks overflowed into the ravine and met in the middle, ringing the plateau with a splendid moat!

Poe established a western outpost in the hilltop buildings of East Tennessee University that overlooked the Kingston Pike, and found there a supply of fodder left by the fleeing Rebels. On the north, he copied the Confederates by placing cannon along Summit Hill. On the east, he put an artillery battery on Flint Hill, and took over the former Confederate command post in Joseph Mabry's house. To protect against artillery bombardment from the south side of the river, or an invasion of raft-borne Rebel troops, he constructed earthworks forts on bluffs beyond the river. A bridge was needed to supply Forts Dickerson and Stanley with ammunition from the central stores, as well as to bring in food supplies from strongly Unionist south Knox County, so the Engineers took up a pontoon bridge that had been built at Loudon, loaded it in sections onto flatcars, and transported it to Knoxville on the patched-up railroad. No sooner was the pontoon bridge in place near the mouth of First Creek than reports came in that the Rebels were planning to float a heavy raft downstream from Boyd's Ferry on the

Holston River, and ram it. Poe ordered a great iron chain stretched across the Tennessee River just above the bridge, and augmented the chain with a boom of logs. Hearing of these defenses, the Confederates abandoned the idea of bridge-ramming.

As a final defense, the Engineers began constructing a large earthworks fort at the tip of a high ridge that separated the railroad from the Kingston Pike; Confederate troops coming from Chattanooga would be forced to pass the fort, on one side or the other. Local history buffs who watched the bastioned fort go up began calling it "Fort Loudon," and the name stuck.

When dispatches announced that Longstreet's army had left Chattanooga, General Burnside went to Lenoir City with 10,000 men to intercept and delay the Confederate advance long enough for Fort Loudon to be finished. The Union forces slowly retreated toward Knoxville, pausing for frequent skirmishes. A hotly contested encounter took place at Campbell's Station, where the defunct historic inn's brick annex had become the residence of Avery Russell. On the morning of the combat, Union General Hartranft had breakfast at the Russell house; as one army fell back, the other moved forward, and Confederate General McLaw arrived in time for supper. (Between meals, while fighting went on around the house, the Russell family retired to the basement— taking with them a valuable white horse that they managed to conceal from both armies!)

Nearing Knoxville, General Longstreet established temporary headquarters in the stately home of Robert Reynolds, on Bearden Hill, while mapping out his plan of action. (Obviously, his map was inaccurate, for he remained convinced throughout the campaign that the French Broad and Holston rivers met *below* Knoxville rather than four miles above.) Told by his scouts that the defenses of the city were well-nigh impregnable, he decided to surround Knoxville on all sides, and place it under siege.

Moving closer to town, he set up permanent headquarters in the residence of Robert H. Armstrong, beside a curve on Kingston Pike. The handsome house of italianate styling had a tall square tower that overlooked the river from one side and the highway from the other— a perfect vantage point for sharpshooters. After ordering siege trenches dug on the west, north, and east sides of the city, Longstreet ferried a force of 1,000 men across the river in an attempt to capture the important Union forts on the southside bluffs. His men succeeded in taking only Cherokee Heights, downstream from their objectives, but by placing an artillery battery there, they were able to shell the Union-held buildings of East Tennessee University. (There was already a large Confederate outpost at Boyd's Ferry on the Holston River above the Forks, but because of his faulty map, General Longstreet failed to blockade the French Broad. This would prove to be his fatal mistake.)

Knoxville was in grave danger, and Fort Loudon was not quite finished, so General Burnside decided to try one more delaying action. General William P. Sanders (the same man who had previously destroyed the railroads) was a member of Burnside's staff, in command of a troop of cavalry. He was ordered to dismount his men and harass Longstreet's headquarters. At nightfall on November 16, Sanders' men dug themselves in on the opposite side of Kingston Pike, some 250 yards east of the Armstrong house. Early the next morning, Confederate General McLaw took up a position directly in front of the house. Throughout the day, Sanders' dismounted troopers fiercely defended their position, knowing that each hour was of the utmost importance to General Poe's Engineers at Fort Loudon. By three o'clock in the afternoon, McLaw had gained the upper hand, and General Sanders rode forward on his snow white horse to organize his men's retreat. He was a conspicuous— though distant— target for the sharpshooters in the tower of the Armstrong house, and one shot found its mark. Mortally wounded, Sanders was carried into the city and taken to the officers' hospital at the Lamar House, where he died the following day. On the night of November 18, he was buried by moonlight in the churchyard of the Second Presbyterian Church, with General Burnside and all staff officers in attendance. His gallant delaying action had enabled Fort Loudon to be completed, and it was rechristened "Fort Sanders" in his honor.

No lights were permitted at General Sanders' funeral, and no volley was fired over his grave, for on the morning of November 18, the siege of Knoxville had begun.

General Burnside had been quick to take advantage of the fact that staunch Unionist farmers lived along the unguarded French Broad River. A detachment of Union soldiers had already set up a shipping point at Bowman's Ferry, where they had been felling trees and making rafts. They now put out a call for fresh and staple produce to feed the beleaguered city, and provisions poured in from the surrounding farms. Rafts piled high with food were set afloat as soon as it was fully dark; during the night, the current carried them swiftly downstream, past the Forks of the River and the eastern end of the Confederate siege trenches, to bump up against the boom of logs held in place by the iron chain. Soldiers waiting on the log jam shunted the rafts ashore, and supply officers sorted the food for distribution to citizens as well as to the military personnel. The rafts were then broken apart, and sawed into firewood for the hospitals.

William Rule's *History of Knoxville* declared in 1900:

> *As is well known, the object of General Longstreet was to starve the Union forces into surrender, in which he would certainly have succeeded had he cut off all supplies from reaching the [city]; but...at the close of the siege,...there was within the fortifications a sufficient supply of food to last...ten days. These supplies were freely furnished by the citizens...who were loyally disposed to the Government of the United States.*

In the final analysis, it was not General Poe who saved Knoxville with his clever fortifications, but the loyal Unionists along the French Broad, with their flotilla of food-laden rafts. Without them, Knoxville might very possibly have been another Vicksburg.

("Mecklenburg," the home of Dr. J.G.M. Ramsey, stood at the very point where the Holston and the French Broad rivers flowed together; the house was built on top of a large Indian mound, and one of its rooms was a museum filled with Indian and pioneer artifacts. Dr. Ramsey was an early and often-quoted apologist for secession, as well as the man who worked for twenty years to obtain railroads for Knoxville. Union soldiers burned Mecklenburg to the ground, destroying the museum *and* the notes and manuscript for a sequel to Ramsey's *Annals of Tennessee*.)

Now that the siege was actually under way, Knoxvillians found themselves living under strict military regulations. Soldiers were quartered in many private homes, and in almost all the public buildings. All the churches were closed, except St. John's Episcopal and Second Presbyterian. The underground fire-cisterns were taken into military custody as an emergency water supply, and the Market House was commandeered for a central powder magazine. The city fathers felt duty bound to protest the seizure of public property without so much as a by-your-leave, and Mayor James C. Luttrell was instructed to call on the Union officer in charge of ammunition supplies, with the request that he immediately distribute the gunpowder stored in the Market House among the various forts and batteries. The mayor informed the general that he should not be storing all his explosives in one place, particularly not in Knoxville's valuable Market House, where an accidental blast would not only destroy the building itself, but would endanger the lives and damage the property of Knoxville's loyal citizens. (While he was about it, the Mayor went on to complain that Federal troops had moved the stalls and benches of the Market House outside, where they had already suffered considerable damage from the weather.)

The siege was almost a week old when General Longstreet was told by General Bragg that starving Knoxville into surrender would take too long. Bragg urged him to move in at once, capture the fortifications by force, and return to Chattanooga where his troops were urgently needed. After thinking it over for a few days (during which time, Bragg lost the Battle of Lookout Mountain) Longstreet decided to comply by attacking Fort Sanders, and he set the assault for Sunday morning, November 29, at daybreak.

Lieutenant General A.P. Stewart, in his sketch of the Army of Tennessee, gives this moving account of the battle:

The weather was bad, misty and freezing. A large number of the Confederates were barefooted and thinly clad...Calmly but quickly with fixed bayonets and with the precision of dress parade, the assaulting columns moved through the mists of the early morning toward the bastions of the dimly outlined fort. The distance was short. The garrison was fully aware that the assault was to be made at daylight, and every man was at his post. The embrasures of the fort bristled with twenty pound Parrotts and twelve pound Napoleon guns, which had been double and triple shotted with shot and shell; and which, almost from the moment the columns moved, had full play upon them. Yet proudly, confidently, heroicly, and defiantly, the gray, grim and grizzled veterans moved into the "jaws of death." Suddenly the head of the assaulting column was broken, the men pitching forward falling over each other. They had struck invisible telegraph wires stretched from stump to stump. The guns of the fort belched forth thunder and lightning into the disordered ranks. Quickly reforming under the galling fire, the Confederates rushed the fort, when once again they halted. They had reached the deep wide ditch about which they were misinformed, and over which they had no way to cross. Only for a moment they paused. Apparently endowed with superhuman activity and determination, they crossed the ditch while volley after volley of artillery and musketry was poured upon them from above, and while "twenty pound shells with fuses cut to explode them at twenty seconds were hurled from the fort into the living mass below." Still onward was borne the flag of St. Andrews.

*The parapet was reached, only to find it covered with ice.
Undismayed, the boys in gray attempted to scale the slippery sides.
A few reached the top only to meet instant death or capture. Three
times the cross-barred flag of the Confederates was planted on the
parapet to float only for a moment...The assault had failed.*

Following a military strategy that was centuries old, General Poe
had cut down all the trees on the hillsides below Fort Sanders to give
the fort's defenders an unobstructed view of the attackers' movements;
what he did with the tree-stumps was something entirely new in warfare.
A Knoxvillian, J.B. Hoxie, had suggested setting a booby-trap for the
advancing enemy by stretching lengths of telegraph wire between the
lopped-off trees, and twisting their ends around the stumps. Poe at
once adopted the idea as the fort's first line of defense. His spiderweb
of wires was difficult to detect in broad daylight, and was totally invisible
in the foggy dawn. (The barbed-wire barricades of later wars were
"improvements" on a device that was first used here.)
General Longstreet's attack was directed at the weakest point of
the fort, the projecting northwest bastion that was in effect a "blind
corner:" If the attackers could reach the ditch below it, they would be
out of range of the defenders' cannon.   But the artillery battery's
commander, Lieutenant Samuel N. Benjamin, had a brilliant inspiration:
His supplies included a number of spherical cannon balls, of the type
ignited by time fuses, and he cut these fuses very short. When the
attackers managed to escape the web of telegraph wire and started
across the ditch, he and his men lighted the fuses and lobbed the time-
bombs over the parapet— Lieutenant Benjamin had invented the hand-
grenade! The Confederates in the ditch assumed that they were being
shelled by their own artillery. General Longstreet thought so, too. He
ordered his artillery, which was in fact raking the flanks of the Federals,
to cease firing.
Of even greater importance than the hand-thrown shells was the
water-filled ditch that surrounded the fort.   General Longstreet
mistakenly believed that this ditch was no more than three feet deep.
He had, through field glasses, watched Union soldiers walk across it, and
presumed that his attacking men would find it equally easy to do so.
What the General didn't know was that the Union soldiers had been
crossing on planks that bridged the moat below the surface of the water,
which was from six to eleven feet in depth, and that the plank bridges
had been removed under cover of darkness.

Longstreet sent his troops into the attack without ladders, or crampoons to aid in scaling the sides of the ditch and the embankment towering above it on the fort side. Floundering in the icy water of the moat, the Confederates found it impossible to gain a firm foothold on the frozen mud of the embankment, and were at the mercy of the murderous bombing from the parapet above. As if this were not bad enough, during the night the Union soldiers had poured water over the sides of the parapet. Freezing temperatures had coated these sheer banks with a thin sheet of ice to make the assault upon cleverly fortified Fort Sanders truly hopeless.

The Battle of Fort Sanders had lasted only twenty bloody minutes. The Confederates had lost a total of 813 men— killed, wounded, or taken prisoner.

Confederate walking-wounded, and soldiers carrying their injured comrades, were able to follow Third Creek from the battlefield to Hazen's Papermill where a field hospital had been set up; but in their disorganized retreat from Fort Sanders, Longstreet's men were forced to abandon the gravely wounded, and the dead. Union soldiers dug shallow trenches into which a great many Confederate bodies were piled; they brought the wounded to hospitals in the city, whether their uniforms were blue or gray. Closest to Fort Sanders was the Deaf and Dumb Asylum, which had been well set up as a military hospital by Confederate doctors, and had become the medical headquarters for the Union Army. By mid-morning, Asylum Hospital was full to overflowing, as was the officers' hospital at the Lamar House. Wounded men were taken to the Court House; the First and Second Presbyterian, Baptist, and Methodist churches; the East Tennessee Female Institute; and the remaining hotels. Only the most fortunate of the wounded had cots or shuck mattresses; the others, wrapped in blankets, lay in rows upon the bare floor.

(In the bitterly cold days that followed, the small amount of fire-wood obtained from the food rafts could not begin to heat so many hospitals. Knoxville's shade trees were cut down, one by one, to warm the wounded.)

Burial of the Union dead began immediately, in a field adjacent to the Gray Cemetery. (After the war, this acreage was enlarged and designated a National Cemetery.)

Two businessmen of Knoxville later visited the battleground, and were horrified at the sight of the Confederate dead half-buried in shallow trenches. Convinced that Christian charity demanded decent burial for any fallen soldier, they commissioned a local undertaker to make simple pine coffins for these dead, and paid for their reburial in the cemetery on Joseph Mabry's land.

Several days after the battle, Confederate scouts captured a Federal courier carrying letters from General Grant to General Burnside; the letters contained the information that Union troops were coming to the aid of the besieged city from the north, the south, and the west. Upon receipt of this unwelcome news, General Longstreet gave up all hope of taking Knoxville, and ended the siege on the night of December 4, 1863, by withdrawing his forces in the direction of Virginia.

Longstreet left not a moment too soon. The Union high command was extremely concerned about General Burnside's plight, expecting momentarily to hear that he had been forced to surrender the city, and they did indeed dispatch three generals to his rescue. The first to arrive was General William Tecumseh Sherman, bringing a sizable army by forced marches from Chattanooga where he had helped defeat General Bragg at the Battle of Lookout Mountain. As Sherman hurried into Maryville on the morning of December 5, he was met with the news that the siege had been lifted only the night before. Suspecting that the enemy's withdrawal might be a ruse of some sort, he left the main body of his troops in Maryville and pressed on to Knoxville with two divisions. Crossing the river on the pontoon bridge provided for their convenience by General Poe's busy Engineers, Sherman's men entered the "starving city."

The first sight that met General Sherman's outraged eyes as he rode ashore into Knoxville was a large pen filled with fine fat cattle. He was escorted to Union Army Headquarters in a spacious and beautifully furnished mansion, where General Burnside was waiting to preside over a belated Thanksgiving dinner that would feature roast turkey, served in high style with fine silver and china on delicate table linen. General Sherman was assured that while he and his staff were feasting at headquarters, his cold and hungry troops were being warmed and fed by the soldiers to whose relief they had come.

Sherman was fit to be tied. He demanded to know who was responsible for tricking him into a forced march of over a hundred miles, in freezing weather, to rescue a "famished" army that was gorging itself three times a day.

He listened open-mouthed as General Burnside explained how raft-loads of provisions had been floated down the river by dark of night, under the very noses of the Confederates. He heard with amazement how the loyal Unionist farmers had provided the citizens and soldiers at Knoxville not just with their daily bread, but with delicacies only dreamed of in cities under siege.

After doing full justice to his turkey dinner, General Sherman returned to Maryville to lead his army back to Chattanooga, quite bewildered by the strange siege he had attempted to alleviate, and still furious that the truth had been concealed from him.

To make doubly sure that Knoxville's railroads remained in Federal hands, General Philip Sheridan was ordered with his troops to the French Broad, and he was no less surprised than General Sherman by the situation in the Knoxville area. He said in his *Memoirs* that "the intense loyalty of this part of Tennessee exceeded that of any other section I was in during the war....So long as we remained in the French Broad region, we lived on the fat of the land." Unfortunately for General Sheridan's comfort, he was soon ordered north.

Until the end of the war, the Union Army retained undisputed possession of a devastated East Tennessee where for three years farm crops had been seized, fields ravaged, and woodlands decimated by first one army, then the other. When Andrew Johnson, who had been appointed military governor of Tennessee, freed his personal slaves on August 8, 1864, many conscience- (or poverty-) stricken East Tennesseans followed his example. As cold weather approached, manumitted slaves and starved-out tenants on small farms converged on Knoxville, expecting the federal authorities to provide for them. The firstcomers slept on the long, uncovered platform at the railroad depot, and roamed the streets begging for food from residents who had none to spare. Shelters for the homeless were hastily set up by the Army in vacated hospitals and the buildings of East Tennessee University, and liberal donations poured in from relief societies in Philadelphia, Boston, and Maine to feed the needy in loyal East Tennessee.

On October 5, 1864, the U.S. Navy's victory at the Battle of Mobile Bay was cause for great rejoicing. In the North and in Knoxville, Admiral Farragut became a hero overnight, and everyone knew how he had rallied his flagging fleet with the battlecry: "Damn the torpedoes— full speed ahead!" West Knox Countians knew something else about David Glasgow Farragut. He was born on July 5, 1801, at Stoney Point, and the first deck beneath his feet was that of his father's ferry-boat on the Tennessee River. Neighbors said that the Farraguts' log cabin was still standing, at the place that had come to be known as Lowe's Ferry.

The dams had been removed from First and Second creeks and the Flag Pond had drained away, this time forever. Quartermaster-supplies and food bundles for the needy were regularly coming in from the North on the Army-supervised ET&V railroad, and farm produce was brought from south Knox County over the pontoon bridge, but all other commodities were in very short supply. Army regulations were relaxed, and Knoxville's Unionist families were invited to attend band concerts and dress parades on the grounds of East Tennessee University. As Thomas W. Humes said of such occasions in his book, *The Loyal Mountaineers of East Tennessee*: "...the weather was fine, the music was better, and the presence of the ladies lent enchantment to the view..."

Jubilation reigned on January 1, 1865, when President Abraham Lincoln's Emancipation Proclamation took effect. Knoxville's freed slaves borrowed an Army drum and paraded joyfully down Gay Street, singing at the top of their lungs. Afterward, having nowhere else to go, most of them returned "home."

There was grief as well as gladness on April 9, 1865, when General Robert E. Lee surrendered at Appomattox Courthouse. While soldiers, civilians, and refugees celebrated in the streets, many Knoxville families closed their window-shutters and sat in semi-darkness, mourning the Lost Cause. Father Abram Joseph Ryan, the Poet-Priest of the Confederacy, was then in charge of the little Catholic mission on Summit Hill; when the sad news came, he began composing his masterpiece, "The Conquered Banner." Unable to find a single sheet of writing paper for sale in the jam-packed shortage-beset city, he flattened out a brown peanut-bag and penned upon it:

> *Furl that banner, softly, slowly!*
> *Treat it gently— it is holy—*
> *For it droops above the dead....*

THE PRESENCE OF THE PAST

After serving as a command post for the Confederate and Union armies in turn, the home of Joseph A. Mabry, Jr. continued to be a family residence at 1711 Dandridge Avenue until the death of its reclusive owner in 1987. Miss Evelyn Hazen's will established an endowment to preserve the Mabry-Hazen House as a museum of family life during and after the Civil War. (Joseph Mabry remained an important figure in post-war Knoxville, and carried on a bitter business feud with a prominent newcomer, Thomas O'Connor. On October 18, 1882, both of the hot-tempered rivals died in an exchange of pistol shots on Gay Street that also killed Mabry's son, Joseph A. Mabry, III.)

Immediately after the War Between the States, the Ladies' Memorial Association of Knoxville took charge of the Confederate Cemetery at 1715 Bethel Avenue. A tall marble monument, crowned by the statue of an infantryman standing at parade rest, was unveiled by the ladies in 1892 as a memorial to the more than 1600 CSA soldiers buried there. In 1886, W.D. Winstead had become the resident manager of the tree-shaded, stone-walled cemetery, and his granddaughter continued to live in the charming superintendent's house. When Miss Mamie Winstead died in 1989, she willed the cemetery (and an endowment for its upkeep) to the Hazen-Mabry Foundation, to be maintained as an essential part of Knoxville's Civil War heritage.

Confederate Memorial Hall, at 3148 Kingston Pike, is the handsome italianate house that served as General Longstreet's headquarters during the siege of Knoxville. (It had been a wedding gift to Robert H. and Louise [Franklin] Armstrong in 1854, from both their families: her father's slaves had come from Jefferson County to build it, on land provided by his father, Drury P. Armstrong of Crescent Bend. The newlyweds named it "Bleak House" after Charles Dickens' popular novel.) Now the property of Chapter 89, United Daughters of the Confederacy, the beautifully furnished house with intricately garlanded plaster ceilings is open to the public as a period museum. Its brick exterior is pocked with shallow bullet holes, and a Federal cannon ball remains imbedded in an *inside* wall. In the room at the top of the square tower are three pencil-portraits, drawn by a sharpshooter stationed there in 1863. Beneath the sketches is the simple epitaph: "Men that were shot up here."

It is coincidence that makes truth stranger than fiction. During the Siege of Knoxville, General William P. Sanders was buried in the cemetery of the Second Presbyterian Church, on Market Street. The church moved in 1906 to the corner of Church and Walnut Streets; it moved again in 1957 to a hill overlooking Kingston Pike. The Tennessee Highway Marker that identifies the spot where General Sanders fell mortally wounded stands on the new lawn of this old church!

During the Civil War Centennial in 1963, dredging operations near the south end of the Gay Street bridge unearthed an enormous anchor attached to a length of a huge rod-and-link iron chain. This was part of the great chain stretched across the river by Union Army Engineers to protect the pontoon bridge that supplied their earthworks forts on the southside bluffs.   The chain played an even more important role during the siege of Knoxville, by stopping the food-laden rafts sent downstream at night by Unionist farmers living along the French Broad River. This unique relic of that strange siege was placed for safekeeping on the grounds of Confederate Memorial Hall.

Fort Dickerson, one of the forts built on the southside river bluffs by the Union Army in 1863, was abandoned at the end of the Civil War, and forgotten— except by generations of South Knoxville boys who played there.   After its existence was recalled in the 1950's, the remarkably well preserved earthworks fort became a city park, and in 1963, the Battle of Fort Sanders was reenacted there as part of Knoxville's Civil War Centennial observance.   Fort Dickerson was substituted for the actual battle site which was (and is) occupied by Fort Sanders Regional Medical Center.

In the 1920's, while the Greek-Revival building of the Tennessee School for the Deaf was undergoing renovation to become Knoxville's City Hall, the rules set by U.S. Army doctors in 1863 for Asylum Hospital were found posted, and still legible, on one wall. The segment of plaster with the rules attached is in the collection of the University of Tennessee's Center for the Study of War and Society, at Hoskins Library.

CHAPTER EIGHT

 # CONTROVERSIAL PARSON BROWNLOW

In the late 20th century, the saying "Life begins at forty" is as much a cliché as "A rolling stone gathers no moss". In the 1840's, however, a man of forty was considered middle aged, and was expected to be well-established in his chosen profession, if he ever hoped to amount to anything.

William G. Brownlow, who arrived in Knoxville in 1849, was forty-four years old and well launched on his *second* career. His first, in which he had achieved a rather widespread reputation in the South, was that of minister of the gospel. Lest anyone should think that this implied a mildness of manner and a kindliness of speech, let it be said at once that Parson Brownlow was a Methodist circuit-riding evangelist, a master of vitriolic oratory, and a passionate advocate of temperance. In short, he was the kind of minister most greatly admired in the South in his day— a real "hell-fire-and-damnation" preacher.

In his late thirties, the Parson became convinced that the pen was not only mightier than the sword, but mightier than the tongue, and he did not so much give up preaching as add to it a new career in journalism. He first published a small newspaper at Elizabethton in 1839, moving to Jonesborough in the following year. Deciding that a larger and more progressive city would offer greater scope for his talents as editor and publisher, he moved his family and his printing press to Knoxville and began the publication of *Brownlow's Knoxville Whig*.

The *Whig*, from its very first issue, was no ordinary newspaper. It carried advertisements, to be sure, and it reported local news and events of national significance; but there ended its resemblance to other journals of the day. The *Whig's* real reason for being was its editorial page.

It was customary for newspapers to carry upon their mastheads mottoes descriptive of the policies they advocated. Two of the mottoes often used by the *Whig* were: *Cry aloud and spare not*, and *Independent in all things, neutral in nothing.* Those were the exact sentiments of the *Whig's* editor. Sometimes it seemed to his readers that he must have dipped his pen in acid instead of ink to write his editorials, but this was the kind of journalism they most enjoyed. The *Whig* was an instantaneous success. Its fame spread through the state and the South until its circulation reached the phenomenal figure, for that day, of 12,000 copies, and the *Whig* became one of very few newspapers in the annals of American journalism to have a circulation greater than the total population of the city in which it was published.

If an election was coming up, the *Whig* was passionately partisan. If a public servant betrayed his public trust, the *Whig* was violently vindictive. If an issue was at stake, the *Whig* could be relied upon to present only one side of it.

William Brownlow was a staunch Unionist, and he was an equally strong believer in the institution of slavery. Although the same was true of many East Tennesseans, the two beliefs were considered absolutely incompatible by the rest of the country. The pro-slavery bias of the *Whig* accounted for a large measure of its popularity in the South, and was responsible for its editor's first taste of national prominence when, in 1858, he was invited to Philadelphia to debate the slavery question with the Reverend Abram Pryne. The public debate lasted for five days, and much Scripture was quoted on both sides of the question by the two ministers. Parson Brownlow, favoring slavery, delivered himself of some fine periods of oratory that were reported in the national press; the entire debate was afterward published in book form, and was widely read in the North as well as in the South.

In the Presidential campaign of 1860, there was a candidate precisely to the liking of William Brownlow. This was his close personal friend (for whom one of his sons was named) John Bell. Bell was campaigning on a platform with a single plank, "Preservation of the Union," and Brownlow's *Knoxville Whig* thundered warning of the dire consequences that would result if the Union were not preserved at all costs. In the famous four-way Presidential race, John Bell and the *Whig* carried the State of Tennessee, but Abraham Lincoln was elected President.

When South Carolina's convention passed the first Act of Secession, Editor Brownlow was galvanized into frantic action. As he had years before denounced South Carolina's Nullification Acts, so he now excoriated her secession. He called it stupidity. He called it treason. In other parts of the South, readers canceled their subscriptions to the *Whig*, and refused to accept copies that arrived addressed to them at their local post offices. East Tennesseans read the *Whig* with nods of approval, and subscriptions began to pour in from the North!

In spite of the efforts of the *Whig* and Brownlow's fellow Unionists, the State of Tennessee seceded from the Union in June of 1861, and an attempt to create a new state in East Tennessee came to naught. A less courageous and determined editor would surely at this point have called it quits and capped his inkwell for the duration, but in the teeth of Tennessee's Act of Secession, the *Whig* continued to print editorials every whit as pro-Union as those of newspapers in New York or Boston. And when Confederate troops arrived to occupy Knoxville, William Brownlow kept the Stars and Stripes floating from a flagpole above his house on East Cumberland Street.

That flag was a thorn in the flesh to the Confederate authorities, as well as to Knoxville's many Southern sympathizers. On a day when Mr. and Mrs. Brownlow were away from home, a rowdy crowd of Confederate soldiers gathered in the street outside the house, demanding that the flag be taken down. With a courage that would have done credit to her intrepid father himself, teenaged Sue Brownlow stepped out on the front porch brandishing a loaded pistol, and invited any man who wanted the flag down to come and get it. The flag stayed put.

Once the city was occupied by Confederate forces, it was no longer possible to send copies of the *Whig* to its thousands of subscribers in the North, and Confederate authorities banned the circulation of the "incendiary rag" in the Southern states. By October of 1861, it was clear to Parson Brownlow that it would be necessary to suspend publication, at least temporarily. The final issue of the *Whig*, dated October 24, announced that its editor expected to be arrested, since he had not the slightest intention of taking an oath of allegiance to the Confederate States of America. He went on to say:

> *I shall in no degree feel humbled by being cast into prison, whenever it is the will and pleasure of this august government to put me there, but on the contrary I shall feel proud of my confinement. I shall go to jail — as John Rogers went to the stake — for my principles. I shall go, because I have failed to recognize the hand of God in the work of breaking up the American government, and the inauguration of the most wicked, cruel, unnatural, and uncalled for war, ever*

*recorded in history! I go, because I have refused to laud to the skies
the acts of tyranny, usurpation, and oppression, inflicted upon the
people of East Tennessee, because of their devotion to the
Constitution and Laws of the Government handed down to them by
their Fathers, and the liberties secured to them by a war of seven long
years of gloom, poverty, and trial! I repeat, I am proud of my
position, and of my principles, and shall leave them to my children
as a legacy far more valuable than a princely fortune, had I the latter
to bestow!*

As it turned out, he did not immediately go to jail. A few days
after the publication of the *Whig's* final issue, Parson Brownlow deemed
it wise to leave occupied Knoxville and seek political asylum in strongly
Unionist Sevier County. He chose to hide in rugged Wear's Valley,
where he lived upon sweet potatoes and wild game. Meanwhile, in
Knoxville, Confederate authorities posted a notice that $2,000 would be
paid for information leading to the apprehension of William G.
Brownlow.

Sevier County's Unionists knew the exact whereabouts of Parson
Brownlow, and they were well aware that he was causing great
embarrassment to his political enemies by hiding in the mountains.
Word went round "by the grapevine" that on a certain Sunday morning,
the Parson would speak in the Court House Square at Sevierville. By
wagon and buggy, on horseback and muleback and on "Shanks' mare",
people came down from the hills and the coves and the valleys, and the
Court House Square was packed. Parson Brownlow made a stirring
speech to the mountain men and women who formed the hard core of
Union resistance in East Tennessee, and he told them what they wanted
to hear: The Federal Union could not fail to win in the end. Back to
the hills and the coves and the valleys went the Parson's friends. Every
one of them knew that there was a price upon his head— he had told
them so himself— but the reward went unclaimed.

News reached Knoxville of this meeting, and of the stiffening
Unionist resistance in the mountains. The Confederate military
authorities sent a message to Sevier County, offering to make a deal
with the fire-breathing parson. If he would agree to go North, and stay
there, they were prepared to offer him safe conduct through the lines
for himself and his family. Parson Brownlow decided to accept the
offer. He left his hiding place and returned to Knoxville to make
preparations for the journey, but as soon as he arrived in the city, he
was arrested and jailed by Knoxville's Confederate civil officials. The

CSA military authorities had kept their promise— a safe conduct pass for the Brownlow family was ready and waiting— but they were unable to persuade the district attorney or the local judge that Brownlow's imprisonment was making him a martyr in the eyes of his political adherents.

From the jail, Parson Brownlow wrote a letter to Judah P. Benjamin, Secretary of War for the Confederate States, and in it he explained how he had come to Knoxville in good faith, to accept a proposition made to him by the duly constituted military representatives of the Confederacy. He told of his arrest and imprisonment by the civil authorities, and asked that pressure be brought to bear upon the local judge to allow him and his family to leave Tennessee. "If you will help me in this", he concluded, "I will do more for your Confederacy than the devil himself, for I will leave it."

During the time it took for the letter to reach Secretary Benjamin in Richmond and his directive to arrive in Knoxville, Brownlow had contracted a serious illness in the jail, and had been removed to his home. He was still under house arrest, and an armed guard was present in his sickroom at all times, when word came from Richmond that it would indeed be in the best interests of the Confederacy if William G. Brownlow left the South. The civil authorities released him to the military, who promptly made good their promise to send the entire Brownlow family through the lines to "exile" in the North.

Invited to speak in several Northern cities, the Parson arrived by train in Cincinnati, where he made an impassioned speech to the large crowd that had gathered to greet him. In the crowd was a Union general on a recruiting mission, and at the end of Brownlow's address, he jumped to his feet and called for volunteers. So great was the response that the general abandoned his own planned tour of the Northern states and followed Parson Brownlow on his tour, signing up recruits at the end of each rousing speech.

The Parson's bitter denunciations of the Confederate cause were music to the ears of his Northern hearers, and great crowds assembled whenever he was scheduled to speak. As soon, however, as word reached him that the Union Army had taken over Knoxville, he set out for home, travelling with his family by military transport— i.e., in a boxcar. By November of 1863, Brownlow's *Knoxville Whig and Rebel Ventilator* was ready to report upon the siege of Knoxville and the Battle of Fort Sanders.

One strange incident that occurred during the battle was not reported in the *Whig,* or in any other publication: it concerned the only Confederate soldier who actually got into Fort Sanders. Lieutenant James O'Brien had led his Louisiana company through the wire entanglements and the deep ditch, and had clambered up the icy embankment. He stood erect upon the parapet for one moment before a rifle bullet hit him; pitching forward, he fell face first into the fort where he was immediately seized and taken prisoner. Although he was seriously wounded, he managed to convey the information that he had a sister living in Knoxville, and to ask that she be notified. And the name of the Lieutenant's sister? *Mrs. William G. Brownlow!* After the battle, the Brownlows took Lieutenant O'Brien to their house, where his sister nursed him back to health. So it was that, during the siege of Knoxville, the city's most passionate Union partisan was harboring in his home an officer in the army of the Confederate States of America. Even the family of Parson Brownlow had problems with divided loyalties.

That Tennessee escaped the full horror of the Reconstruction Era is well known, but the reasons for her preferential treatment are not always clearly understood, The long road back to statehood began in 1862, when the Confederate state government was forced to abandon the capital at Nashville. President Lincoln then appointed a military governor for Tennessee, and his choice was a logical one: Andrew Johnson had been governor of Tennessee before his election to the U.S. Senate, and he was the sole representative of a Southern state who demonstrated his loyalty to the Union by remaining in his Senate seat on the fateful day when the members of Congress from the South left the Capitol in a body. That Johnson accepted the assignment was a tribute to his bravery and devotion to duty, for no man could have found himself in a more equivocal situation. As a Tennessean whose home area felt the scourge of battle and alternate occupation by the warring forces, he had the deepest sympathy for the people of the divided state he was called upon to govern, but the people of Middle and West Tennessee looked upon him as a renegade and a traitor, and flouted his authority on every possible occasion; and this made necessary more stringent measures of control than would otherwise have been used.

While Andrew Johnson was serving as Military Governor, he made a public statement to which Parson Brownlow took immediate exception. Addressing a large meeting of blacks in Nashville, Johnson announced the freeing of his personal slaves on August 8, 1864, and called himself the hope of the black people of the South. He went further. He likened himself to Moses, who would lead them "out of the house of bondage".

In Knoxville, Parson Brownlow addressed an equally large crowd of blacks, but the tenor of his remarks was different. He informed his hearers that if Andrew Johnson proposed to be their Moses and lead them to the Promised Land, he, Brownlow, would be their Pharaoh to drive them right straight back to Egypt. These two speeches created great amusement in the North, and Parson Brownlow chose to keep the jest alive for years by frequently referring to himself as "Pharaoh Brownlow".

Andrew Johnson was rescued from his untenable position as Military Governor by his nomination to the Vice Presidency in 1864, when Abraham Lincoln was running for a second term. The selection of Johnson as a running mate for the President was not a popular one. It is said to have been the choice of Lincoln himself, who felt that Johnson, a native of the South and a man who had experienced the anger of defeated Southerners in his capacity as governor of a conquered state, would be able to give wise counsel about the rehabilitation of the South when the war came to an end. Certainly, Abraham Lincoln and Andrew Johnson were not thinking in terms of the punitive measures advocated by many Northern statesmen. Each of them felt that the South, having greatly suffered during the war, would suffer sufficiently in defeat without additional punishment from the victors.

When the war ended and the prayed-for peace began, Knoxville faced a new set of problems. The federal troops were withdrawn and most of the commandeered public and private buildings were returned to their rightful owners, but First Presbyterian Church (which was viewed as a stronghold of Confederate sympathy) became the headquarters of the Freedmen's Bureau. First Presbyterian's elders protested, but were told by Major General Stoneman: "There is plenty of room in the loyal churches of this city for all those who wish to attend the worship of the Most High God."

Once the Market House was provided with new stalls and benches, it reopened. The Court House, the University buildings, the School for the Deaf, the Female Institute, the hotels and churches, and many private homes had seen service as headquarters, barracks, hospitals— even stables; all of them had suffered major damage, and some were in unusable condition.

The Reconstruction Era would be just that, for Knoxville, and some U.S. Army veterans stayed on to help with the rebuilding process. In 1865, Captain W. W. Woodruff advertised in the *Whig* that his new store on Gay Street was offering a full line of hardware, plus the tools and machinery urgently needed to revitalize East Tennessee's war-ravaged farms. Colonel Hiram S. Chamberlain, who had been chief quartermaster at Knoxville during the Union occupation, established the Knoxville Iron Company on Second Creek, and brought in experienced Welsh iron-mongers to supervise his foundry, rolling mill, and machine shop.

On the other hand, the founder of Kern's Bakery was a former Confederate soldier. Peter Kern had emigrated from Heidelberg, Germany to the United States at the age of eighteen, and was living in Georgia when he enlisted in the Rebel army. After recovering from a wound, he passed through Knoxville on his way to rejoin his unit in Virginia— just when the city was taken over by General Burnside's troops. Trapped here for the duration, he formed a partnership with a German baker (whom he soon bought out) and began supplying bread and cakes to Knoxville's housewives.

During the final year of the war, residents with Confederate and Union sympathies had made a start at living together in what passed for amity, but old bitterness resurfaced when the soldiers of both armies began coming home. One Confederate, Abner Baker, was a very small man with a very large score to settle: he was the son of Dr. Harvey Baker, who had been killed by Union raiders inside his own home on Kingston Pike. At the Knox County Court House, Abner accused the large and muscular court clerk, William Hall, of having been a party to his father's murder. When Hall struck Baker across the face with a heavy cane, Baker whipped a pistol from his pocket, and killed Hall on the spot. Witnesses seized Baker, and hauled him off to the county jail. That night, an unruly mob broke into the jail, and dragged the prisoner outside to a nearby tree. A noose was placed about his neck, and he was asked if he had any last words to say. Drawing himself up to his full five feet three, Abner Baker shouted: "Yes! Now watch a Rebel die!"

This was the situation in Knoxville in 1865, when William G. Brownlow was elected governor of the still-divided state of Tennessee. Soon afterward, upon the assassination of President Lincoln, Andrew Johnson became President of the United States.

The U.S. Army's pontoon bridge was still in place in Knoxville and, having been declared war-surplus property, was for sale. The Knox

County Court was anxious to keep this convenient link with the area south of the river, and hoped to buy the bridge at a nominal price, so Governor Brownlow was petitioned to use his influence with the U.S. Quartermaster General on the County's behalf. This he did, and having bought the span, the County expended an additional $1,000 to install a draw that permitted steamboats to travel up and down stream. Sad to say, the following spring, the bridge was washed away by an unprecedented flood.

President Andrew Johnson was determined to get his home state back into the federal union without delay, and on the most favorable terms possible. Governor Brownlow was another man whose primary objective was Tennessee's readmission to the Union. Although they had at one time been personal enemies, these two men had worked side by side as leaders of the Unionist sympathizers in East Tennessee and they joined forces once again to promote their common cause. The records of the U.S. War Department showed that Tennessee's First and Second Congressional Districts (comprising Johnson's upper East Tennessee and Brownlow's Knoxville area) had furnished more recruits to the Union Army *per capita* than any other two congressional districts in the entire nation, and they planned to use the loyalty of this section of the state as the entering wedge to obtain the entire state's reacceptance into the Union.

Almost the first act passed by Tennessee's reorganized legislature was a law denying the franchise to former Confederate sympathizers for from five to fifteen years. Most of the voters qualified under this law were from East Tennessee, and there was naturally a storm of protest from the rest of the state. So intense was the opposition to this first postwar government that the term "Brownlow's Legislature" was used as an epithet of opprobrium.

Governor Brownlow, who was looking for the first favorable opportunity to apply for Tennessee's readmission to statehood, recognized such an opportunity in 1866. The Fourteenth Amendment to the Constitution had been sent to the various states for ratification, and the Radicals in Congress had implied that the acceptance of this controversial amendment by the legislature of a seceded state would be a strong point in favor of its readmission to the Union. Six days after the amendment was sent to the states by Congress, Governor Brownlow called a special session of Tennessee's legislature to consider its ratification.

The amendment that guaranteed the civil rights of citizens

"regardless of race, color, or previous condition of servitude" was totally unacceptable in the South, and President Johnson had advised the Southern states to reject it. Even Parson Brownlow, the most avid of pro-Union men, found it difficult to swallow. The members of the legislature wanted no part of it, and enough of them stayed away from the special session to prevent the bill's passage for lack of a quorum to act upon it. Governor Brownlow was livid. This was Tennessee's chance to avoid much greater difficulties than the Fourteenth Amendment would imply, and he was determined that the amendment should be ratified. He took a step that accomplished his purpose, but enraged the citizens of his state.

A sufficient number of the absent legislators to constitute a quorum were arrested and brought to Nashville, where they were announced to be in attendance, and a quorum was declared present. The Fourteenth Amendment was then voted upon and passed, although the members brought in by force refused to vote. Governor Brownlow telegraphed the news of the ratification to the Radicals in the Congress, and Tennessee became the third of all the states, North or South, to ratify. Largely on the strength of this ratification, Tennessee— the last state to secede and join the Confederacy— became the first Southern state readmitted to the federal Union.

The United States Congress had, in 1862, passed an act that set aside certain public lands to be sold for the benefit of colleges and universities which would undertake to establish departments of agriculture. Unfortunately for Tennessee, the act stated that colleges must apply for these benefits within two years, and 1866 was too late. However, William G. Brownlow was Governor of Tennessee, Andrew Johnson was President of the United States, and Horace Maynard, a former professor at East Tennessee College, was the U.S. Congressman from the Knoxville district. Through their good offices, the Congress was persuaded to make an exception, and in 1867, a special act entitled Tennessee to qualify for benefits under the Land Grant Act; the legislature designated East Tennessee University the state's Land Grant College in 1869. The University's trustees purchased, as the law required, a large farm on the north bank of the Tennessee River just west of Third Creek, and established the College of Agriculture that is still there. As a result of a second requirement of the Land Grant Act, the University became a military school. Its students were called cadets, and their uniforms were exactly like those worn at West Point.

The University's buildings had been used by Confederate and

Union forces alternately, and during the siege of Knoxville, they were shelled repeatedly by the Confederates from the heights across the river. When the property was returned to the trustees at the close of the war, the classrooms and dormitories were so dilapidated that extensive restoration was necessary. There was not a tree left standing on The Hill.

The man selected to undertake the task of rebuilding the University was Dr. Thomas W. Humes, who resigned as rector of St. John's Episcopal Church to accept the appointment. Dr. Humes had been a strong and vocal advocate of the Union cause, and it was he who recited the Episcopal burial service from memory at General Sanders' moonlight funeral.

East Tennesseans had breathed a sigh of relief when Tennessee resumed its place among the states of the Union, knowing that there would be no further military occupation of its territory, and that the Freedmen's Bureau would henceforth have less than total power. (As the first evidence of that fact in Knoxville, the First Presbyterian Church was relinquished, in deplorable condition, by the Freedmen's Bureau to its elders.)

The rest of the state was unconditionally opposed to anything that smacked of Governor Brownlow's machinations. The Ku Klux Klan was organized in Pulaski, and as it spread, lawless acts and demonstrations became commonplace. Declaring that a state of emergency existed in Middle and West Tennessee, Governor Brownlow placed nine counties under martial law.

William G. Brownlow was perhaps the only man in Tennessee who would have sought reelection to the governorship under such circumstances, but he proclaimed his willingness to see his state through her hour of deep distress. He was reelected in 1867, and continued to fight fire with fire in the disordered western counties.

Pragmatic Knoxvillians, regardless of their stance in the late war, had begun "pulling themselves up by their own bootstraps." When the Gay Street merchants subscribed almost all of the $8,250 needed to purchase the city's first steam-powered fire engine, the aldermen could do no less than provide a place to keep it. Knoxville's first City Hall, completed in 1868 at the north end of Market Square, contained a fire station on the first floor with offices and a meeting room above; a cupola on top of the square brick building held a huge bell that summoned the volunteer firemen.

Far-reaching consequences resulted from the merger of Knoxville's two railroads in 1868. The new East Tennessee, Virginia, and Georgia Railway built short lines and connectors that gave access to Kentucky and the midwest, as well as to western Tennessee; and endless rows of tall and slender poles carried telegraph wires along the railroad right of way. Locally, the ETV&G's own yards and shops provided steady employment, and increased the output of East Tennessee's iron and coal mines by spawning such industries as a railroad-wheel-and-car works, and foundries that manufactured spikes and rails.

In 1869, William G. Brownlow resigned as governor to accept another office: Tennessee's legislature had elected him to the United States Senate. No sooner had the controversial Reconstruction Governor been booted upstairs than a constitutional convention was called.

Tennessee's first constitution had been a praiseworthy document in 1796, and the Constitution of 1870 was a remarkable achievement under the existing conditions. It extended the right to vote and hold office to all citizens, regardless of race, creed, or color, and specified that this provision applied to American Indians as well as to Negroes. (On the subject of suffrage for former Confederates, it was silent; however, all rights were restored to them by Congress through the General Amnesty Act of 1872.)

Even before the Constitution of 1870 granted blacks the right to vote and to hold office, David Brown was elected to Knoxville's Board of Aldermen. He represented Parson Brownlow's home area, East Knoxville, which was annexed to the city proper in 1869.

East Tennessee's newly enfranchised blacks allied themselves with the party of the Great Emancipator, Abraham Lincoln, and voted the straight Republican ticket. However, in Tennessee and Kentucky, Emancipation Day was not celebrated on January 1 as in the rest of the nation but on the Eighth of August— and the date was always written out and capitalized, like the Fourth of July. This tradition originated on August 8, 1864, when Tennessee's military governor, Andrew Johnson, freed his personal slaves and urged his fellow Southerners to follow his example; it persisted because it gave black citizens their own special holiday, in addition to New Year's Day which was a "day off" they shared with whites. (East Tennessee's Unionists also voted Republican, and they persevered in doing so. The Second Congressional District, which includes Knoxville, has not sent a Democrat to the U.S. House of Representatives since 1854, and the First Congressional District of upper East Tennessee has broken the tradition only once.)

Meanwhile, Senator Brownlow had been using his considerable political influence on behalf of Knoxville, and he was aided in his endeavor by Representative Horace Maynard, another former leader of East Tennessee's Unionists. They pointed out to all and sundry that Knoxville was the *only* city to withstand a Civil War siege, and that the loyalty of its citizens had been neither recognized nor rewarded by the federal government. As a result of their strenuous efforts, Knoxville received a new Post Office and Customs House that was far superior to such structures in other Southern cities. Its architect, Alfred Bult Bullett, had gained national fame by designing an over-ornamented French Second Empire building for the State, War, and Navy departments in Washington, but he chose a simple italianate styling for Knoxville's federal building, and faced the outer walls with locally quarried white marble. When construction began at the corner of Clinch and Market streets in 1871, a railroad-spur was built to bring the marble to the site from east Knox County quarries. (The railroad bridge crossed the Holston at the Forks of the River, and the freight trains rumbled directly above the ruins of Mecklenburg, which had been the home of railroad enthusiast J.G.M. Ramsey.)

The railroads had opened up a world-wide market for Tennessee marble, and Bullett had brought it to the attention of other architects. Demand increased, and marble mills were established to cut the great quarried cubes into slabs, and polish them, before they were shipped away.

Tennessee's Senator William G. Brownlow, one of the foremost orators of his time, made not a single speech on the Senate floor during his entire term in office. Illness had left him with a permanent throat disability, and in the last years of his life, he was unable to speak except in a hoarse croak. The voice of Parson Brownlow may not have echoed in the Senate chamber, but his words were heard. His speeches were written and, although the vigor of his style was somewhat weakened by the substitution, they were read aloud for him by the clerk of the Senate.

His term in Washington completed, Senator Brownlow returned to Knoxville and to the newspaper business. He had sold the *Whig* when he became governor, so he now purchased a half interest in the *Knoxville Daily and Weekly Chronicle*, and wrote an occasional editorial for it. But Parson Brownlow had fought, and he had won; there were no dragons left to slay. He was willing to let others take on the uninspiring task of "binding up the wounds of war" while he watched from the sidelines, an interested observer and caustic critic of their efforts.

In 1876, the aging Parson Brownlow made his last public appearance at the dedication ceremony of Knoxville College for Negroes, which had been established by the United Presbyterian Church. He was escorted to the platform by a black alderman of Knoxville, William F. Yardley, who was then running for governor of Tennessee as an independent candidate. Yardley was a renowned public speaker, and as he stumped the state, many of his hearers likened his oratorical style to that of the fiery Governor Brownlow. (Even so, he received almost one percent of the total vote.)

During the 1870's, two buggies— one large and one small— regularly met each passenger train that pulled into the Knoxville depot. The smaller buggy carried passengers to the hotels; the larger conveyed travellers to the Brownlow home on East Cumberland Street. It was a rare day when at least a double dozen friends and allies of the Parson were not surrounding him on the porch or in the parlor.

William G. Brownlow died in 1877, and was buried in Gray Cemetery, but the stream of visitors did not cease. Every President of the United States who visited Knoxville in the period from Johnson to Taft paid his respects to Mrs. Brownlow, who lived to be ninety-five.

Tennessee's Reconstruction Governor was still a controversial figure in 1987. In that year, the legislature ordered Parson Brownlow's portrait removed from the newly renovated State Capitol.

THE PRESENCE OF THE PAST

The foundry built in 1868 by the Knoxville Iron Company took a new lease on life when the Second Creek Valley was chosen as the site of Knoxville's International Energy Exposition in 1982. The huge building that then became the Strohaus is now a permanent feature of the World's Fair Park.

When the beautiful Baker-Peters house was bought by an oil company in 1988, and was slated to be replaced with a filling station, preservationists rallied to save the Kingston Pike landmark. Officials of the Phillips Petroleum Company listened to the story of Dr. Harvey Baker's death, and of Abner Baker's attempt to avenge his father's murder, and graciously offered a compromise: They moved the proposed filling station to one side of their purchased property, and sold the historic house to a local investor for adaptive use.

Knoxville's reward for withstanding a Confederate siege was the imposing building of locally-quarried white marble that served as the main Post Office and Customs House until 1933, when a new pink-marble Post Office and Federal Building was completed on Main Street. The upper floors of the old Post Office then became the headquarters of the newly established Tennessee Valley Authority. In the early 1970's TVA moved into its own Towers, and transforming the steel-framed Customs House into a repository for local archives dating back to Territorial days was the first project approved by the Greater Knoxville American Revolution Bicentennial Commission. The building also houses the renowned McClung Historical Collection of the Knox County Public Library, and a major project of Knoxville's Bicentennial observance is the transformation of the East Tennessee Historical Center's street floor into a museum of local and area history.

In 1875, Dr. John Fouché remodeled his antebellum Gay Street home and dental office into a rental property, extending the brick structure westward along Clinch Avenue to the alley beside the Customs House. For more than a century, the Fouché Block's street level shops and upstairs offices remained fully occupied, but its prime corner location made the small two-story building an obvious target for "tax-increment financing." In 1989, Gay Street's second oldest building was condemned by the City, vacated, and turned over to the Knoxville Community Development Corporation for disposition. Demolition seemed inevitable until, in 1991, a proposal for its rehabilitation and reuse was accepted from Marylyn Bullock, the same developer who had salvaged the Southern Railway Station.

CHAPTER NINE

 ## INFLUENTIAL PEREZ DICKINSON

The final quarter of the 19th century would go down in history as a time of exceptional prosperity and progress. Knoxville, with railroad main lines and connectors raying out in all directions, was the wholesale distribution center for the upper South, supplying not only East Tennessee but large areas of Virginia, North and South Carolina, Georgia, Alabama, and Kentucky. Jackson Avenue warehouses backed up to the tracks for easy unloading, and the east side of Gay Street was lined from the railroad ravine to Union Avenue with capacious buildings that had street-level showrooms and stockrooms on the upper floors.

Each of the great wholesale houses specialized in one type of commodity. To name but a few examples, M.L. Ross & Company sold groceries; C.M. McClung & Company, hardware and farm equipment; Sanford, Chamberlain, & Albers, drugs; Daniel Briscoe Bros. Company, drygoods and notions; McMillan, Hazen Company, hats; Sterchi Bros., furniture and carpets; Arnold, Henegar, & Doyle, boots and shoes; Cullen & Newman, glass and china; McArthur, Sons & Company, musical instruments; and Hooker, Littlefield, & Steere, candy and confectionery.

Together, Knoxville's wholesale dealers offered all the merchandise a general store might conceivably carry, and on Gay Street, every day was like a trade fair. Each passenger train brought merchants from near and far, eager to replenish their stocks. Competition was keen, and the major firms sent their own hacks and drivers to meet incoming trains, with friendly "drummers" who drummed up trade by buttonholing prospective customers and escorting them back to the showrooms. Travelling salesmen went by hack to communities off the railroad, armed not only with bulky catalogues but with horsehide trunks crammed full of sample merchandise.

Mind you, this happy state of affairs was attained within twenty years after Knoxville was prostrated by the Civil War, but it was by no means an accidental occurrence. Former enemies had buried their differences and worked side by side, under the exemplary leadership of a man named Perez Dickinson.

The wholesale trade had begun in a small way before the war, and the most important of the antebellum companies remained a leader to the end of the century. When Cowan, McClung & Company opened in 1858, it was a store owner's one-stop shopping center containing everything from ladies' shawls to baling wire, and even after specialization became the order of the day, it continued to handle a wide range of items by maintaining several departments under one roof. Perez Dickinson was a silent partner in this firm, and he also engaged in undercover activities of quite a different sort.

He had spent two years at Amherst College before joining his family in Knoxville, where his brother-in-law, Joseph Estabrook, was principal of the Knoxville Female Academy. In 1830, after teaching for a year at Hampden-Sydney school for boys, he entered East Tennessee College where he earned a Bachelor of Arts degree and made a congenial friend in Thomas W. Humes. Thomas' father had died young, while building the handsome Gay Street residence and store that became Knoxville's best hotel. His mother was charming Margaret Russell, who had been married in turn to James Cowan, Thomas Humes, and Francis Alexander Ramsey. She was widowed three times, and to each of her deceased husbands she bore a posthumous son! (After Colonel Ramsey's death in 1820, she wisely declined to re-wed.)

The two friends regarded themselves as "progressive thinkers," and they thoroughly approved of a newspaper called *The Liberator*, first published in Massachusetts in 1831 by William Lloyd Garrison, which advocated the abolition of slavery. Most college students find, sooner or later, that their utopian goals are either out of reach, or out of reason. Not so Perez Dickinson and Thomas Humes.

Perez was not only idealistic but extremely canny, and he seemed to possess the Midas touch. In 1832, he formed a business partnership with another brother-in-law, James H. Cowan, (the eldest son of Margaret Russell Cowan Humes Ramsey) whose uncles had been Knoxville's first merchants forty years earlier. The new firm, Cowan & Dickinson, occupied a three-story brick building at the corner of Gay and Main streets, and prospered mightily. It was not long before Perez bought a Main Street lot, two blocks from the store, and built for himself and his mother a veritable mansion with wide and spacious rooms, broad porches, and deep cellars. (One of the cellars, and the porch above it, would later be of great importance.)

Back in Massachusetts, the Dickinsons had hired their household help; since this was not possible in Knoxville, Perez purchased well-trained house servants. This placed him in a quandary that was not uncommon among wealthy Southerners of the day: although he owned slaves, he was unalterably opposed to the concept of human bondage.

In 1838, he found himself dissatisfied with the editorial policies and the literary shortcomings of Knoxville's weekly newspapers, and felt inclined to start a new and different journal. To appease his transplanted New England conscience, he proposed to publish an anti-slavery paper. There were other young men in Knoxville who shared his qualms and who agreed to help finance a newspaper of literary merit that would introduce their little city to some inspiriting ideas. But in the year 1838, abolitionism was still radical thinking, even in Massachusetts. In the South, it was considered unparalleled effrontery. Upon mature reflection, one after another of the group withdrew their names and their financial support from the venture, leaving Perez Dickinson to underwrite its entire cost.

He made a trip to Philadelphia, where he purchased the best available printing press, and went on to Boston in search of a printer. There he found James C. Moses, whose credentials were excellent, and who was willing to come south as foreman for the *Knoxville Times*. He found an editor closer to home in Thomas Humes.

Thomas and Perez had no intention of producing an inflammatory gazette like the *Liberator*. Their bi-weekly newspaper (the first in Knoxville to appear more than once a week) was more than a collection of news items and advertisements: it was an scholarly publication, artistically printed on best-quality paper, and even its advertisements were couched in polished prose. In this form, disguised to be sure but still recognizable, appeared Perez Dickinson's idea of an abolitionist newspaper for the South. Its anti-slavery views were partially hidden in general moralization, but they were there— a strange anomaly in Knoxville, Tennessee.

After some months, the *Times* was allowed to merge with its rival, the *Knoxville Register*; the *Register's* name was retained, but James C. Moses became the owner of the combined papers. Perez Dickinson had decided that it was too soon for even a watered-down version of abolitionism in Knoxville, but his personal convictions upon the subject remained unchanged.

Those convictions were heartily endorsed by a new literary club called the "Junto", whose members included the defunct *Times'* owner,

Perez Dickinson; its editor, Thomas Humes; its foreman, James C. Moses; John L. Moses, a lawyer, who had joined his brother James in Knoxville; and Horace Maynard, a recent Amherst graduate who was teaching at East Tennessee College. They looked upon themselves as Knoxville's intelligentsia, and each of them would justify that exalted opinion. Thomas Humes entered the Episcopal ministry, and founded St. John's Episcopal Church; he wrote a book about the Civil War entitled *The Loyal Mountaineers of East Tennessee*; he was president of East Tennessee University and its successor, the University of Tennessee, and came out of retirement to be the first librarian of Lawson McGhee Library. James and John Moses organized the First Baptist Church, and acted in turn as chairman of the board of the Tennessee School for the Deaf in the pre- and post-war years. Horace Maynard was a recognized leader of East Tennessee's Unionists, and the county seat of Union County is named Maynardville in his honor. He served in the U.S. House of Representatives before and after the Civil War. He was appointed U.S. Ambassador to Turkey by President Grant, and was Postmaster General of the United States under President Hayes. Perez Dickinson continued to be a moving force behind the scenes.

In 1845, Perez returned to Massachusetts to marry Susan Penniman of New Braintree. After the wedding on April 10, the Dickinsons set out at once from Boston, by way of New York and Washington, to Raleigh, North Carolina. This much of the journey was accomplished in the comparative comfort of steamboat saloons and railroad cars, but the rest was not so easy. Boarding a stagecoach in Raleigh, they jolted slowly westward to Greensboro, to Salisbury, to Asheville, to Warm Springs...Finally, through the glorious green of East Tennessee's countryside, they arrived in Knoxville where a joyous welcome awaited them, and began a pleasant and leisurely life.

It would be nice to buy a hilltop, Susan suggested, and plant some fruit trees and a flower garden. Perez listened smilingly as she planned a square white summer home with cool, high-ceilinged rooms, and talked of the entertaining they would do there. As soon as they found the right hilltop, Perez promised, they would build the house and plant the gardens.

The next year, a baby was born in the house on Main Street; the next day, Susan Dickinson and the baby both were dead.

Perez was exceedingly fond of children, and he had built the Main Street house with a family in mind. He and his mother would have found it echoingly large had it not been constantly running over with Estabrooks and Cowans— to say nothing of New England relatives who, having made the long trip to Tennessee, paid visits lasting several months. (Cousin Emily Dickinson, the shy and retiring family poetess, was regaled with descriptions of East Tennessee's rough-hewn hills and misty mountains by many a returned traveller.) After the death of Lucinda Dickinson Cowan, her daughters came to live with their grandmother in Uncle P's hospitable home. Grandmother Dickinson died in 1855, and from then on, the misses Mary and Lucy Cowan took over the management of Uncle's household. Lucy stayed on after her marriage to Charles Alexander, and to Uncle's great delight, two healthy babies were born in the Main Street house.

In the period preceding the outbreak of the Civil War, Perez was an avowed Union sympathizer, and an undercover abolitionist. Opponents of slavery were considered traitors in the rest of the South, and even in East Tennessee, it was best to make no mention of such radical sentiments, so he did not bruit his views about. He acted upon them, and in so doing, he took advantage of a natural phenomenon, the honeycomb of caves that underlies Downtown Knoxville.

His house, with its extensive cellars, was a scant two blocks from the north bank of the river; across the river and downstream, the mouth of a deep cavern on Cherokee Bluffs was just above the waterline. When his preparations were complete, a secret tunnel connected one of his cellars with a cave extending almost to the river's edge, and a small "servants' house" covered the exit of the passageway. From this point, the current would carry a skiff to within a few yards of the cavern at Cherokee Bluffs.

The Dickinson nieces were sometimes called upon to sit on the side porch with their needlework. Who would suspect, seeing them placidly sewing there in plain view of passers-by on Main Street, that below the porch floor was a cellar where frightened runaways were huddled? Not until it was pitch black dark could they pass through the tunnel and cross the river to the next hiding place on the "Underground Railroad."

After Tennessee seceded from the Union, and Confederate troops arrived to occupy Knoxville, Perez Dickinson's reputation as a Unionist suspected of anti-slavery leanings placed every member of his household in grave danger. Lucy was devastated by divided loyalty when Charles Alexander volunteered for the Confederate Army and was commissioned a major. When, in the summer of 1861, all East Tennesseans were required to sign an oath of allegiance to the Confederacy or quit the country, Perez Dickinson had no choice but to leave and take his family— Mary, Lucy, and the beloved children— with him.

A hack was piled high with trunks of clothing, folding chairs, cushions, and bundles of bedding; and a cow was tied behind to furnish milk for the toddlers on the way to Jonesborough, where they would reach a section of the railroad that was not in Confederate hands. Abandoning the hack, but not the cow, they set up housekeeping in a box-car for the long trip to Syracuse, New York, where they remained until it was safe to come home again.

After the publication of the Emancipation Proclamation, the Dickinson household returned to Knoxville wearing deep mourning for Major Alexander, who had been killed in battle. The Main Street house was little better than a shambles, having been commandeered by the Confederates as officers' quarters and used by Union forces as a hospital. In renovating it, Perez decided to leave the tunnel.

The end of the war was in sight, but the shelves of the city's stores were empty, and all the banks were closed. As the first step in reestablishing Knoxville as a business center, a group of citizens formed a new bank that began extending credit to merchants for replenishing their wares. Perez Dickinson was named president of the First National Bank, and he offered the best possible proof that the bank was solvent and its stock "gilt-edged" by paying all stockholders' dividends in gold.

In 1865, the absence of war did not mean the immediate presence of peace. Although Knox County was never terrorized by the Ku Klux Klan, there were bound to be racial incidents as freed slaves competed with returned soldiers for scarce jobs. Several times, the Dickinson nieces sat and stitched on the side porch while some family friend took refuge in the cellar until it was time to escape through the secret tunnel.

The Emancipation Proclamation had brought freedom, plus a whole new set of problems. For the first time in their lives, freed slaves were expected to provide their own clothing, food, and shelter. Those who had no marketable skills stayed on in domestic service, and for the first time, newly impoverished former slaveowners found themselves paying wages to their household help. It was mutual courtesy and forbearance that made the situation tolerable.

In the community at large, a major social revolution was quietly taking place. It required great self-confidence, and enormous courage, for Knoxville's freed slaves to put their new-found independence to the test; but blacks fared far better here than in other Southern cities—

primarily because they were so few in number. Most of them had been house servants, or trained artisans who worked alongside their owners at various trades, and there was therefore a close personal relationship between the races. At the close of the war, the skilled carpenters, smiths, and bricklayers were hired to help repair the city's ravaged buildings. Butlers, valets, and coachmen had acquired the manners and the speech patterns of the households where they lived and worked; they were sought after by the reopening hotels, restaurants, and livery stables. Many former slaves embarked upon new careers with the aid of their former masters, who never ceased to feel responsible for the people who had belonged to them. For instance, Benjamin Maynard was helped to buy a tract of South Knoxville land which he turned into a flower farm. He operated a colorful and popular stall in the Market House as an outlet for his blossoms and greenery, and was for many years East Tennessee's only black florist. (Emancipated slaves were permitted to choose their own surnames, and Benjamin had elected to keep the name of his owner and benefactor, Horace Maynard.)

Before the war, the balconies of Knoxville's churches had been reserved for servants attending services with their white families. Mount Zion Baptist Church was organized in 1864, during the Union occupation of the city, and two more black churches were established in 1865. One was Logan Chapel, AME Zion; the other was Shiloh Presbyterian Church, which met on the rear porch and the lawn of Perez Dickinson's Main Street house until a lot was purchased and a sanctuary built.

One of the Shiloh Church's organizers was James Mason, who had been Major James Swan's valet and favorite servant. He had learned to read and write, and was permitted to earn money on the side, so long as his outside work did not interfere with household duties. Every penny of his earnings had been saved to purchase his wife Betty's freedom because, under Tennessee law, the children of a slave mother were born into slavery. James Mason wanted his children to be born free. When his own freedom, and his family's, was assured by the Emancipation Proclamation, he used his savings to buy a house and lot on West Cumberland Avenue, and became Knoxville's first black taxpayer in 1866.

Unlike other Southern states, Tennessee had no laws prohibiting education for non-whites. James Mason was one of many slaves who were taught the 3 R's in their Knoxville owners' households, and for some years before the war, Reverend Thomas Humes conducted a school for free black children at St. John's Episcopal Church. During the Union occupation, Knoxville was overrun by black refugees. With the permission of General Burnside, a school for their children was opened by Mrs. Laura Scott Cansler, who had attended the school at St. John's.

Leaders of both races looked upon free public education as the only lasting remedy for the postwar period's social and economic woes, and under a revised school law passed in 1867, Tennessee became the first Southern state to mandate public schools for white and black children in each county. Knox County's school system was established in 1868. In 1871, when Knoxville's first public schools opened in rented houses scattered throughout the city, three of the nine were for black children. The president of the Board of Education, Jesse A. Rayl, stated that the schools' purpose was "to educate white and black, rich and poor, Catholic and Protestant, exactly alike, giving no advantage to the one that you do not give to the other, and making all conform to the same rules."

One of the teachers in those first city schools was Miss Emily Austin, a Philadelphia lady past the first blush of youth who had decided to devote her life to black children. In 1879, a new school was planned for her pupils, and her friends in Philadelphia and Boston contributed $6,500 toward the building of the Austin School on Central Avenue. But Emily Austin had discovered that her pupils' special needs were not met by the regular curriculum that was the same for white and black children. It was largely through her efforts that the Slater Training School opened in 1885 with 200 black pupils and $6,000 in funds, of which $5,000 had been contributed by northern friends. In addition to the first three grades of the city's school program, useful trades were taught: carpentry and printing for boys; sewing, cooking, and housekeeping for girls.

When Emily Austin died in Philadelphia in 1897, memorial services were held at Knoxville's Logan AME Temple, and a plaque was placed in the Austin School. The plaque, transferred to succeeding schools that have borne her name and most recently at Austin-East, reads:

In Memory of
Miss Emily L. Austin
Born October 1, 1829; died May 4, 1897
Founder of the Austin School in Knoxville, Tennessee, and for

thirty years a devoted friend of the freedmen, fearless of criticism, shrinking from no duty, unswerving in fidelity, coveting only Divine approval. She is gratefully remembered by those whose elevation she sought by educating mind and heart.
"She has done what she could."

Knoxville College was founded by the United Presbyterian Church in 1875, for the purpose of educating young black men and women for the teaching profession; the following year, its first building was dedicated on a hill still scarred by Confederate siege trenches. The school's president, Dr. J. S. McCulloch, complained to the board of the sponsoring church in 1877 that the institution he headed could hardly be called a "college", since its most advanced students were barely able to cope with fractions and percentages. The secretary of the church board replied: "It is a College, and a College it shall be." Dr. McCulloch took those words to heart.

The Tennessee School for the Deaf had reopened in its renovated building that had seen hard usage as Asylum Hospital, and was adding new dormitories and classrooms as enrollment escalated, but no provision was being made for black deaf-mutes. James Mason took the first step toward education for the children of his race who could neither hear nor speak, when he opened a school for them at his home on Cumberland Avenue in 1879. Once this school was in existence, John L. Moses, Chairman of the Board of TSD, was able to persuade the state authorities to take over its support. In 1881, the beautiful old house built by Melinda White Williams was purchased by the State of Tennessee, and James Mason moved his ten pupils into the new Colored Branch of the Tennessee School for the Deaf.

With the expansion of the railroads during the post-war period came a corresponding rise in employment, on rail line construction and in railroad-related heavy industries. Word went out through Alabama, Georgia, and South Carolina that good-paying jobs were available in Knoxville, where schooling was provided *free* for every child, and families flocked to take advantage of these dual opportunities. Two primarily black postwar communities, developed by landowners John L. Moses and Colonel Charles McGhee, merged into the busy suburb of Mechanicsville with a population of 2000. Mechanicsville was annexed to Knoxville on its own petition in 1883, bringing with it Fairview School which had been built by the citizens themselves on land donated by John L. Moses.

From 1869 to 1890, Knoxville had at least one black alderman, and in some years two. At least three black lawyers were admitted to the bar, after reading law in the offices of white attorneys, and many ambitious citizens— women as well as men— were going into business for themselves. More than one outstanding family cook became a cateress whose services were engaged weeks in advance for important social functions. Skilled seamstresses took up dressmaking, moving from household to household in order to refurbish the ladies' wardrobes. Several former lady's maids became "hairdressers," and paid weekly visits to the homes of their regular clients, while former valets were in great demand as barbers. The 1883 City Directory listed nine black-owned and operated barbershops, plus four saloons, four blacksmith shops, two shoemaker's shops, a restaurant, and a boardinghouse. (One of the saloon-keepers, Caledona F. Johnson, was already a city alderman, and was destined to be among Knoxville's wealthiest men.)

While the black community was making such remarkable strides, white Knoxvillians were fitting together the shards of their shattered world. Music lovers of whatever political persuasion rubbed elbows at the Philharmonic Society's vocal and instrumental concerts that began in 1867, and the windows of every house were opened to the serenades of the Martingale Club's strolling singers. The whole city took pride in the opulently appointed Staub's Opera House, which opened (in Knoxville's first permanent theatre building) at the southeast corner of Gay and Cumberland in 1872, with a locally-cast production of *William Tell*.

Business recovery was underway, and considerable entertaining was going on. No one played host more often, or more lavishly, than Perez Dickinson who had acquired a new hobby and a new summer home.

There was great need to rebuild the productivity of East Tennessee's war-wasted farms, and he was setting an example. Purchasing a large level island in the river just above the city in 1869, he bought also a mile or two of nearby southshore land. On a hilltop overlooking the property, he built a country home in a setting of fruit trees and flower gardens, exactly as Susan had planned so long ago. The house was square and white, and beautiful with the architectural simplicity of New England; he named it "Island Home."

No other Knoxville house was ever the scene of more parties, or sheltered a greater number of distinguished guests, but Island Home's owner never spent a night beneath its roof.

As the seasons passed, elm trees overarched the carriage drive that led through the riverside property to the house. There were apple and peach trees in the orchards, and sweet cherry, pear, and plum trees on the lawn. Flowers bloomed all year around in the outdoor gardens and the greenhouses, and Perez quietly assumed the responsibility of furnishing the altar flowers for Second Presbyterian Church. Every week, his carriage arrived from Island Home in time for morning worship, bringing the best of whatever was in bloom. Experience taught him that exactly enough blossoms to fill the two marble urns on the pulpit would fit upright in a large oval cardboard hatbox, and the box of flowers was a familiar Sunday morning sight for almost thirty years.

He took great delight in driving out to Island Home with a carriage full of friends, or in entertaining Sunday School groups there; every guest received a gift of fruit or a posy of flowers to take home. So many people came out of curiosity, uninvited, that Perez posted a sign of his own composition at the point where the carriage drive divided to encircle the house. It read:

Welcome to view the beauties of this place
Raised by the gardener's skill on nature's face,
But no rude hand should fruit or flower pull.
For pulling fruit without the Gardener's leave,
Mankind was ruined by our Mother Eve.

In 1875, a group of young men organized a rifle company, intending to entertain themselves not only with drills and target practice, but with the more congenial pursuits of picnics and supper parties. It made no difference that some of them were scions of families that had supported the Confederacy while others belonged to families that had been pro-Union: they unanimously elected Perez Dickinson their honorary colonel, and called themselves the Dickinson Light Guard. Perez was tremendously complimented, and responded (as they had hoped he would) by entertaining the Dickinson Rifles often. Soon everyone was calling him "Colonel Dickinson", and very much the portly Southern colonel he looked with his twinkling eyes, his pleasant smile, his broad-brimmed planter's hat.

Only the best would do for a man who went to Boston for a printer and to Philadelphia for a printing press: Colonel Dickinson had sent to Switzerland for a farmer. Under the management of Henry Ebnoether, Island Home turned into a showcase for the latest developments in agriculture, and crowds of people came to watch the region's first mechanical reaper in operation. Part of the property was a model stock-farm, and thereby hangs a tale.

Island Home had produced a monstrous hog, weighing upwards of a thousand pounds, that was the envy of neighboring farmers. A parade of fine livestock was arranged in Knoxville, and it was a foregone conclusion that Colonel Dickinson's giant porker would have a place of honor in the line of march. Up Gay Street, past the reviewing stand in front of the Fouché Block, came spirited horses, balky mules, fat cattle, and finally, the Colonel's thousand pound hog. After a quarter century of hard use, the river-rock pavement was pitted with holes, and an overnight rain had left them filled with muddy water. At the Clinch Street corner, the weary hog paused to wallow in a convenient puddle, and there the exertion of the march overcame him. Before the very eyes of the judges, he flopped over on his bulging side, and died!

After the pontoon bridge washed away in 1867, the only way to reach South Knoxville was by ferry, from the mouth of First Creek; but the ferry was exasperatingly slow and traffic grew heavier every year. In 1874, the County Court supposedly solved the problem once and for all by building a toll bridge at the foot of Gay Street. Massive stone piers supported the wooden box-bridge with high solid sides that kept horses from "spooking" at the sight of the water far below. This bridge opened with great fanfare in 1874, and cut the time required to drive from Colonel Dickinson's Main Street house to Island Home in half. *HOWEVER*, on May 2, 1875, the wooden superstructure was blown off its piers by a sudden gust of wind! So it was back to ferries while the County Court debated what to do with the empty stone piers.

A car-line had been planned to run the length of Gay Street from the bridge to the railroad, and the Board of Aldermen did not allow the County Court's misfortune to delay public transportation on the city's principal business street. Tracks were soon laid, and horsecars ran on schedule, past Perez Dickinson & Company's retail store on the Main Street corner and Cowan McClung & Company's imposing new wholesale house at Union Avenue.

The car-line was not the only innovation in 1876. Knoxville had its first ice plant where, wonderful to relate, river water was transformed into huge blocks of crystal-clear ice even on the hottest summer day! Peter Kern was quick to see the possibilities of manufactured ice. He moved his flourishing bakery into the back of a new building on Market Square at Union Avenue, reserving the front for Kern's Ice Cream

Parlor.   There, white metal chairs and tables stood about the checkerboard floor of black and white marble, and delectable cakes and candies were displayed in a tall glass case along one wall. Above the ice cream parlor was a ballroom presided over by a French dancing master, where young ladies and gentlemen learned to waltz to the strains of a gilded harp.

In 1879, East Tennessee University was elevated to the dignity of a state university and Colonel Dickinson, the longtime friend of its president Dr. Thomas Humes, was appointed to the University of Tennessee's first Board of Visitors. He repaid the compliment by offering gold medals for superior scholarship, and made it a practice to entertain each year's senior class. As many as 200 guests attended these annual banquets at his home on Main Street. Engineering was then called "Mechanical Arts."   When a handsome new building was constructed for this popular program, it was named for the University's outstanding former president, Joseph Estabrook.   Perez Dickinson presented the portrait of his brother-in-law, by Lloyd Branson, that hangs in Estabrook Hall (now the second oldest academic building on the UT campus.)

For several years, the city had had a Library and Reading Room, supported by private subscription and open to members only. In 1879, it was decided that the privileges of the library should be extended to all citizens of Knoxville, and that its collection should be greatly expanded— in fact, its governing body avowed for the library the object of acquiring every book and pamphlet ever published in the State of Tennessee! When this first public library was established, the chairman of its board was none other than Colonel Perez Dickinson.

He was among the merchant princes who doubled as the city's civic leaders, and were successful in both roles. "What's good for business is good for Knoxville", they reiterated, "and vice versa." The Board of Trade, whose president was Perez Dickinson, had enormous political influence, and did not hesitate to use it: advantageous new developments came thick and fast.

In 1880, the County Court was persuaded to lease its empty piers to a private developer for construction of a wooden toll bridge, this time with latticed sides. One block of Gay Street, extending almost perpendicularly upward from the riverside, was permanently closed and the bridge ended at the Hill Street level. Consequently, the new span sagged in the middle. The grade was so steep at the Gay Street end that signs were posted, warning: "$5 fine to ride or drive faster than a walk on this bridge!" Even so, the way to Island Home was made much easier.

The first telephone wires were strung on tall poles along Gay and Main Streets in 1880, and long distance lines were added in 1884. (In 1894, a second telephone exchange was created, and the two companies continued to compete until 1925, when they merged into the Bell System. All the banks, and many businesses, found it expedient to subscribe to both the Old Phone and the New Phone, and W.W. Woodruff & Company was listed as Number 1 in both directories.)

The blessing of "city water" arrived in 1882, with the completion of an intake station on Riverside Drive and a tall cylindrical water tower, with an attendant standpipe, on Mabry's Hill. Untreated river water was pumped uphill to the settling tank, and distributed through the network of water mains by gravity flow.

In 1883, the state legislature made a generous appropriation of $80,000 to build a hospital for the insane, at Knoxville. Its turreted and crenelated building, on property settled in 1809 by Captain William Lyon, overlooked a horseshoe bend of the Tennessee River with four tiers of the Smoky Mountains in the distance; so, although its official title was the East Tennessee Insane Asylum, its euphemistic local name was "Lyon's View."

The city's skyline was dramatically altered in 1884 by the addition of two tall clock towers at opposite ends of the plateau. Together, they remedied the lack of a "town clock" in the bell-tower of the City Hall. (Public timepieces were urgently needed, because a pocket-watch was beyond the means of the average working man, and the wristwatch had yet to be invented.) High above Market Square on Summit Hill, a fine brick Church of the Immaculate Conception replaced the tiny Roman Catholic mission, and the City of Knoxville paid for the very large clock that was installed in its soaring steeple. Eight blocks away, Knox County's government left its 1840's Greek Revival Court House, and moved across Main Street to a stylish red brick Queen Anne Revival structure with Civil War naval cannons flanking its entrance; one wall of the entry hall held a painting by Knoxville artist, Lloyd Branson, of the 1793 Blockhouse on whose site the new Court House stood. In the square central tower that ended in a copper-roofed cupola, a clock with four faces not only told time visibly, but struck the quarter-hours loudly and authoritatively. (Construction of both the church and the Court House was delayed by the fact that they were competing for building materials from the same brickyard.)

City services increased by leaps and bounds under the Board of Public Works that was established in 1883 to create new city departments for specific purposes. The first was a Street Department responsible for pavement maintenance, and for the installation of sanitary and storm sewers. Within two years, the City Health Department had begun building the handsome, well-equipped Knoxville General Hospital near North Broadway, and the new Knoxville Fire Department was staffed by paid professional firemen instead of volunteers. One year later, Knoxville's first Police Department had three officers including the chief, and eighteen patrolmen. (James Mason was one of two black policemen, and retired from the force after eighteen years of service.)

The first electric streetlight caused a sensation when it was switched on at the southwest corner of Gay and Clinch streets in 1885. (A new set of wires carried current from a coal-fired generating plant to the ornamental clusters of large white globes borne upright on heavy cast-iron posts.) A few merchants "modernized" their premises with ceiling fixtures, but the bright new lights were deemed far too garish for home use.

There was no room in the City Hall for all the new divisions of Public Works, so the original building was replaced in 1888 by a larger and more elaborate structure on the same Market Square site. Huge doors opened onto Wall Street, allowing the horse-drawn fire engine to make a quick exit from the ground floor Fire Hall, and once again the building was topped by a bell tower. (The fire bell was an anachronism, for there was no longer any need to summon volunteers.) An electric alarm system was something new: to report a fire, one simply twisted the handle of the numbered metal alarm box wired into a corner light post.

Perez Dickinson was a member of the commission that raised funds to return the body of Tennessee's first governor to the State's first capital, and he made the journey to Alabama on the special train that brought John Sevier's flag-draped casket home in 1889. He sat on the platform during the lengthy and loquacious reinterment services on the Court House lawn, and he was on the platform eight years later when the Sevier Monument was dedicated.

Knoxville's first electric streetcar line was formally opened on May 1, 1890, and Colonel Dickinson was among the "leading citizens" who rode in the procession of trolley cars to Lake Ottosee. (The host on that occasion was William Gibbs McAdoo, the president of the

Knoxville Street Railway Company, who later lost a vicious fight for control of the city's streetcar system, and went on to greener pastures. He became Secretary of the Treasury under President Woodrow Wilson, and was married in the White House in 1914, to the President's daughter, Eleanor Wilson.)

Lake Ottosee was on the eastern outskirts of the city, and access to it had been made possible by the granting of a 100-foot right of way through the extensive property of the Branner family. Knoxville Mayor H. Bryan Branner named that wide street Magnolia Avenue in honor of his mother, Mrs. George Branner, née Magnolia Bryan, who was instrumental in establishing a local Audubon Society.

To mark the 25th anniversary of the Civil War's end, both Union and Confederate veterans of the Battle of Fort Sanders attended a reunion in Knoxville in October of 1890. Some out-of-town dignitaries were guests at Island Home, but many more were entertained in the Cumberland Avenue mansion of Perez Dickinson's nephew, James D. Cowan, that stood in the very shadow of the Fort. The reunion lasted through three days of speeches, reminiscences, band concerts, and poetic readings. General Longstreet was present, and had prepared an address that was read for him by a friend: a bullet wound in the neck, received during the last days of the war, made it impossible for him to speak above a whisper.

Veterans revisiting Fort Sanders were surprised to find that the trees cut down before the battle had never grown back. The bare hillsides below the eroding earthworks had been divided into building lots, and Clinch Street ran the length of the ridge crest, stopping at the Fort's western palisade. The southeastern bastion of Fort Sanders had become the corner of Clinch and Sixteenth streets, and there a massive granite monument was erected to honor the 79th New York Highlanders who were responsible for the Fort's defense in 1863. A number of former Highlanders had come for the unveiling ceremony, and afterward, they walked diagonally across Sixteenth Street to a reception at the castle-like Cowan home. (Entering a side gate of the grounds that covered a city block, they passed several greenhouses, and the water tower that made the mansion's indoor plumbing possible, on their way to the "vestibule" front door that faced Cumberland Avenue. They were particularly impressed by the full-size bowling alley in the basement.)

Colonel Dickinson had begun to use his advancing years as an excuse for declining committee chairmanships and tedious public functions, but Island Home was still the scene of innumerable picnics and garden parties for church and civic groups. He was always happy to entertain the Dickinson Light Guard, the students of the University, his family, and his friends. Still the hatbox of flowers arrived each Sunday at the Second Presbyterian Church, and on his eightieth birthday in 1893, there was an interesting reversal. His florist friend, Benjamin Maynard, brought eighty lilies to the man who had given so many flowers to so many people, for so many years.

That year, in front of the Colonel's house, a new set of overhead wires cross-hatched Main Street from pole to opposite pole, supporting an electrical cable above the trolley tracks in the center of the new brick pavement. High-backed, forward-facing benches stretched all the way across the open-sided electric streetcars that were mounted by means of running boards, and at the end of the line, the conductor reversed the position of the bench backs so that passengers could face forward on the return trip. Many families decided that keeping a horse and buggy was a needless expense, now that it was possible to "take the trolley" to all parts of town.

South Knoxvillians (and Perez Dickinson) convinced the County Court in 1895 that the sway-backed fifteen foot wooden toll bridge was unsafe for the "heavy traffic" of carriages, wagons, pedestrians, and farm animals that used it daily. The County floated a bond issue of $225,000, and reclaimed its stone piers for construction upon them of a fifty-foot wide steel span whose superstructure would rise more than a hundred feet above the water and would therefore be level at both ends. (During construction, a temporary wooden bridge was supported by the lower scaffolding, and ended on Front Street.) When the wide and wonderful— and free to the public— Gay Street Bridge opened in 1898, Colonel Perez Dickinson's carriage was one of the first vehicles to cross it.

Another amenity of the waning century was the splendid two-story Market House, completed in 1897, that filled the center of Market Square from Union Avenue to the City Hall. Permanent stalls inside the building specialized in bakery products, fresh meats and fish, staples, and "shipped produce", while pats of country butter and homemade cottage cheese were sold from tables in the center of the floor. Outside, bushel baskets of hickory-cane corn, market baskets of ripe peaches, coops of plump live chickens, and buckets of rainbow-hued zinnias from Knox County's once-again flourishing farms were temptingly displayed in wagons backed up to the curb. (Fruits and vegetables were sold by the peck or by the dozen, rather than by the pound.) A large public hall on the second floor of the Market House provided needed space for political rallies, official ceremonies, and meetings of the Chamber of Commerce.

But the 19th century went out in a blaze that was far from a blaze of glory. On April 10, 1897, smoke billowed from the windows of a wholesale house, and flames soon spread along the east side of Gay Street from Commerce to Union avenues. Alerted by telegraph, the Chattanooga Fire Department loaded men and equipment on railroad flatcars, and highballed to the aid of Knoxville's embattled firemen. Despite the efforts of the combined crews, the fire burned for days, feeding on the contents of eight multi-story buildings crammed with furniture and carpets, groceries, hats, shoes, hardware, china, and paper products. Far worse than the material destruction was the loss of four lives in the collapse of the Knox Hotel.

Although all the buildings leveled by the blaze were replaced and reoccupied within a year, Gay Street's "Million Dollar Fire" marked the beginning of Knoxville's change from a center of wholesale distribution to a retail shopping center: the city's first department store, the M. M. Newcomer Company, filled all five floors of a former jobbing house, and spilled over into a tiny adjoining building with Newcomer's Pharmacy.

Another era ended four years later. In Old Gray Cemetery, a simple monument of finest quality bears the inscription: "Perez Dickinson. Born Feb. 25, 1813, Died July 17, 1901. A resident of Knoxville for 71 years."

During those years, Knoxville had changed from a town torn asunder by conflicting loyalties to a progressive and cohesive city. Perez, the radical young newcomer, had become Colonel Dickinson, Knoxville's most influential and beloved citizen; only a few years after he was exiled from Knoxville because of his anti-slavery beliefs, his return from a lengthy business trip was hailed by a brass band playing "Welcome, Welcome Home."

THE PRESENCE OF THE PAST

Colonel Dickinson would be pleased that his model farm is now the campus of the Tennessee School for the Deaf, and he would rejoice with James Mason and John L. Moses that the school is fully integrated. His knot-gardens and greenhouses have long since given way to dormitories and classrooms, but square white Island Home belies its age as the lovingly cared for Superintendent's Residence. Since 1930, Dickinson's Island has been the Downtown Island Airport. A portion of the Colonel's riverside property, developed into a series of gardens and a bird sanctuary by Mr. and Mrs. Harry P. Ijams, has become the city-owned ecological treasure, Ijams Audubon Nature Park.

In the McClung Historical Collection is a portrait of Susan Dickinson that is said to have been painted by Samuel Shaver in 1846. Behind the seated figure of a pale, dark haired young woman is the likeness of Perez Dickinson's Main Street house that was razed for a parking lot after World War II.

Cowan McClung & Company's mammoth wholesale house, built in 1873, was spared when Gay Street's "Million Dollar Fire" stopped on the opposite side of Union Avenue. The building was extensively remodeled by Fidelity Bankers Trust Company in the 1920's; since then its appearance has hardly changed.

Between Union and Wall Avenues are the architecturally significant buildings erected in 1897, after the disastrous fire. This portion of Gay Street's east side became the "Promenade Block" in 1960, when the structures were connected by a covered walkway at the rear, reached by stairways from a multi-level parking lot with a State Street entrance. One of the buildings is still occupied by its original owner, Woodruff's, which has been in business on Gay Street since 1865.

Peter Kern's Ice Cream Parlor on Market Square was Knoxville's meeting place from 1875 through World War I, and three generations of brides planned their receptions around Kern's tiered wedding cakes and white grape ice. Ice cream, individually molded into pink roses, bluebirds with spread wings, or golden slippers, was available until Kern's Bakery moved to Chapman Highway in the 1930's. Two restaurants, and an executive-suite hotel, now occupy the building at the Union Avenue corner.

Since 1876, Knoxville College has occupied its hilltop campus that is centered by the belfry tower of McKee Hall. The four-year liberal arts institution continued to flourish until the 1970's when it shared the nationwide revenue decline of small private colleges. Through the efforts of its determined alumni, it weathered the financial crisis to remain an outstanding member of the National Negro College Association. (The college campus encompasses the former home of famous author, Frances Hodgson Burnett, who lived in Knoxville from 1869 to 1875; it was during this time that her short stories began to appear in print.)

There have been many improvements in the attitude toward, and the treatment of mental illness since the East Tennessee Insane Asylum was established on Lyons View Pike in 1883, and to reflect them, the hospital's name has been changed several times. It is now the Lakeshore Mental Health Institution, and its tall iron entrance gates stand open.

The 1884 Knox County Court House was greatly enlarged in the 1920's to make room for expanding governmental functions. The cannon that originally flanked its entrance were donated to the World War II scrap drive, along with the cast iron picket fence that surrounded its lawn; Lloyd Branson's painting of the 1793 Blockhouse on its site now hangs in the McClung Historical Collection. A recent total renovation has restored the youth of Downtown Knoxville's most distinctive landmark, and the Old Court House still serves its original purpose of housing County offices.

The Church of the Immaculate Conception, completed on West Vine Street in 1884, seats Downtown Knoxville's last-organized congregation in the area's oldest church building. The sanctuary was saved in the 1970's, when several nearby streets were obliterated to make way for Summit Hill Drive, but its parish house and parochial school were casualties of that construction.

The steel Gay Street Bridge, which opened in 1898, replaces two former wooden spans on the same stone piers. Until the Henley Street Bridge opened in 1932, it provided the only access to South Knoxville; passenger traffic has been carried across it by horse-drawn hacks and carriages, trolley cars, and chauffeured limousines, as well as by diesel buses and compact cars.

Above: A prehistoric Indian burial mound on the campus of the UT College of Agricultural Science and Natural Resources.

At left: Sequoyah, the only man in history who invented an entirely new alphabet, lived in a Cherokee town on the Little Tennessee River.

Above: In 1786, James White erected a log house on the future site of Knoxville.

Below: It was sold after 1800 to James Kennedy, Jr., who built this handsome residence facing State Street. Protected with weatherboard, James White's house became the kitchen wing that linked the mansion with the servants' quarters.

Above: James White's house as the Kennedy kitchen.

Below: When the Kennedy home was razed in 1906, its historic wing was bought by Isaiah Ford who removed the clapboards and numbered each log as it was lifted down.

Above: **The house, reassembled south of the river on Woodlawn Pike, was the Ford family home for over 50 years.**

Below: **In 1970, Knoxville's oldest house was moved again, to its present location near the James White Memorial Auditorium/Coliseum.**

At right: In 1791, Governor William Blount selected White's Fort as the site of the Southwest Territory's capital.

Below: This 1976 photograph of Blount Mansion shows the detached kitchen, the Governor's one-room office that was the Territory's seat of government, and a small cooling cellar for milk and wine that had been unearthed during a recent garden restoration.

At left: Blount named the territorial capital for Major General Henry Knox, a hero of the American Revolution, who was Secretary of War in President Washington's cabinet.

Below: Charles McClung, who planned and surveyed the town of Knoxville in 1791, and his wife Margaret, the eldest daughter of James White.

At right: One of Tennessee's representatives in the national capitol's Hall of Fame is Governor John Sevier. (The other is President Andrew Jackson.)

GENERAL JOHN SEVIER
of
TENNESSEE

First Governor 1796-1801, 1803-1809
Governor of the State of Franklin, 1785-1788
Representative in Congress 1790-1791, 1811-1815

Below: Sevier's Plantation, Marble Springs, is maintained by the State of Tennessee as an historic shrine.

At right: The sanctuary and cemetery of First Presbyterian Church occupy the plot of ground first cleared (and planted to turnips) by James White in 1786.

At left: Hugh Lawson White, who helped his father clear the turnip patch, became a judge, a banker, a U.S. Senator, and a presidential candidate.

Above: The 1848 Deaf and Dumb Asylum (Old City Hall) was a Confederate military hospital in 1862. In 1863, it was taken over by U.S. Army doctors.

Below: The Lamar House was commandeered for an officers' hospital during the Siege of Knoxville. (The hotel was 61 years old when President Rutherford B. Hayes spoke from its balcony in 1877.)

Above: Confederate Memorial Hall was General James Longstreet's headquarters during the battle for Knoxville. Union general William P. Sanders was fatally wounded by a sniper's bullet from the tower.

Below: These pencil portraits on the tower's plastered wall depict three sharpshooters killed there by an exploding Union shell.

At left: This 9-foot anchor, part of the great chain stretched across the river in 1863, was dredged up a century later during the Civil War Centennial.

Below: In 1987, the Tennessee Legislature ordered Governor William G. Brownlow's portrait removed from the newly-renovated state capitol.

At right: James Mason was Knoxville's first black taxpayer in 1866. In 1879, he opened the first home for black deaf-mutes in his home on West Cumberland Avenue.

Below: In 1868, this huge brick foundry was built on Second Creek by the Knoxville Iron Works. It turned into the Strohaus during Expo '82, and is a permanent feature in the World's Fair Park.

At right: Dr. Thomas W. Humes, the postwar president of East Tennessee University, shored up its bombarded buildings and replanted The Hill with trees.

Below: The 1873 Customs House held TVA's headquarters for 40 years, and is now the East Tennessee Historical Center. (The plainer wing at left was added in 1910.)

Above: In the 1890's, aging Col. Perez Dickinson welcomed visitors to his knot-garden at Island Home. The house is now the superintendent's residence of the Tennessee School for the Deaf.

Below: This handpainted plate, sold during the Tennessee Centennial in 1897, pictures the Knox County Court House with a new marble shaft marking the grave of John Sevier.

Above: A memento of Knoxville Day at the Tennessee Centennial: a pendant showing the city flag designed for the occasion by Lloyd Branson.

At left: Lawson McGhee (Mrs. Shelby Williams) died in 1883 at the age of 23. In memory of his beloved daughter, Col. Charles McGhee presented a public Library to the City of Knoxville.

Below: Bettie McGhee (Mrs. L. D. Tyson) headed the women's committee that had the Knoxville Building moved from Nashville's Centennial Grounds to Knoxville's Main Street in 1898.

At right: Brigadier General Lawrence D. Tyson, a hero of World War I, had been president of the 1911 Appalachian Exposition. He became a U.S. Senator in 1925.

Below: Tyson House, shorn of one portico and hemmed in by dormitories on Volunteer Boulevard, now contains the Alumni Affairs and Development Offices for UT's Knoxville campus.

Appalachian Exposition,
Knoxville, Tenn.

Above: In Chilhowee park, the octagonal marble bandstand is the only vestige of the early Appalachian and Conservation expositions.

Below: Cal F. Johnson, one of Knoxville's wealthiest men, posed in 1922 beside the marble fountain he presented to Cal Johnson City Park.

Above: In 1909, a group of Knoxvillians turned Elkmont Logging Camp into a summer resort high in the Great Smokies.

Below, left: Mrs. W. P. Davis (Annie L. May) suggested the Great Smoky Mountains National Park in 1922. In 1925, she was elected to the Tennessee Legislature, and introduced the first state appropriations bill for the Park.

Below, right: Colonel David Chapman, for whom Chapman Highway is named, was chief purchasing agent for all land on the Tennessee side of the Park.

At right: After the Park was opened in 1933, a scenic loop brought Knoxville sightseers to the mountains via the new Chapman and Alcoa highways.

This 1937 souvenir plate features major attractions in the Knoxville area: Norris Dam; the National Park; Blount Mansion; Old City Hall; the U.S. Post Office; UT's Ayres Hall; and the Henley Street Bridge.

At left: When Fort Loudoun Dam was completed in 1943, it had the highest single-lift locks in the world.

Below: "Crackerbox houses" formed a residential area of Oak Ridge in 1944.

The restored L&N Station

Above: During Expo '82, the Candy Factory's 7 floors were filled with shops and restaurants.

At right: The theme-structure Sunsphere and the Tennessee Amphitheatre are lasting reminders of the 1982 World's Fair.

Above: Immediately after the Fair closed, its Technology and Lifestyle Center reopened as the City's new Convention Center.

Below: A 1989 addition to the World's Fair Park: The Knoxville Museum of Art.

At right: After the collapse of the Butcher banking empire, the United American Bank Building was renamed *Plaza Tower*.

At left: During the holidays, Market Square becomes an outdoor ice-skating rink. In the background are the TVA Towers.

At left: "Little Diamond", the first African elephant born in captivity in this country, is a star attraction at the Knoxville Zoo.

Below: In 1955, the first Dogwood Trail in Sequoyah Hills was only a few blocks long. Now the Dogwood Arts Festival's 6 Trails and 5 Garden By-Ways cover more than 60 miles of residential streets.

CHAPTER TEN

 ## AT THE TURN OF THE CENTURY, THE TYSONS

(Watermelon... firecrackers... patriotic speeches... The South's traditional Independence Day was in abeyance during the Civil War).

On July 4, 1861, Lawrence Davis Tyson was born on the family plantation near Greenville, North Carolina. His father was an officer in the Confederate Army, and his childhood memories were of the Reconstruction Era in which his native state was far less fortunate than neighboring Tennessee. Lawrence had "a head for figures," and at seventeen, he went to nearby Salisbury hoping to find work as a book-keeper; instead, fate stepped in to change his life. Hearing that a competitive examination for the United States Military Academy would soon be held, he crammed for it, took it, made the highest grade in mathematics, and was awarded the appointment. He entered West Point in 1879, a Southerner who had snatched at his only chance for a college education. He left in 1883, a Second Lieutenant in the United States Infantry sworn to preserve, protect, and defend the country whose birthday he shared.

The federal territory of Wyoming was still in the throes of Indian warfare and Geronimo, the great Apache chieftain, was at the height of his fame and power. Lieutenant Tyson was ordered to Cheyenne, and was sent out immediately to take part in the two year campaign that criss-crossed the Southwest and ended with Geronimo's capture.

In 1885, the tall and handsome lieutenant from North Carolina was back on the Army post in Cheyenne where he was a great favorite with the ladies. One day, he was flirting with a charming belle on the front porch of a house on Officers' Row when a high-spirited horse came galloping down the dusty street. In front of that very house, the skittish mount reared, and the rider was thrown from her sidesaddle. Lieutenant Tyson cleared the porch steps in a flying leap, and gathered a beautiful girl in his arms. (Fate, again.)

The Governor of the Wyoming Territory was Colonel George Baxter from Knoxville, Tennessee, and the Governor's Lady had brought her younger sister with her to Cheyenne. Miss Bettie McGhee might not have been the most accomplished horsewoman in Wyoming, but to Lawrence Tyson, she was far and away the best thing that had ever happened to the Territory. His courtship began on the day of the accident, and continued through her visit with the Baxters; when Bettie went home to Knoxville, it was to make preparations for her wedding. In 1886, Lieutenant L.D. Tyson arrived in Knoxville for the first time, but not to stay. Immediately after his marriage, he returned to Wyoming with his bride.

Colonel Charles McGhee was not at all sure that his daughter Bettie would be safe and comfortable in a frontier Army post, and her letters did nothing to allay his fears. She described the post as "remote," and their quarters as "primitive," and the words had an ominous sound when read aloud in Knoxville. Then she wrote that her husband had been ordered away on a foray, leaving her alone except for a half-breed Indian servant, and Colonel McGhee was more worried than ever. This was not the same thing as having a daughter in Wyoming as the wife of the Territorial Governor!

Fortunately for the Colonel's peace of mind, Bettie's husband was ordered east, to upstate New York. (Mrs. McGhee complained that though New York must surely be more civilized than Wyoming, it seemed just as far away from Knoxville.) When a telegram brought the happy news that a son, McGhee Tyson, had been born at Clifton Springs, Colonel and Mrs. McGhee agreed that it was high time Bettie came home. So, at the Colonel's request, the University of Tennessee appointed First Lieutenant L.D. Tyson its Professor of Military Tactics in 1891.

Reporting for duty, Lt. Tyson found that he would be teaching duplicate courses in Military Tactics on two campuses. In 1890, the United States Congress had passed an act requiring all Land Grant Colleges to provide separate but equal facilities for white and black students. From that time until 1909 (when Tennessee Agricultural and Industrial Institute opened in Nashville) Knoxville College was a branch of the University of Tennessee, and its male students were uniformed cadets.

The University itself was in the midst of growth and change. Dr. Charles Dabney had become its president in 1887, and in a sweeping program of reform, he promptly fired all but two of the faculty. There was a strong movement in educational circles to broaden the liberal arts curriculum by including specialized career training, so Dr. Dabney established a College of Law in 1889, and was preparing to open a Department of Home Economics in 1893, when women were scheduled to be admitted to the University.

The Tysons were cordially welcomed to Knoxville, where everyone told Lawrence how fortunate he was to have such wonderful in-laws. Mrs. Cornelia McGhee was the daughter of Knoxville's most distinguished citizen, Hugh Lawson White, and the second wife of Charles McGhee. His first wife had been her sister, Isabella. After serving in the Confederate Army, Colonel McGhee amassed a sizable fortune through a variety of enterprises that included meat packing, banking, coal mining, railroads, and manufacturing. He firmly believed that "Much is expected of those to whom much has been given." In 1883, when the ladies' sewing society of his church suggested establishing a home for foundlings, he underwrote St. John's Orphanage. In 1885, he gave Lawson McGhee Library to the city of Knoxville as a memorial to his beloved daughter, Mrs. Shelby Williams, who had died in childbirth at the age of twenty-three. Lawrence wondered how Bettie, brought up by such cultured parents in their luxurious home, had put up with the makeshifts and inconveniences of Army life.

In the tastefully appointed parlor of the McGhee house on Locust Street, the consensus was that "women can do anything they set their minds to." The talk frequently turned to the recent advances made by women in Knoxville: Everyone took pride in the fact that Ossoli Circle was the first women's club in the South when it was founded in 1885, and that Knoxville had appointed the South's first Police Matron in 1891. Coeducational Holbrook College opened in the new summer resort of Fountain City, and during the off-season, the fashionable Fountain Head Hotel doubled as its women's dormitory. At this first school in the Knoxville area to offer business training, the courses in double-entry bookkeeping, shorthand, and "type-writing" were open to all students. It would not be long, predicted the McGhees, before women were employed as stenographers in offices all over town.

Bettie's sister Annie (Mrs. Calvin M. McClung) was determined to establish a haven for what were euphemistically called "unfortunate young women in need of a few months' shelter," and her family was delighted (although not at all surprised) when she succeeded in opening the Florence Crittenden Home in 1896. Lawrence was curious to know what the next McGhee project might be.

He had long since decided that it would be easier for him to leave the Army than for Bettie to leave Knoxville, and while teaching Military Tactics, he had been attending classes at the College of Law. In 1895, he resigned his commission, and left the University to enter the law firm of Lucky and Sanford. The Tysons bought a large frame antebellum house, just west of the University hill, and gave a series of entertainments to repay their numerous social obligations. (One particularly pleasant family party followed the christening of baby Isabella at St. John's Episcopal Church.)

Tennessee's hundredth birthday was celebrated one year late, because the Centennial Exposition Grounds in Nashville were not ready in 1896. "That's typical," Knoxville's aldermen grumbled, but all the same, they sent crews of workmen to Nashville in 1897 to construct the handsome Knoxville Building that displayed the city's business, industrial, and educational advantages. Proudly flying above its front entrance was the official flag of the City of Knoxville, designed in honor of the occasion by Lloyd Branson. (The flag was plainly dated 1791, but Tennessee's first capital had forgotten to celebrate its own Centennial. The only mention of Knoxville's hundredth birthday appeared in the *Chattanooga Times* whose editor, Adolph Ochs, was a Knoxvillian; he began his newspaper career as a reporter on the *Knoxville Journal*, and ended it as owner of the *New York Times*.)

On Knoxville Day at the Centennial Exposition, a highlight of the entertainment was the soprano solo presented by Mrs. John Lamar Meek, who had represented the State of Tennessee at the Chicago World's Fair in 1893. Mary Fleming Meek, a founder of the Tuesday Morning Musical Club, was not only a renowned singer but a talented composer: she created the music for the University of Tennessee's Alma Mater, and also wrote the lyrics beginning "On a hallowed hill in Tennessee..."

All structures on the Exposition Grounds were scheduled to be razed when the Centennial observance ended, but the women's organizations of Knoxville had other plans for the handsome building belonging to their city. Mrs. Lawrence D. Tyson was chairman, late in 1897, of the Ladies Committee that had the Knoxville Building dismantled in Nashville and re-erected as the Woman's Building on Knoxville's Main Street, across from the Court House.

When the Battleship Maine was sunk in Havana Harbor, Lawrence Tyson felt a sense of outrage and an upsurge of patriotism. After the United States declared war on Spain, West Point graduates were urgently needed to train the raw recruits and he was among the first to volunteer his services. In response to his telegram to the War Department, First Lieutenant L.D. Tyson found himself a full colonel, assigned to command the Sixth United States Volunteer Infantry— just as soon as he finished recruiting it. (As usual, recruiting was easy in the Volunteer State.) After hasty training, the Sixth Infantry was ordered to Puerto Rico and spent the rest of the brief war there. When peace came, Colonel Tyson remained in Puerto Rico as Military Governor.

On the island, there was plenty of time to think about the future, and he decided not to return to the practice of law. Knoxville was growing, geographically and numerically; the city's population of 36,537 in 1900 was six times as large as at the outbreak of the Civil War. The city's economy, balanced at the moment between business and industry, was shifting— he thought— toward industry; and textile manufacturing seemed to be the coming thing. He resolved to put his judgment to the test by organizing not one but two manufacturing plants, the Knoxville Cotton Mills and the Knoxville Spinning Company, and by being president of both.

He came home in 1899 to find a bronze statue of a Spanish-American War infantryman guarding the Court House lawn, and Bettie deeply engrossed in a new project. The Woman's Building was undeniably an asset to the city, and although the cost of moving it was higher than anyone expected, the Ladies Committee had come up with a sure-fire way to raise the extra money. Knoxville's most renowned hostesses had been invited to contribute their favorite recipes for publication in a cookbook, and the ladies were so pleased and flattered that they were divulging all their best-kept culinary secrets!

Copies of the *Knoxville Cookbook* sold like the proverbial hotcakes in 1900. Dessert must have been the favorite course at the Tyson table, since Bettie was represented by eight mouth-watering recipes— for pie crust, lemon pie, molasses custard, suet pudding, pineapple jelly, delicate cake, and Quaker sponge cake.

Considering the menus that the cookbook also included, it is nothing short of miraculous that so few turn-of-the-century Knoxvillians succumbed to apoplexy. This menu is by no means the most elaborate:

A GENTLEMEN'S DINNER
"Hungry as the sea, and can digest as much"

Oyster Cocktails
Salted Almonds   Olives

Green Sea Turtle Soup

Fillet of Lamb, Sauce Tartare   Shoestring Potatoes
Sherry

Lobster a la Newberg   Crackers

Fillet of Beef with Cauliflower and Potatoes
Claret

Stuffed Quail with Chestnuts   Asparagus Tips
Roman Punch

Sweetbreads, Mushrooms, Etc., in Ramekins   Celery
Champagne

Individual Ices and Cakes

Coffee   Cigars
Benedictine with Cracked Ice in Smoking Room

(How could all those dishes be prepared at the same time, in a home kitchen? The answer is, on a mammoth cast-iron coal range whose entire top was cooking surface, red-hot above the fire-box and simmer-temperature at the back. In addition to the cavernous bake-oven, there was a warming oven fitted around the stove-pipe; heat from the pipe, and steam from the cooking pots below, kept food hot and moist until serving time. And Kern's Ice Cream Parlor was around to furnish those individually molded ices and petit fours.)

The Cookbook went into a second printing in 1902, when it became the favorite souvenir of Knoxville for teachers attending an innovative summer session at the University of Tennessee.

Convinced that teacher-training was the quickest and best way to improve the quality of public education, Dr. Philander P. Claxton established the Summer School of the South for the expressed purpose of teaching the region's teachers how to teach. He sent letters throughout the southern states, explaining the purpose of the project, and felt that if as many as 300 teachers would attend his classes, a good start could be made toward raising the level of education in the South. On opening day, the registration desk was swamped with applicants for admission. Determined not to turn away a single would-be participant, Dr. Claxton somehow managed to accommodate more than 2,000 teachers. Those who came from flat country were alarmed and discouraged by the steepness of The Hill, but Dr. Claxton solved this problem by hiring a string of hacks to transport them from Cumberland Avenue to the University's classrooms on the hilltop. A vast majority of the students were women, ranging in age from the early twenties to the mid-fifties, and Lawrence Tyson brought home a joke that was going the rounds downtown: "Have you seen the Summer School girls?" . . . "Yes, summer school girls and some are not." Bettie failed to find this funny.

(Until it was discontinued in 1918, the Summer School enrolled more students than did the University's regular sessions. Dr. Claxton then became the U.S. Commissioner of Education, and the University of Tennessee extended the school year to include a regular summer quarter.)

In this first decade of the 20th century, Americans were beginning to realize that the riches of their nation were not inexhaustible. The great herds of buffalo that once roamed the western prairies had been hunted almost to extinction, and the passenger pigeons that formerly migrated by the millions had all but disappeared; the unbroken forest that covered the eastern continent in colonial days, from the Atlantic seacoast to the Mississippi River, had retreated to the upper reaches of the Appalachian Mountain chain.

Theodore Roosevelt was then President of the United States. "It is not enough," declared the hero of San Juan Hill, "to defend this country in wartime. We must preserve our national prosperity, and protect our natural resources."

Lawrence Tyson gook a good look at prosperous Knoxville and at resource-blessed East Tennessee, and made up his mind that Teddy Roosevelt was right. In 1903, a delegation called upon him to request that he run for the state legislature on the Democratic ticket, and he felt duty bound to accept. There should be new hunting laws to prevent the wanton destruction of wildlife.

(Bettie was unable to vote for him. Advocates of "Women's Rights" pointed out that the only United States citizens excluded from the suffrage were women, and convicted felons.)

After his election, Representative Tyson from Knox County was chosen Speaker of the House, and his prominent position entailed a great deal of political entertaining. Compared to the palatial new homes on Cumberland and Laurel Avenues, the Tysons' square white house was looking plain and antiquated; but since the interior arrangement of its large, high-ceilinged rooms exactly suited them, Bettie decreed that they should remodel rather than rebuild. After facing the frame exterior with stylish pale-yellow brick, they added clusters of tall white Corinthian columns on two sides— plus entablatures, balustrades, and a *porte cochere*. Inside, they turned the third floor attic into a stately ballroom.

By 1907, the Temperance Movement was rapidly gaining strength across the nation. In that year, Knoxville's breweries, distilleries, and saloons were put out of business by a city referendum that prohibited the manufacture or sale of "spiritous liquors."

The Woman's Building, paid for with such effort, burned to the ground in 1907, but Knoxville's ladies were not about to let their club activities go up in smoke. A modern annex was added to a residence at the corner of Cumberland and Walnut to create the Women's Lyceum, jointly owned and operated by four prestigious organizations: Ossoli Circle; Bonny Kate Chapter of the DAR; Chapter 89 of the UDC; and the Tuesday Morning Musical Club. On the site of the Woman's Building, the city erected a large auditorium with an arched roof requiring no interior post supports, and this precursor of World War II quonset huts was ready and waiting for the important event that took place in 1910. (It was later turned into the Streetcar Barn.)

Knoxville civic leaders who attended the 1904 Louisiana Purchase Exposition had been much impressed by the business benefits it brought the city of St. Louis, and they made up their minds to copy it on a smaller scale in their smaller community. Realizing that their exhibition would be more attractive to out-of-town visitors if it were built around some timely topic, they cast about for an appropriate peg on which to hang it.

President Roosevelt was preaching "Conservation." (This word had recently been coined by Gifford Pinchot, the Director of the National Forests, to mean "the *wise use* of natural resources.") The Southern Appalachian Region was rich in the very resources that the President most often mentioned: rivers and streams; wildlife; forests; coal; and mineral deposits. Why wouldn't Knoxville be the ideal place to hold an exposition with a conservation theme?

A lot of hard work (and hard cash) went into site-preparation for the Appalachian Exposition that opened on September 12, 1910, in Chilhowee Park on the eastern outskirts of the city. Enclosed within the Park was Lake Ottosee, the popular boating and picnic spot to which Knoxville's first electric streetcar line was built in 1890. The small natural lake had been reshaped, and enhanced with a boardwalk-bordered bathing beach at one end; a nearby amusement area featured a towering wooden roller-coaster, and a splendid merry-go-round with a steam calliope. The lake was ringed with rustic exhibition halls, one of which (as Knoxville ladies had demanded) was a Women's Building. Knox County's marble producers contributed a large octagonal bandstand, strategically located on a central promontory, and as a special drawing card, the log cabin birthplace of Admiral David Farragut was moved from Lowe's Ferry to the Exposition grounds.

The last stop on the streetcar line was Burlington, where large crowds regularly gathered for the Saturday harness-racing at Cal Johnson's racetrack (now a residential street called Speedway Circle). Two highlights of the month-long Exposition originated here, and both were firsts for East Tennessee. From the racetrack's center oval, a dirigible-airship was launched to float above Chilhowee Park; and Phil Parmalee used the track as a runway for his fragile airplane whose upper and lower wings were held together by slim wooden struts. Spectators gladly paid the extravagant sum of fifty cents to watch the plane take off, circle the track once, and wobble to a landing.

The real climax of September, 1910, was the visit of a national hero, President Teddy Roosevelt, who gave the Appalachian Exposition his highest praise when he pronounced it "Bully!" He spoke to a capacity crowd at the City Auditorium, where the arched ceiling dripped huge American flags, and a palmleaf fan waited with the evening's program on the seat of every folding chair.

Regional advertising attracted visitors from all over East Tennessee and from neighboring states, and the 1910 Exposition proved such a boon to business that it was repeated in 1911 with additional exhibits, expanded entertainment, and a parade of motor cars. This time, President William Howard Taft honored the occasion with his presence.

The President of the 1911 Appalachian Exposition was Lawrence D. Tyson, who had come to equate conservation with love of country.

After these preliminary try-outs, Knoxville volunteered to stage a national conservation exhibition in 1913. Startled by the temerity of this proposal, experts in the field objected that "the undertaking [was] too great for so small a city." Nevertheless, Knoxville's offer was accepted by the National Conservation Association and Gifford Pinchot, the father of the conservation movement, agreed to serve as chairman of the exposition's National Advisory Committee.

The federal government gave its blessing to the Exposition, scheduled for September and October, 1913, with an advance appropriation of $50,000. The Southern and L&N railroads arranged excursions; the Knoxville Street Railway Company purchased new electric trolley-cars. The business community donated $100,000 to expand the simple structures of the Appalachian Expositions into large white-stuccoed exhibition halls.

Largest of these was the Machinery and Liberal Arts Building, with 80,000 square feet of floor space, that overlooked the lake from the present site of the Jacob Building. Exhibits provided by the mining interests of Tennessee and Kentucky were housed in an unusual edifice faced with chunks of iridescent black coal. The official report of the Exposition recorded that the handsome Negro Building "was designed by a Negro architect, built by a Negro contractor and Negro workmen, with money subscribed by Negro citizens of Knoxville."

The greatly enlarged Women's Building exhibited exquisite needlework and traditional handcrafts; there were flower shows and tea-time musicales, as well as demonstrations of the "chafing-dish cookery" that anticipated woks. The Nicholson Art League filled the Fine Arts Building with imported statuary and masterpiece-copies from the collection of Eleanor Deane Audigier, and with the works of local artists that included several women. Ella Bolli VanGilder's intricate wood-sculpture was featured, as were massive oil paintings by Adelia Armstrong Lutz, portraits by Eleanor Wylie, and impressionistic canvasses by Catherine Wylie who would become internationally known. Lloyd Branson's action-filled scenes balanced the quiet landscapes of Thomas Campbell and Charles Christopher Krutch, and "Art Photography" centered around the world famous Knaffl Madonna created in 1899 by Joseph Knaffl. (Miss Emma Fanz, who had posed for the mother, was by now Mrs. Albert Hope; the baby, Josephine Knaffl, had yet to become Mrs. David Baker.)

Evening banquets for visiting dignitaries were held aboard an enormous gaily-decorated houseboat, moored beside the lake whose surface mirrored the exhibition buildings outlined with electric lights.

The first National Conservation Exposition was an unqualified success. It attracted visitors from the North, East, South, and West who were (in the parlance of the day) edified by the educational exhibits, fortified with refreshments from the booths assigned to women's groups of various churches, and entertained by concerts emanating from the marble bandstand.

In the published report of the two-month event, Gifford Pinchot had high praise for Knoxville:

This Exposition would have been a worthy under-taking for any city, and that so small a city as Knoxville should venture to stage the enterprise and then carry it through must in itself have been inspiring.... The beauty of the Knoxville region, and the initiative, energy, and hospitality of the people, who blend the vigor of the North with the warm-hearted generosity of the South...combined to make the city an ideal place for the purpose.

There was indeed a serious purpose behind the Exposition, and visiting conservationists were duly impressed by the region's natural resources. However, they deplored the fact that the neighboring Great Smoky Mountains had been invaded by large lumber companies. It might be possible, they suggested, to save at least a remnant of the primeval eastern forest by turning the Smokies into a National Park.

On January 10, 1917, the opening of the new Lawson McGhee Library was an event of special significance to the Tysons. In 1885, Colonel Charles McGhee had built as his gift to the city a structure that not only housed the public library but provided its endowment: the first and third floors of the building were rented for income purposes, while the library occupied the second floor. After the death of Colonel McGhee, the property at Gay and Vine streets was sold and the funds were used to build the white marble library on Summit Hill that would henceforth be maintained by the city. At its dedication, Lawrence D. Tyson, the president of the Library's Board of Trustees, presented the building to the city on behalf of the McGhee family.

Lawson McGhee Library's dedication preceded by only a few months the declaration of war on Germany, and Colonel L.D. Tyson immediately volunteered for active duty. President Woodrow Wilson appointed him the only brigadier general from Tennessee.

In Knoxville, fluttering flags on every lamp-post fanned the fire of patriotism that engulfed the city. Young men lined up to enlist; men too old to go to war sold Liberty Bonds, or bought them. Women rolled lint bandages at Red Cross headquarters, and took home knitting-kits containing khaki-colored wool and directions for making the Balaclava helmets that were the ancestors of ski-masks. Wearing white wrapper-uniforms and caps embroidered with the Red Cross emblem, they staffed canteens at both the railroad stations day and night—meeting every troop train with free coffee, doughnuts, apples, cigarettes, and stamped postcards ready to be written home.

Everywhere, bands were playing "Over There," and "It's a Long Way to Tipperary." Isabella Tyson teased her father by saying that George M. Cohan had written a song about him:

> *I'm a Yankee Doodle Dandy—*
> *Yankee Doodle, do or die!*
> *I'm a real live nephew of my Uncle Sam,*
> *Born on the Fourth of July....*

The Tysons had spent months planning a joint gift to the neighborhood around his cotton mills: a community center designed to provide day-care for the children of working mothers, and to offer programs for the elderly. After Lawrence left for training camp, Bettie presided at the formal opening of the Dale Avenue Settlement House that would be operated by the Junior League of Knoxville until the 1960's.

By a quirk of fate, the 59th Infantry Brigade, commanded by Brigadier General L.D. Tyson, trained at Camp Sevier near the site of the Revolutionary War's turning-point Battle of King's Mountain. Landing at Calais in May of 1918, the men of the 59th were the first Americans to enter Belgium, and the Battle of Ypres, fought there on July 4, was General Tyson's birthday celebration for that year. Tyson's troops were constantly in combat, in Belgium and France, until September 29, the turning-point of World War I.

The evening before, General Tyson had made a speech to his men in which he told them that they were facing one of the decisive battles of history, and history proved him right: His 59th Brigade demolished the "impregnable" Hindenburg Line, the vaunted stronghold of German defense. When the Hindenburg Line broke, the resistance of Germany broke with it, and the war ended a short six weeks later. It was then possible for General Tyson to leave the Army and return to Knoxville, where he received a hero's welcome marred by deep personal sorrow.

McGhee Tyson had been one of the first Tennesseans to volunteer, but had not followed his father into the infantry; he chose a brand-new type of warfare by enlisting in the Naval Reserve Flying Corps. After receiving flight-instruction at Boston and Pensacola, he was commissioned in the Navy and sent overseas, arriving in England in August of 1918.

On a mission over the North Sea one chilly early-autumn day, Lieutenant McGhee Tyson's plane was shot down. Official notification of his death was sent to General Tyson in France, and to Mrs. Tyson in Knoxville; from the circumstances of the crash, it was presumed that his body could never be recovered.

General Tyson was handed the death notice at the height of the battle for the Hindenburg Line. As soon as the German defenses crumbled, he took leave and went to England to search for his son's remains. It had turned bitterly cold, but he scoured the beaches and ventured out to sea in a small boat, searching for signs of the wreckage of a Navy plane. After several days, the body of McGhee Tyson was found and identified, and started on the long journey home that would take months to complete.

A strange coincidence attended the final stage of the journey. James M. Meek, McGhee's boyhood friend, was released from the Army at Camp Lee, Virginia; as he boarded the train for home, he noticed a flag-draped coffin being loaded on it. At the station in Knoxville, he saw through the Pullman car window a guard of honor standing at attention, and he stepped from the train to join the group waiting to receive his closest friend, whose body he had unknowingly escorted home. Full military honors attended the burial in Old Gray Cemetery of Naval Lieutenant McGhee Tyson, the first Tennessee aviator killed in battle.

On Armistice Day in 1919, Knoxville's returned soldiers and sailors paraded down Gay Street to the strains of "I'm a Yankee Doodle Dandy", and Tennessee's only Brigadier General, recipient of the Distinguished Service Medal, rode tall and straight at the head of the procession. In front of the Knoxville High School stood the statue of a doughboy, a memorial to Knoxvillians who gave their lives "to make the world safe for democracy."

General Tyson had resumed the presidency of his mills and of Lawson McGhee Library's board, and was giving much time to the American Legion. A fellow trustee of the library was Calvin Morgan McClung, a man of literary tastes whose first wife Annie had been

Colonel McGhee's daughter. C. M. McClung devoted a lifetime to compiling a collection of historical and genealogical books and manuscripts that was unequalled in the South. Upon his death in 1919, his personal library was presented by his widow, Barbara Adair McClung, to Lawson McGhee Library. This was the nucleus of the constantly expanding, nationally important McClung Historical Collection, now housed in the Customs House.

Another trustee of Lawson McGhee Library, Edward Terry Sanford, became Knoxville's first (and so far, only) member of the United States Supreme Court in 1923. Justice Sanford had delivered the oration at the University of Tennessee's Centennial Celebration in 1894, and since 1908, had served as Federal District Judge for Middle and East Tennessee. He was Lawrence Tyson's former law partner.

As though the library, two mills, and the American Legion were not enough to keep him busy, General Tyson had bought a newspaper which he planned to operate himself. The *Knoxville Sentinel* prospered under his direction, and supported his candidacy when he ran for the United States Senate, to which he was elected in 1925. By now, as the result of a 1913 amendment to the state constitution, Tennessee's Senators were chosen by popular ballot. And this time (thanks to the Woman's Suffrage Amendment of 1920) Bettie voted for him! Senator Tyson concerned himself with legislation to protect the rights of veterans, and he was there when President Calvin Coolidge signed the Enabling Act for the Great Smoky Mountains National Park in 1926.

The entire nation was ecstatic over Charles A. Lindberg's solo transatlantic flight in 1927, and pundits predicted that the forty-eight states would soon be linked by a chain of airports. Feeling that Knoxville should not lag behind while other cities were preparing for the coming of the "air age," City Council purchased an existing private airfield on Sutherland Avenue in 1929, and named it McGhee Tyson Airport in memory of Knoxville's first flying officer.

Americans were beginning to take an interest in the appearance of their cities. Bettie Tyson was a founder of Knoxville's City Beautiful League, whose members urged the city to clear away unsightly shacks and polluting industries from the downtown waterfront, and replace them with a well-landscaped scenic drive. Then as now, riverfront redevelopment was a slow process.

In the meantime, Bettie envisioned a new city park that would rejuvenate winding Third Creek in West Knoxville; after the extensive tract was purchased and cleared, she selected blossoming shrubs and perennial flowers to beautify it, and supervised their planting. Tyson Park was to be her own memorial to her son, and the deed of gift (recorded in December, 1929) required the property to revert to the heirs of her daughter Isabella (Mrs. Kenneth Gilpin of Virginia) should the city's principal airport ever cease to bear the name of McGhee Tyson. (The airport moved from congested West Knoxville to Blount County in 1937, and the name moved with it.)

When the Senate recessed for the summer in 1929, the Tysons came home to Knoxville. The Senator was pleased that the new Tyson Junior High School on Kingston Pike was to be named in his honor, but he didn't look well, and he complained of the heat. The American Legion was holding its state convention in Greeneville, and he had agreed to be the principal speaker; against all advice, he kept the commitment. Ill in Greeneville, he was worse when he returned to Knoxville. A visit to specialists in Philadelphia brought temporary improvement, but he died there, unexpectedly. In Knoxville, there was an outpouring of praise for the patriot who served his country well, in war and peace.

Lawrence D. Tyson— early conservationist, Brigadier General, and United States Senator— is buried in Old Gray Cemetery. (He had suggested buying a hilltop lot in the new Highland Memorial Cemetery, with a view of the Great Smoky Mountains where a National Park was finally taking shape, but Bettie would have none of it. Lawrence persisted. He reminded her that Old Gray was seriously overcrowded, and stressed the importance of Highland Memorial's perpetual care fund. "I'm looking ahead to the distant future," he said.

"So am I," Bettie retorted, "and that's exactly why I'm going to be buried at Old Gray. *When I rise, I want to rise among friends!*")

THE PRESENCE OF THE PAST

The Tyson's opulent Temple Avenue residence now faces Volunteer Boulevard, in the midst of the University of Tennessee's main campus. "Tyson House"— encroached upon by dormitories, shorn of its balustrades, and minus one columned portico— is occupied by UT Knoxville's Alumni Office and its Development Office. (At the rear of the original property, a smaller and more recent red-brick Tyson House faces Melrose Place; this is an Episcopal Center for the University.)

Still in existence on Locust Street, although disguised beyond all recognition, is the veranda-encircled frame residence built by Colonel

Charles McGhee in 1873. The porch was replaced with massive white columns in 1912, when the house was faced with brick and enlarged by the addition of a fourth floor. It then became the [Old] Masonic Temple.

"Greystone", on North Broadway, has been the home of WATE Radio and TV since 1962. When Major Eldod Cicero Camp built the stone mansion in 1890, for the astronomical sum of $125,000, Broadway ended at an ornamental lake in the center of a new summer resort called Fountain City for its multiplicity of springs and streams. Fountain City Park had just replaced the Methodist Campgrounds, in use since 1845 for protracted revival meetings.

St. John's Episcopal Church was founded in 1844, and waited 142 years for its elevation to St. John's Cathedral. The stone sanctuary that looms like a medieval English fortress on Cumberland Avenue, at Walnut Street, was constructed in 1893. A courtyard, entered by a lych-gate, separates it from the recent additions built of matching but less weathered stone.

In 1904, the buff-colored, Dutch-gabled Southern Railway Station was erected in the deep ravine that had held railroad tracks for exactly half a century. In that sunken location, its clock tower had to be disproportionately tall; a pedestrian overpass joined Depot Street to the formal entrance on the second floor. Until passenger trains were discontinued in 1970, the Southern offered overnight Pullman service to Washington and New York. Then the clock tower was removed, and the station was abandoned until 1988, when it was painstakingly restored for adaptive office use. Its new owners were careful to preserve the fumed-oak staircase, and the marble plaque above a waiting room fireplace with the Biblical adjuration: "Be ye not unmindful to entertain strangers."

(In 1919, a narrow bridge above the Southern tracks was replaced by the Gay Street Viaduct. In the process, the north end of Gay Street was raised some fifteen feet, half-burying several small buildings on the west side of the 100 block, and making their second floors level with the new sidewalk. Their former street floors went underground, and are still there.)

In the red-brick-and-white-stone Louisville & Nashville Station, completed at Henley Street and Western Avenue in 1906, the waiting rooms were floored with tiny tiles laid like wall-to-wall carpeting in colorful Oriental designs. A separate Ladies' Entrance opened into a waiting room furnished in oak with writing desks and rocking chairs.

The building stood empty after passenger trains to Chicago and New Orleans ceased to run, until it became one of the on-site structures rehabilitated for the 1982 World's Fair. The restored L&N Station is one of the Fair's lasting benefits: At the rear, a soaring wrought-iron staircase provides access to two restaurants that overlook the World's Fair Park.

From 1910 until the last class graduated in 1951, students from all over town converged on Knoxville High School where home economics, manual training, and business classes were offered in addition to the college preparatory course. The block-square building on North Fifth Avenue then housed administrative offices of the Knoxville Board of Education until 1987, when the city schools were turned over to Knox County.

After the First National Conservation Exposition in 1913, the lake at Chilhowee Park shrank to a fraction of its former size, and the transplanted birthplace of Admiral David Farragut was destroyed by fire; one after another, the handsome exhibition buildings burned to the ground. The sole legacy of the Appalachian and Conservation expositions is the octagonal marble bandstand, whose restoration was a major project of Knoxville's Bicentennial Commission in 1976. But each September, Chilhowee Park relives the early expositions by hosting the ever-popular Tennessee Valley Fair.

CHAPTER ELEVEN

THE GATEWAY TO THE GREAT SMOKIES

"Botany's antique shop," naturalists have nicknamed the Great Smokies. These highest mountains in the eastern United States were already old when the Rockies and the Alps were mere young upstarts; eons of rain and snow have softened their sharp outlines, and given them a rich topsoil that supports an amazing variety of plant life. Because the Smokies were spared the ravages of a destructive glacier, a number of plants persist here in the same form as their fossilized ancestors; some are species that elsewhere vanished during the last Ice Age.

Toward the end of the 18th century, the Smokies' marvelous profusion of flowers was reported by such world-famous botanists as William Bartram of Philadelphia and André Michaux of France. Since then, more than 1500 native species of blossoming plants, shrubs, vines, and trees have been identified. During the 19th century, foresters found that more varieties of trees were indigenous to these mountains than to all of northern Europe; furthermore, the rich soil and abundant rainfall in the Smokies produced specimens of enormous height and girth.

Settlement began on the western slopes of the mountains around 1800, and since the only roads into the uplands were narrow Indian trails, the firstcomers brought with them only what they could carry themselves, or strap on the backs of farm animals. Their basic equipment consisted of tools, and seeds. Only a man who was sure he could produce, with his own two hands, a livelihood for his family would have attempted to carve out a homestead in the midst of an unbroken forest; and only those settlers whose self-confidence was justified would manage to survive. Succeeding generations encountered the same problems and found the same solutions as had their forebears, and it has been said of the people in these mountains that "heredity and environment conspired to keep them pioneers."

Their education may have been minimal, but mountaineers were as far from ignorant as it is possible for people to be. Every settler was his own carpenter, stone mason, and cabinet maker. He tanned the leather from which he then made his horse's harness and his family's shoes. He was a "good provider"— a dead shot with a long rifle, and a setter of ingenious snares; he caught the wily brook trout on hooks, or with his bare hands. He domesticated swarms of wild bees in hollowed gum-tree logs, and he managed to wrest a corn crop from a few impossibly steep hillside acres.

His wife was equally versatile, if not more so. Not only did she card, spin, and weave the material from which she made her family's clothes, she also dyed her homespun cloth with wild indigo, walnut hulls, and sourwood bark. She was the family doctor, and concocted her own medicines. She had no way of knowing that the sweet-scented native spicebush is a natural source of benzoin, a medicament prized by physicians for its soothing qualities, yet she boiled spicebush twigs, and used the fragrant steam arising from the kettle as a remedy for croup and whooping cough. She was a step ahead of scientists when she brewed a tea from the bark of the black willow (Salix nigra) to reduce fevers: her home remedy contained salicylic acid, which is the active ingredient of aspirin. She also put the 19th century's inch-wide copper pennies in a damp place until they were covered with green mold, and applied them to stubborn sores that refused to heal; this primitive ancestor of penicillin is said to have worked remarkably well.

Even the mountain children were attuned to their environment: in the sap of the sweet-gum tree, they found the old original chewing gum!

The ruggedness of the mountain terrain kept settlement sparse and development at bay until the 1890's, when America's eastern timberlands had all but disappeared. Wood was then in great demand for frame houses and fine furniture, as well as for paper pulp, and the lumber industry turned to the Great Smokies as a last resort.

The largest tract of timberland on the Tennessee side of the mountains belonged to the Little River Lumber Company, chartered in 1901: those 86,000 acres extended from Tuckaleechee Cove to the foot of Clingman's Dome. The company established its headquarters at Townsend and set up an outpost in the highlands at Elkmont, a logging camp where housing was provided for the lumbermen and their families. In theory, it should have been possible to float logs down the Little River from Elkmont to the sawmill at Townsend, but in practice, the logs were much too long and bulky for the narrow, sharply angled stream. To get the timber down to the lumberyard, and supplies up to the logging camp, the company built a narrow-gauge railroad alongside Little River. Its tracks clung precariously to the rocky cliffs, and crossed the river more than once on spindly wooden trestles; the engine labored mightily to haul a string of empty flatcars up the steep grade, and the loaded logging train came down the mountain with the speed of a roller-coaster.

Knoxvillians heard about the railroad's scenic route through the Little River Gorge, and fabulous tales were told of the trout fishing to be found at Elkmont. Sportsmen began riding up in the caboose of the logging train to try their luck at fly-casting.

By 1909, the timber around Elkmont had been cut-over, and the logging operations moved to a new location. The fishermen happily formed the Appalachian Club, bought the abandoned logging camp, and converted the lumbermen's houses into rustic summer cottages. They also built East Tennessee's first condominium: The Appalachian Clubhouse contained a communal dining room, and individually owned apartments. A small passenger train made a daily round trip during the summer season, and Wonderland Hotel was built nearby to accommodate early tourists. In 1912, the hotel was purchased by other Knoxvillians, and became a second private club.

Mothers and children went to the mountains for the entire summer, taking with them trunks of clothes and crates of canned goods; fathers came up for the weekends, bringing fresh vegetables and stale newspapers. During the week, a small combination store and post office provided such necessities as stamps, and kerosene for the lamps that were the only form of lighting. The devoted adherents of Elkmont and Wonderland claimed that nowhere in the world was the scenery so beautiful and the air so invigorating as in the heart of the Great Smokies.

They were not the only Knoxvillians who thought so. Many lovers of the mountains scorned the shelter of summer cottages, preferring to camp out beside a rushing stream. Hikers followed the Indian trails, and the cow-paths that led up to natural grass balds where the settlers' cattle grazed in summer. Geologists studied the striated formations of the rocky cliffs, taking fossil samples, while botanists returned year after year to the secluded coves where wildflowers congregated, to collect specimens of blossoms, leaves, and seedpods in their flower-presses. Artists (notably, Charles Christopher Krutch) sketched mist-shrouded peaks, and returned home to depict the thrilling scenery in oils, on canvas.

At the First National Conservation Exposition, held in Knoxville in 1913, the scenic wonders of the Smokies were displayed in scale models and enlarged photographs, alongside pictures of enormous trees being felled by logging crews. Nearby, the National Conservation Association's educational exhibit explained the major difference between a national forest and a national park: Judicious timber cutting was permitted in a national forest to improve the quality of the remaining stand, in the same way that thinning increased the yield of a vegetable crop; but in a national park, nature was allowed to take its course without human interference of any kind.

Obviously, said visiting conservationists, turning the Great Smoky Mountains into a national park was the *only* way to stop the ruthless clear-cutting that would eventually destroy not only the forests but the shade-loving wildflowers and the native wildlife. Conservation-minded Knoxvillians agreed in principle, but they knew that the national parks in the Rocky Mountains had simply been set aside by the federal government from public lands, whereas all the targeted area in the Smokies was privately owned, under the jurisdiction of two sovereign states. Before a national park could come into being there, every acre of timberland would have to be bought, from an owner unwilling to sell. (Not until the 1920's did the park's proponents seriously consider invoking the "dangerous" principle of eminent domain.)

In 1916, Willis P. Davis came from Louisville, Kentucky, to take over the management of the Knoxville Iron Company, and was soon a "booster" of his adopted city. He and his beautiful wife loved the Smokies, and visited them often. After vacationing in the western national parks in 1922, Mrs. Davis suggested that the Great Smokies would be a splendid place for a new eastern park. W.P. Davis wholeheartedly agreed. He was the organizing president of the Great Smoky Mountains Conservation Association in 1923, and some very helpful people were among its charter members: Edward J. Meeman, the editor of the Knoxville News, gave the park project not only local publicity but national exposure through the Scripps-Howard newspaper chain. The proposed wilderness reserve was enthusiastically supported by the manager of the Knoxville Chamber of Commerce, Carlos Campbell, who was a dedicated mountain hiker and a knowledgeable naturalist. Magnificent photographs of mountain scenery were made by James E. Thompson, a charter member of the Smoky Mountains Hiking Club; they were widely published, and were of great importance in promoting the Smokies as a national park site. A retired Army

Engineer, General Frank Maloney, was an expert cartographer whose maps of the areas to be purchased were accepted without question by the National Park Service; he originated the idea of the Foothills Parkway, and charted its (eventual) 72 mile route.

The most active and effective of all the Association's members was Colonel David Chapman, the president of a wholesale drug company, who became the purchasing agent for property on the Tennessee side of the park.

The timing was perfect. All of the existing national parks in the far west were inaccessible to the vast majority of Americans, and public sentiment favored a new park in a mountainous area east of the Mississippi. Accordingly, in 1923, the U.S. Department of the Interior appointed a commission to study possible park sites in the Southern Appalachian region. The five commissioners announced plans to visit several North Carolina areas, including Mount Mitchell and the Linville Gorge, but the Great Smokies were not on their itinerary. W.P. Davis and David Chapman headed the committee of Knoxvillians who drove to Asheville, met with the commissioners, and convinced them that they should not decide on a park location without first seeing Mount LeConte, Elkmont, Cades Cove, and Gregory Bald.

As a result, on December 12, 1924, the commission reported to the Secretary of the Interior:

> *We have found many sites which could well be chosen, but...of these several possible sites, the Great Smoky Mountains easily stand first because of the height of the mountains, depth of valleys, ruggedness of the area, and the unexampled variety of trees, shrubs, and plants.*

Unfortunately, the federal government decided not to act upon the report.

Conservationists then put forward a startling scheme. Since the boundary line between Tennessee and North Carolina followed the crest of the Great Smoky Mountains, dividing the projected park area in half, they proposed that the two states use their powers of condemnation to purchase 512,000 acres of park land, and then deed the property to the federal government as a gift. The idea caught on, and in response to an appeal for private contributions, $1,000,000 was raised in North Carolina and Tennessee.

In 1925, the Little River Lumber Company announced its willingness to part with 76,507 acres of cut-over timberland, for the sum of $273,337.

In that same year, Mrs. W.P. Davis became the first woman elected from Knox County to the state House of Representatives, and she promptly introduced a bill authorizing the purchase of the lumber company's property. Tennessee's lawmakers balked. Knoxvillians were the people pushing for a national park, and before a single dollar of state money was committed, the City of Knoxville would have to come up with one third of the purchase price. ("That'll settle it, once and for all," agreed the legislators. "Knoxville's not about to spend $91,000 in tax money for a tract of land 35 miles outside the city limits, and then give the land away.")

Indeed, the park project might have stalled right there, if Knoxville's mayor had not been a far-sighted civic leader and a member of the Great Smoky Mountains Conservation Association.

In 1923, Knoxville had adopted a new form of government, and Mayor Ben Morton persuaded the first City Council to make the first public appropriation for the new national park.

With considerable reluctance, Tennessee's legislature kept its side of the bargain. Governor Austin Peay (who owned a cottage at Wonderland) signed the state appropriations bill with a gold-pointed ostrich feather pen, which he presented to Mrs. W.P. Davis, the Representative from Knox County.

So the first tax money for the Great Smoky Mountains National Park didn't come from the federal government, or from the states of Tennessee and North Carolina, but from a prosperous little city with a population inching toward 100,000. In 1925, a large billboard on Gay Street correctly described Knoxville as "The City of Homes." Every family that could possibly do so owned a home and lived in it, quietly and contentedly— with a sneaking suspicion that people who were content to be "renters" had a screw loose, somewhere.

"Home delivery" made life easier. The milkman appeared at the unlocked kitchen door each morning with sweet milk in glass bottles, and buttermilk in a gallon jug from which he filled the housewife's own container. An order for chicken salad telephoned at 9 a.m. to Knoxville's favorite "fancy grocery," T.E. Burns & Company, was delivered in time for lunch. Laundry and dry cleaning picked up on Monday were returned on Tuesday. The mail came twice a day, and the garbage was collected twice a week.

Gay Street was the retail shopping mecca for a 150 mile area. There were two "first class" department stores— Miller's, and S.H.

George & Sons— and three "economy" stores— Sears Roebuck, J.C. Penney, and Knox Drygoods— in addition to specialty women's wear shops for dresses, hats, shoes, and lingerie. There were two top-rate men's clothing stores, Hall's and Schriver's, and a number of "for men only" establishments that included barber shops, cigar stores, a billiard parlor, and a Turkish bath.

At the curb in front of Hope Brothers Jewelers stood a tall iron clock, and gilded musical instruments marked the entrances to two music stores. There were six large furniture stores; five drugstores; three ten-cent stores; two photographers' studios; two delicatessens; a specialty bakery; and a fruit stand— plus numerous shops selling stationery, books, and candy, and a few pawnshops and repair shops near the railroad.

Grocery stores were concentrated around bustling Market Square. M.B. Arnstein's elegant seven-floor department store stood on Market Street at Union Avenue; one block away at the Clinch Street corner, Todd & Armistead's Drugstore had dispensed not only a million prescriptions, but enough ice cream sodas to snow-cap a mountain.

Automobiles had hardly replaced horse-drawn vehicles on Knoxville's streets, but already there was a parking problem: in 1925, it was announced that Blount Mansion was about to be razed and replaced by a row of garages. Throughout the 19th century, the Mansion had been the cherished home of the Boyd family; then, after declining steadily as rental property, it had become a tenement. The front door was missing, and the inside stairway was visible from the street. Looking at the dilapidated structure, most Knoxvillians shook their heads and said: "Good riddance. It's nothing but a fire-trap."

But Miss Mary Boyce Temple was outraged at the thought of destroying the first 2-story frame house west of the mountains, the birthplace of Tennessee history; she gave her personal check for an option on the property. Under her leadership, and through the efforts of the Bonny Kate Chapter of the DAR and the newly formed East Tennessee Historical Society, Blount Mansion was purchased, restored, and opened to the public as Knoxville's first house museum in 1930.

Mary Boyce Temple was 65 when she set out to save Blount Mansion, and for 40 of her years, she had had a finger in every Knoxville pie. In 1885, she was the first president of Ossoli Circle— daringly named for a controversial early feminist, Margaret Fuller, the Countess Ossoli. When the National Federation of Women's Clubs was organized in 1890, she was elected its first recording secretary. In 1893, she turned her attention to genealogy, and established the first of Knoxville's many DAR chapters which she named Bonny Kate for Tennessee's first "first lady," the wife of Governor John Sevier. In 1900, Governor Benton McMillin appointed Miss Mary Boyce Temple of Knoxville as Tennessee's official representative at the Paris Exposition, and in 1921, Lincoln Memorial University conferred upon her an honorary doctorate of law.

It is "characters" that give a city flavor, and Mary Boyce Temple was a character if there ever was one. After graduating from Vassar College in 1877, she travelled widely in this country and abroad. Returning to her native city, she appointed herself Knoxville's official hostess, and entertained each and every visiting celebrity from Frances E. Willard, who came in 1883 to organize a chapter of the WCTU, to General John J. Pershing, who received a hero's welcome after World War I.

(One of the most amusing anecdotes about her concerns an invitation to a "celebrity" dinner party, which was hand-delivered by her butler to a distinguished professor at the University of Tennessee. Surprised that his wife's name was not included on the invitation, Dr. McIntire called upon Miss Temple to explain why he was forced to decline. "I make it a rule," he said, "*never* to attend a social function to which my wife is not invited."

"But my dear Doctor," cried the astonished Mary Boyce Temple, "when one is having a party, one simply *has* to draw the line somewhere!")

There was one form of entertainment from which no one was excluded. Knoxvillians young and old turned out to watch the parades that formed on Main Street, pivoted around the corner by the streetcar-barn, and marched the length of Gay Street to the Southern Depot. Something was missing from the Fourth of July, circus, Shriners, Labor Day, and Armistice Day spectacles in 1925: for the previous quarter of a century, Cal Johnson's high stepping trotter harnessed to a two-wheeled sulky had brought up the rear of every parade.

The death of Cal Johnson caused newspapers in Knoxville and New York to take a retrospective look at the life of a former slave whose career might have served as a model for one of Horatio Alger's success stories. With the first money he earned at the end of the Civil War, he bought a horse and dray, and contracted to gather and bury the bodies of the dead from the battlefields near Cumberland Gap; eighteen years later, he was elected a member of Knoxville's Board of Aldermen.

Cal Johnson was an uneducated man with a phenomenal memory, who kept his extensive business records in his head. A non-drinker, he became the proprietor of Gay Street's most popular saloon, and invested his considerable profits in downtown rental properties. He was an excellent judge of horseflesh and owned a livery stable on Central Avenue where White's Fort once had stood; he also owned the city's only racetrack, at Burlington, where he kept a string of pure bred trotting horses. By 1920, he was one of the city's wealthiest men, universally liked and respected. To provide a park and playground for the black community in crowded East Knoxville, he bought up a strip of land that bordered the east side of First Creek from Cumberland Avenue to Vine Street, and sold it to the city for a nominal sum. In 1922, he had the pleasure of presenting a magnificent marble fountain to Cal Johnson City Park.

The same procedure of buying land for public enjoyment, and turning it over to a government able to maintain it, was being followed in the Smokies. President Calvin Coolidge signed the Enabling Act for the Great Smoky Mountains National Park in 1926, and the states of North Carolina and Tennessee appropriated matching funds that added up to $4,000,000. Private contributions raised the total to $5,000,000, but even in Coolidge dollars, that was not enough to buy 800 square miles of land. Conservationists appealed to John D. Rockefeller, Jr., whose interest in the preservation of natural and historic resources was well known. He responded by doubling the funds in hand with a munificent gift of $5,000,000 from the Rockefeller Foundation, made in memory of his mother, Laura Spelman Rockefeller.

Land acquisition began in earnest, and was relatively easy in North Carolina where few people actually lived on the eastern slopes of the Smokies and most of the land was owned in large tracts by individuals or corporations. The largest property owner in what is now the Park was Champion Fibre Company, whose 93,000 acres straddled the summit of the mountain chain from Clingman's Dome to Mount Guyot.

Things were different on the western side of the boundary line, where there were 6400 land owners for Tennessee's purchasing agent, Colonel David Chapman, to contact and dicker with. He found himself up against rugged individualists, who refused to believe that the state had any right to force them to give up their homes when they most emphatically didn't want to do so. Tennessee's laws of eminent domain required all title holders to sell their land at an agreed upon fair price, but there was a loophole: An owner could receive the full purchase price for his property while retaining a life estate in it. This meant that, so long as the person who signed the deed was living, a family could continue to occupy its home.   Members of the Appalachian and Wonderland clubs availed themselves of this option, as did many of the more than eighty families then living in Cades Cove.

When 150,000 acres had been deeded to the federal government, the National Park Service took charge of turning the Smokies into a national park, accessible (as the donor states insisted) to people of all ages and physical strengths. To this end, all man-made structures were torn down so that the forest could reclaim the farms; existing roads were erased, and new roads constructed in areas unmarked even by a footpath.   The main highway that crossed the mountain crest at Newfound Gap was a marvel of modern engineering, and a welcome replacement for the century-old dirt road through Indian Gap. A Park Headquarters had to be built, and public facilities provided, et cetera. These improvements were paid for with a federal appropriation of $1,550,000 from Public Works funds, and much of the work was done by the newly created Civilian Conservation Corps.

When the still-unfinished Park was opened to the public in 1933, billboards on Cumberland Avenue and North Broadway proudly proclaimed:

KNOXVILLE—
THE GATEWAY TO THE GREAT SMOKIES!

A 100-mile scenic loop drive began at the new Henley Street Bridge and followed the Chapman Highway, so named in 1929 by Tennessee's legislature to honor Colonel David Chapman whose tireless efforts brought the park project to a successful conclusion. Chapman Highway ended at Gatlinburg, a tiny hamlet in the process of turning into a thriving town. Tennessee and North Carolina had given the land for the Great Smoky Mountains National Park with a string attached: The agreement between the states and the federal government prohibited commercial development within the Park boundaries. This meant that the entrance communities of Gatlinburg and Cherokee would have the privilege of providing lodging, food, and filling stations for an ever-increasing number of tourists. (An exception to this rule is made for LeConte Lodge, the highest "resort" in the eastern United States with an altitude of 6,593 feet, which opened in 1925. Since it can only be reached on foot, and the shortest route up Mount LeConte via the Alum Cave Bluff Trail is five and a half miles one way, the Lodge poses no threat to fringe-area motels.)

Inside the Park boundary, at the river-stone Park Headquarters, visitors came face to face with oil portraits of Willis Perkins Davis and Mrs. Davis, née Annie Lovella Patrick May; in a nearby glass case was the ostrich-plume pen used by Governor Austin Peay to sign Tennessee's first Park-appropriation bill. The scenic loop climbed Sugarland Mountain to Maloney Point, offering the view of Mount LeConte that was General Frank Maloney's favorite. Beyond Fightin' Creek Gap, the drive descended the Little River Gorge on the roadbed of the early logging train, through the first land purchased for the National Park. Leaving the Park at the erstwhile logging town of Townsend, the loop returned by way of Alcoa and Maryville to Knoxville, passing within 200 yards of Colonel Chapman's home on Topside Road.

By another of the interesting coincidences that abound in Knoxville's history, the national park that was an outgrowth of President Theodore Roosevelt's conservation movement was officially dedicated by another President named Roosevelt. Franklin D. Roosevelt, a victim of polio, always travelled in a private Pullman car especially equipped for his needs. On the morning of September 2, 1940, he was lifted down from its observation platform at the Southern Railway Station in Knoxville, and transferred to a limousine for the drive to Newfound Gap where the tiered stone Rockefeller Memorial stood on the high point of the boundary line between Tennessee and North Carolina. Speaking from the Memorial's lower terrace to a crowd of 10,000 that packed the parking lot, President Roosevelt accepted the gift of the Great Smoky Mountains National Park from the people of North Carolina and Tennessee, on behalf of the people of the United States.

The early conservationists' dream had become reality. Lumbering in the Smokies was a thing of the past, and more than 100,000 acres of virgin forest had been saved for incorporation into the new national park. It remained to be seen whether time and nature could restore the cut-over timberlands, but a second-growth forest was already erasing former cornfields and obliterating early settlers' homesites. In mountain-ringed Cades Cove, the cleared land was shrinking fast, but six pioneer log houses were still occupied on "lifetime leases," and three churches were surrounded by their cemeteries; a water-powered gristmill, in operation since the 1870's, was still grinding corn.

By the 1940's the concept of conservation was expanding to include historic preservation, and the National Park Service made a momentous departure from established policy: officials wisely decided to reverse the return-to-nature in Cades Cove, and to preserve the area (five miles long and less than two miles wide) as a unique open-air museum of mountain life.

Elsewhere, the regeneration of the ravaged timberlands took place far more rapidly than anyone had dared predict; once more, the Park's steep slopes were nurturing every type of forest that occurs on the eastern American continent from Georgia to Newfoundland. Because of the astounding diversity of these Cove-Hardwood, Hemlock, Northern-Hardwood, and Spruce-Fir forests, the Great Smoky Mountains National Park was named an International Biosphere Reserve in 1976.

Meanwhile, small blossoming trees and shrubs had returned to the forests' understory, and the once-muddied streams ran crystal clear; in sheltered coves, the glorious wildflowers had miraculously reappeared. Once again, the Smoky Mountains were America's garden spot.

The Great Smoky Mountains National Park differed from all others by being a gift from the people to their government, rather than the other way around. Interstate highways have made these mountains readily accessible to the great mid-section of America, and (as its donors intended) this most popular of all the national parks is designed to be enjoyed by young and old. It has paved roads and developed campgrounds, picnic shelters, and short wildflower walks; well marked hiking trails lead to its spectacular views and foaming waterfalls. In addition, it has vast areas of untrammeled wilderness beloved of backpackers, and 70 challenging miles of the Appalachian Trail are within its borders. The Park Service does a magnificent job of protecting this national treasure from some 10,000,000 annual visitors.

A great many of those visitors are Knoxvillians, who take a proprietary pride in the National Park to which their city was— and is— the gateway.

THE PRESENCE OF THE PAST

After the First Baptist Church on Gay Street burned in 1922, the city's largest congregation moved to a Main Street sanctuary that is patterned after London's St. Martin's-in-the-Fields. During the 1920's the church owned and operated one of Knoxville's earliest radio stations: Sunday services were broadcast live over Station WFBC, whose call letters stood for First Baptist Church. Masquerading as a weather-vane, the radio antenna was mounted on the tip of the steeple.

John Fanz Staub, a native of Knoxville, became "the dean of America's residential architects." In 1924, before he moved to Texas, he designed his first house for his aunt, Mrs. Albert G. Hope, who wanted "a Cotswold cottage." Fanz Staub won several architectural awards for the house, and started a national trend toward historic-preservation-by-incorporation when he built it around the ancient rafters, beams, and lintels from a barn on Admiral David Farragut's birthplace farm, and used the original doorstep of the Sevier-Park House as its hearthstone. "Hopecote," on Melrose Place, is now the guest-house for the University of Tennessee's Knoxville campus.

Since 1926, the front door of the handsome neo-Georgian YWCA Building has faced West Clinch Avenue. For many years, a separate entrance on Walnut Street (opposite the prestigious men's Cumberland Club) opened into an unexcelled Tea-Room whose profits helped support the residential facility for young women.

Downtown Knoxville gained two high-rise office buildings in the mid-1920's. Doctors' and dentists' suites filled the upper floors of the stylish art-deco Medical Arts Building on Main Street at Locust, the first office building in Knoxville to have a built-in parking garage. The Renaissance-style General Building, at Market and Church Streets, offered all the up-to-date amenities— for instance, each office was equipped with a direct-line buzzer that instantly summoned a Western Union messenger.

The existing buildings of Knoxville's oldest country clubs were under construction at the same time. In the new eastern subdivision of Holston Hills, the charming English-style Holston Hills Country Club opened in 1927, overlooking its challenging 18-hole golf course. Cherokee Country Club had been founded twenty years earlier: In 1907, its rustic wooden clubhouse was built on the opposite side of Lyons View Pike from the Knoxville area's first golf course, at the mid-point of the Tennessee River's horseshoe bend. The original structure was torn down, and replaced with an elegant French-provincial clubhouse that was acclaimed "the finest in the South" when it was completed in 1928.

The Tennessee Theatre that opened in 1928, on the original Gay Street site of Blount College, was one of the nation's great "movie palaces." (It occupied the newer half of the Burwell Building, whose corner segment had been Knoxville's first skyscraper in 1907.) A long lobby, floored with marble terrazzo and walled with mirrors, led to the ornate Spanish-moorish theatre with 2,000 seats, a full proscenium stage, and a mighty Wurlitzer organ that rose majestically from the orchestra pit. Movies are still shown at the Tennessee, which has been the scene of several world-premiere performances, and the fully-restored theatre also serves as a showcase for concerts and stage productions.

CHAPTER TWELVE

 ## THE GREAT LAKES OF THE SOUTH

Knoxville in 1929 was the same sort of city it had always been— comfortable, friendly, and well satisfied with a diversified economy that produced no really great wealth, but permitted very little abject poverty. Business was conducted in an atmosphere of confidentiality and trust, and a man's word was as good as his bond. Manners were more important than money in social circles: A cultured family's fortunes might wax or wane, but its position in "polite society" remained unchanged.

Only a few citizens were directly affected by the September stock market crash, but when the markets for marble, textiles, and coal collapsed in 1930, everyone began to feel the pinch. The University of Tennessee's new graduates had no high-salaried positions waiting for them; they were happy to find work in filling stations at $18.00 a week. Would-be construction workers lined up for the jobs on the Henley Street Bridge that paid twenty cents an hour. In response to public pressure, their hourly wage was increased to twenty-five cents, and that meant something. Five cents would buy enough dried soup beans to feed a family; only the affluent could afford to waste a nickel on an ice cream cone or a Hershey bar.

Caught in the backlash of a Nashville banking scandal, the Holston-Union National Bank went into receivership in December. The laws governing nationally chartered banks required that all stockholders pay in to the receiver *twice* the face value of their stock, so that no depositors would lose their money. It was good news when the new Hamilton National Bank took over the tall office building at the corner of Clinch and Gay streets in April, 1931, but eight months later, the East Tennessee National Bank closed its doors at the corner of Gay and Union. Again, the stockholders paid the value of their stock twice over. Tax revenues declined so sharply that the City of Knoxville was forced to pay part of its employees' salaries in "City Scrip." Those small-denomination promissory notes were accepted at a discount by local stores. Money was scarcer than hens' teeth during the nationwide Bank

Moratorium in October of 1933, but the resulting new federal banking laws removed the double penalty for stock ownership, and established a new type of protection with the Federal Deposit Insurance Corporation. Knoxvillians breathed a sigh of relief when the Park National Bank, capitalized at $1,000,000, opened in the East Tennessee Bank's former headquarters that December. They were convinced that when it came to a financial crisis, their city could weather the storm as well as any and better than most, and it was a shock when their area was singled out by the national press as being in dire need of charitable assistance from the federal government.

During World War I, a dam with a hydroelectric generator had been built on the Tennessee River at Muscle Shoals, Alabama, to furnish power for munitions and fertilizer plants; after the war, the no-longer-needed dam became the largest white elephant in United States history. Various schemes for its use were suggested in the 1920's, and rejected as impractical; it was offered for sale, but attracted not so much as a nibble.

Then Senator George Norris of Nebraska introduced a bill that solved the problem of what to do with Muscle Shoals by making it part of a series of dams and locks on the mainstream of the Tennessee River that would turn the river into a navigable inland waterway. This was not the first time such a plan had been proposed. A century earlier, in 1830, President Andrew Jackson had dispatched Colonel Stephen H. Long of the U. S. Army Corps of Engineers to make a detailed study of the alternately deep and shallow stream. Long's report, submitted in September, 1832, compared the potential capacity of the Tennessee River favorably with that of the Ohio, and stated that its optimum usefulness could best be attained by building a series of dams and locks. (In view of the high cost of such a project, Long made a stopgap suggestion that was acted upon by the Tennessee legislature: dredging the riverbed to create a continuous channel with a minimum depth of 24 inches at extreme low water.)

The presence of a hydroelectric generator in the dam at Muscle Shoals inspired Senator Norris to recommend that similar power plants be installed in all the other dams, thus creating an abundance of electricity for the entire Tennessee Valley.

While Senator Norris' plan was under discussion, President Franklin D. Roosevelt was advised by the Army Corps of Engineers that spring flooding on the lower Tennessee, the Ohio, and the Mississippi rivers could be significantly reduced by building storage dams on the

Tennessee's upper tributaries.   The engineers hailed the Tennessee River System as an excellent choice for such an experiment, for two reasons: First, the western slope of the Unaka Mountains, where the upper tributaries rose, enjoyed the highest annual rainfall average in the eastern United States. Second, in that region, each newly created lake would be contained by a ring of high hills, and there would be no spillover into surrounding areas if it became necessary to raise the water level for downstream flood control.

President Roosevelt saw an even wider application for the proposal than did Senator Norris or the Corps of Engineers. The President sent a special message to Congress urging the passage of the Norris Act, in which he set forth his own interpretation of its implications:

> *It is clear that the Muscle Shoals development is but a small part of the potential public usefulness of the entire Tennessee River. Such use, if envisioned in its entirety, transcends mere power development; it enters the wide fields of flood control, soil erosion, afforestation, elimination from agricultural use of marginal lands, and distribution and diversification of industry. In short, this power development of war days leads logically to national planning for a complete river watershed involving many states and the future lives and welfare of millions. It touches and gives life to all forms of human concerns.*

The Norris Act, passed May 18, 1933, established a single agency called the Tennessee Valley Authority to buy land, design and build dams and hydroelectric power plants, construct transmission lines, and market the electricity produced. As the inevitable result of damming rivers, TVA would also create the "Great Lakes of the South" with a combined shoreline of more than 10,000 miles.

President Roosevelt appointed TVA's first directors: Arthur E. Morgan, Chairman; David E. Lilienthal; and Dr. Harcourt A. Morgan, who resigned as president of the University of Tennessee to become the Authority's authority on agriculture. They announced that twenty new dams would be constructed, and that five dams already in existence would be improved or modified. As the largest city in the area where the first dams would be built, and the hub of railroad transportation, Knoxville was selected as the headquarters for the Tennessee Valley Authority.

The entire nation was now in the depths of the Great Depression, and to people outside the Tennessee Valley, the "squandering" of federal

tax money on a grandiose project that would benefit only one small area
was a bitter pill to swallow. To make the dose more palatable,
Americans were encouraged to feel that the inhabitants of the chosen
area were far more in need of aid from a benevolent government than
were their more fortunate compatriots. So many newspaper and
magazine articles were written about barefoot children, tumbledown
shacks, semi-starvation, ignorance, ringworm, and pellagra that the
Tennessee Valley was viewed from a distance as a sort of gigantic
Tobacco Road.

When the first stories appeared, Knoxvillians were startled and
annoyed. They wrote letters to editors, pointing out that while such
conditions might exist *somewhere* in the Tennessee Valley, extreme
poverty was certainly not characteristic of the Valley as a whole.
Protesting was a waste of time and postage stamps. The adverse
publicity continued for years, in a succession of articles that were at best
biased, often patently untrue, and sometimes so far fetched as to be
ludicrous.

A preliminary survey by U. S. Army Engineers had resulted in the
decision to build TVA's first dam on the Clinch River, twenty miles
from Knoxville, and to name it for the author of the Act that created
the agency. Norris Dam was begun in 1933 and completed three years
later— years that were filled with turmoil for the Clinch River Valley,
and for Knoxville.

TVA Headquarters replaced the United States Customs offices in
the Old Post Office on the corner of Market and Clinch Streets. (Since
the 1870's, Knoxville had been a "port of entry", where local wholesalers
and retailers paid the duty on their imported merchandise, but in the
deepening Depression, imports had fallen almost to the vanishing point.
Chattanooga also had a Customs Office, and there was no longer a need
for two so close together. Since Knoxville was to be the headquarters
of TVA, the Customs Service felt it would only be fair for Chattanooga
to be the port of entry for all of East Tennessee.)

The fact that TVA began its operations during the Depression
meant that it was able to hire outstanding experts in various fields who
could not, in more prosperous times, have been lured away from
industry. These specialists chose to join TVA for two reasons: first, to
be a part of the largest engineering and construction project ever
undertaken in United State history; and second, in a missionary spirit,
to aid in enriching the lives of the Tennessee Valley's hapless residents.
Therefore, TVA brought in a group of highly trained (and highly

motivated) persons to direct its wide-ranging affairs.   These early
executives found it difficult to reconcile what they had read about the
Valley with what they actually saw and heard.   Here they were, engaged
in a great social crusade to improve the quality of life in a desolate and
deprived area, but the people they met in Knoxville refused to admit
that their area was desolate, and certainly did not consider themselves
in any way deprived. After all, in 1934, the University of Tennessee was
celebrating the 140th anniversary of its chartering and Knoxville College
was in its 67th year. Statistics previously compiled by Dr. Philander P.
Claxton, the United States Commissioner of Education, showed that
Knoxville had a larger number of college-educated women *per capita*
than any other city in the country! Ossoli Circle, a member of the
National Federation of Women's Clubs, was making preparations for its
50th birthday party; the Junior League of Knoxville had been part of a
national network since 1921. The Knoxville Garden Club had become
an affiliate of the Garden Club of America in 1932. Those national
women's organizations had long been in the forefront of advances in
continuing education, welfare, and conservation. Men's civic clubs, such
as Rotary and Kiwanis, were numerous and active; the Mens Cotillion
Club was 45 years old; and the Knoxville Chamber of Commerce was
right on hand to welcome TVA.

TVA's firstcoming families quickly adapted to Knoxville, finding
congenial friends who shared their interests, and making their presence
felt in the community. They fostered the efforts of the Melrose Art
Center that maintained classrooms and a gallery in an antebellum
mansion near the University. They swelled the crowd at travelling
productions of Broadway plays, as well as at the national champion
Tennessee Volunteers' home football games. Their financial support
and encouragement were vital to the success of the Knoxville Symphony
Orchestra that evolved in 1934 from a chamber music group formed by
Bertha Walburn Clark in 1910.

As the scope of the agency increased, additional offices were
rented in the downtown area, and a wave of middle-management
employees arrived to fill them. These new residents, who converged on
Knoxville from all the compass points of the United States, were firmly
convinced from what they had read in newspapers and magazines that
they were going to the nation's most backward region. People usually
see what they expect to see, and the newcomers all too often said that
Knoxville was a one-horse town where the sidewalks were rolled up
every night at 9 p.m. "What do you people do for entertainment?" was

the question they most frequently asked.

Made touchy by this condescending attitude, Knoxvillians always began by mentioning the Tennessee Theatre which was ranked among the nation's most opulent movie palaces. Then they went on to speak of radio. WNOX, one of the oldest stations in the country, had been on the air since 1921 at 1010 on the dial; the station was broadcasting live from the penthouse at the Andrew Johnson Hotel, and the public was welcome to watch. The Andrew Johnson's free postcards proclaimed it "The South's Newest and Finest Hotel," and Mrs. Roosevelt was just one of its famous guests.

Of course there was Chilhowee Park, where the Tennessee Valley Agricultural and Industrial Fair was held every September. In addition to all kinds of machinery and livestock exhibits, the TVA&I Fair had a large midway. The Park's permanent merry-go-round and roller coaster operated all summer, and the big indoor roller-skating rink was open all year around. The Knoxville Zoo was there, too, but— the natives felt duty bound to admit— it was nothing to write home about. There was just one thing to remember: Chilhowee Park was reserved for Knoxville's black citizens on Emancipation Day. (It was hard to convince incredulous Yankees that, in Tennessee and Kentucky, Emancipation Day was not New Year's Day, but the Eighth of August.)

"Prohibition" was (supposedly) in force, and the newcomers refused to believe that a city the size of Knoxville had no speakeasies. Natives enlightened them about home delivery, and rather reluctantly passed on the name of a reliable bootlegger.

Before long, most of the new residents were revising their preconceived notions of the Tennessee Valley. They began to find the leisurely life restful, and the lush green countryside beautiful. They came to love the mist-clad mountains, the rugged hills, and the swift-flowing rivers of East Tennessee; and they began to love Knoxville, too— for its obvious faults as well as for its sometimes hidden virtues. Natives sensed a change in the atmosphere, and relaxed their defenses. By the time Norris Dam was completed, Knoxville's old and new residents were able to laugh together at some of their misapprehensions about each other.

Meanwhile, the construction of the dam was going on apace, and the jobs it provided were a God-send to the region. So many day-laborers were employed at the site that TVA built a model town to house those not commuting from Knoxville and the surrounding area. This town called Norris was the pioneer experiment in the field of public housing, and its planners tried out all sorts of innovative ideas. (For example, a few houses were constructed of cheap and sturdy corrugated iron.   When the hot summer sun turned them into uninhabitable sweatboxes, corrugated metal was hastily crossed off the list of building materials.)   In the end, most of the houses at Norris were modifications of a pattern long found satisfactory in East Tennessee: one story, farmhouse-type homes with steeply pitched roofs for rain run-off and snow dispersal, cross-ventilation for cool summer sleeping, and shady porches to sit on in the long twilight of the hill country.

If the building of the dam had been TVA's sole end and aim, there would have been no problem: the best engineering minds in the country were in charge of it. The trouble was, once the dam was finished, it was going to hold water! When that happened, farms and roads and towns were going to be down at the bottom of a lake; the cool springs and the age-old shade trees were going to be drowned. This was very difficult for East Tennesseans to accept.   In the Great Smoky Mountains National Park, houses and barns had been torn down and fences removed, so that the land would look the way it did before the people came; but the land itself had remained.   There was something frightening— almost sacrilegious— about erasing the very contours of the Clinch River Valley that the good Lord had seen fit to put there.

TVA's Land Acquisition Division was in a hurry to get the property bought and the people moved before the water rose, but the people were in no hurry at all. Selling a farm that had come down in the family was a big responsibility, and the owners intended to do considerable dickering before signing on the dotted line. As time grew short, condemnation proceedings were instituted in the Federal District Court against all the landowners who had not yet signed agreements. Now, East Tennesseans had never been averse to going to court to protect what they believed to be their rights, but they were stunned to find that "the law" could not only force them to sell their land; it could also set the price they had to take for it. They were "mad enough to chew nails and spit tacks!"

There was one question on which the federal and state laws were in direct conflict. Many churches with adjoining cemeteries, and many fenced-in graveyards on the valley's farms, were in the area to be flooded. TVA offered to move the thousands of graves in the hundreds of burying grounds to new locations selected by the churches or families concerned, but several plot owners brought suit to halt the graveyards' desecration. One of the cemeteries to be moved was the last resting place of a former judge and U.S. Senator, John K. Shields. Judge Shields had once decided a case that involved moving a cemetery against the wishes of the family who owned it, and whose ancestors were buried there. The judge's landmark decision, unquestioned in the courts of Tennessee for more than half a century, ordered that "the wheels of progress must stop at the grave." Neither Judge Shields' decision nor his grave could halt the removal of the cemeteries in the Clinch River Valley. Federal District Judge Xenophon Hicks pointed out that if the graves were not moved with their title-holders' consent, they were doomed to be covered by the waters of Norris Lake; and that was that.

People took the money paid them for their land, and set out to buy farms beyond the reach of the water, but Norris was not the only dam planned for the Knoxville area. A glance at the map as it was destined to be when all the lakes were filled showed plainly that there would be almost no river bottomland left in the whole of the East Tennessee Valley. The displaced farmers were mad all over again!

TVA bought outright only the bottomlands that would be covered by the lake, and paid extra for easements on the nearby acres that could conceivably be under water if the dam's flood-gates were closed to prevent the flooding of populated downstream areas. Some farmers were left with hilly land that they had not previously cultivated, preferring (as the University's County Agents advocated) to leave it in timber or use it for grazing. They built new homes on these wooded hilltops, and dug wells to replace their clear spring water— and at this point, quite a few of them gave up farming, and went to work for TVA.

The houses on the floor of the valley were razed, the trees felled, the cemeteries moved. And then the water came. It built up gradually behind the great white bulk of Norris Dam, and Knoxvillians drove out often to watch the landmarks disappearing one by one. Within weeks, there was the lake, looking as though its fingers of clear water had been reaching deep into the hills from time immemorial. For awhile, people would say: "Back from the dam apiece was the house my great-grandpappy built way back in 1805," or "Right over yonder used to be the town of Loyston." (Twenty years later, when the water in Norris Lake was at an unprecedentedly low level, the site of Loyston suddenly reappeared with houses and trees gone, streets and foundations silted over. Former residents hurried out to see, and held an impromptu reunion where their homes had stood; but they were not sorry when the lake began to rise and their dead town was decently reburied beneath the shining water.)

Tall transformer-towers, looking like the products of some giant-child's Mechano set, marched away from the Norris generating plant in all directions, and in a surprisingly short time, TVA's Rural Electrification Program brought the blessings of inexpensive electricity to scattered hamlets and isolated farmhouses throughout mid-East Tennessee. But not to Knoxville. The Tennessee Public Service Company, a private corporation, refused to relinquish its profitable franchise that brought in almost six cents a kilowatt hour. In 1934, construction was begun on a city-owned electric distribution system for TVA power, but TPS brought suit to halt it, challenging the constitutionality of the Norris Act. Knoxville's legal battle was finally won in 1938, when the United States Supreme Court declared TVA and all its programs constitutional; and Knoxvillians' electric bills dropped 40% after the switch was made to TVA power.

(Once the dams were built and their generators installed, reliable, non-polluting hydroelectric power was very inexpensive to produce. Federal money allotted to TVA for building the dams and power plants was not an outright gift from the government, but a long-term, zero-interest loan with yearly payments due on the principal. Everywhere it operated, TVA paid state and local taxes; but since it paid no federal taxes, its rates could be markedly lower than those of competing private utilities).

While Norris was under construction, other dams were in the planning stages. Soon there was Cherokee on the Holston; Douglas on the French Broad; Melton Hill on the Clinch; and Fort Loudoun on the Tennessee River itself. When Fort Loudoun Dam was built in 1943, it towered an incredible 130 feet above the riverbed, and had the tallest single-lift locks in the world. Since then, their height has been exceeded only by the locks at Egypt's Aswan Dam on the River Nile.

Each of these dams was within twenty-five miles of Downtown Knoxville, and each had created a beautiful new lake; from an airplane, these first Great Lakes of the South looked like huge free-form sapphires set in prongs of bright green hills. Knoxvillians took to the water like new-hatched ducklings. Small speedboats troubled the placid surface of Norris Lake above the town of Loyston; white-winged sailboats skimmed past the birthplace of Admiral David Farragut, on a promontory overlooking Fort Loudoun Lake. Bass fishermen came home from Douglas Lake to talk about the great dike TVA had built to protect the charming old town of Dandridge.

Lower power rates, water sports and year-around fishing were the good news. The bad news was that East Tennessee's best river bottomlands were gone forever. Gone, too, were the many canneries (including Stokely Brothers) that had been the mainstay of the rural economy. East Tennessee was no longer the nations's most important poultry-producing area, and in Knoxville's grocery stores, fresh fruits and vegetables were "shipped in" rather than homegrown.

In the mid-1960's, Knoxville was pinpointed on the map in the center of a five-pointed star of lakes whose combined shoreline totalled 2,322 miles, and Downtown Knoxville was bordered by the headwaters of a nine-foot shipping channel that extended 900 miles to the Gulf of Mexico at New Orleans. (The Tennessee-Tombigbee Waterway now cuts the distance to the Gulf in half).

Enough's enough! East Tennesseans chorused when TVA announced plans for a sixth dam in the Knoxville area. The new lake would inundate the lower reaches of the Tellico and Little Tennessee rivers, and would be connected to Fort Loudoun Lake by a canal, but Tellico Dam would not contain a power plant. Instead, the canal would funnel in more water to increase the power-capacity of Fort Loudoun Dam. Conservationists protested that America had no wild rivers to spare. Archeologists and historians deplored the destruction of ancient Cherokee townsites and pioneer landmarks. Energy experts questioned the need for, and the efficiency of, the canal as a power-booster. Objections were of no avail.

Tellico Dam was almost complete when a supposedly unique species of fish was discovered in the Little Tennessee River, and the three-inch long "snail darter" accomplished what humans could not do: under the provisions of the Endangered Species Act, its presence halted TVA. (Foothills fishermen laughed when pictures of the extremely rare fish were shown on television and printed in the Knoxville newspapers. "'Endangered snail-darter,' my fat foot! I've been usin' those minners for bait all my life.") Court battles between environmentalists and engineers dragged on. Ultimately, TVA was allowed to finish the dam, which had already been in progress when the Environmental Protection Act was passed. (Afterward, the snail-darter was found swimming happily in other fast-flowing East Tennessee rivers.)

Because flood control is one of TVA's mandated purposes, all the dams on the upper reaches of the Tennessee and its tributaries have flood gates that hold back vast quantities of water during periods of heavy rainfall. By raising the water level of these storage lakes, TVA spares downstream towns and cities— such as Chattanooga— from disastrous flooding.

HOWEVER, the six lakes within twenty-five miles of Downtown Knoxville have *permanently* inundated 131,180 acres of East Tennessee's best farmland. That's enough water-surface to cover the entire city of Chattanooga, PLUS the District of Columbia, Manhattan Island, the Principality of Monaco, and Vatican City— and still have 10 square miles of lake left over!

No one can deny that the Knoxville area is (as TVA's early advertising matchbooks boasted)

"THE BEST DAM PLACE IN THE COUNTRY!"

THE PRESENCE OF THE PAST

In 1929, broad Chapman Highway replaced the narrow, winding Old Sevierville Pike with a shorter, more direct route to the Great Smoky Mountains. For access to it, the Henley Street Bridge was built across what was then the Tennessee River, but is now the headwaters of Fort Loudoun Lake. The water, controlled by downstream Fort Loudoun Dam, is deeper than it used to be, but no wider: both the 1890's Gay Street Bridge and the new bridge completed in 1932 were in place before the dam was built in 1943.

The skeletal structure of what was to be the "Tennessee Terrace Hotel" stood unfinished on Gay Street for two years after its Atlanta developer went into bankruptcy. Refinanced and renamed, it opened as the Hotel Andrew Johnson on New Year's Eve in 1929. Unlike most hotels, the Andrew Johnson prospered during the Great Depression because its views of the river and the mountains combined with elegant appointments and superior services to attract 130 resident guests. The 16-story building, now renovated as an office plaza, was the tallest in Knoxville until 1982.

In 1930, the YMCA moved from its large State Street building into an even larger, Mediterranean-style structure at the corner of West Clinch and Locust Streets. The new "Y" was like a men's athletic club with attractions that included an indoor swimming pool and handball courts. Those facilities are being retained and improved upon as the building's upper floors become downtown condominiums.

Unlikely though it seems, the Church Street United Methodist Church is situated on Henley Street, between Main and Hill Avenues. It moved to this location in 1931, after its Church Street sanctuary was destroyed by fire. The cathedral-style stone church stands on the site of the 19th century Knoxville Female Academy.

A row of 19th century Main Street residences, and the Women's Lyceum Building on Cumberland Avenue, were demolished to make way for the block-square Main Post Office that opened in 1934. The classically simple structure is a treasury of Tennessee marble: Its outer walls look white in dry weather, but turn rose-pink on rainy days. Many varieties of locally-quarried "cedar" marble, in variegated patterns of beige, maroon, and brown, appear in the exterior foundation, the curbing, and the interior walls and floors.

CHAPTER THIRTEEN

 # SPLITTING THE ATOM

In 1941, Knoxville was 150 years old, and in spite of the lingering Depression, this time the city's milestone birthday was suitably celebrated. On a beautiful Indian-summer Sunday afternoon, Shields-Watkins Football Field was the scene of the Sesquicentennial Pageant that began with a reenactment of the signing of the Treaty of Holston, featuring a delegation of costumed Cherokee from the Qualla Reservation. Puffs of black-powder smoke hovered above a make-believe Civil War skirmish, and the ceremonies ended with a stirring medley of patriotic marching songs presented by massed school bands. (UT's President James D. Hoskins chaired the Sesquicentennial Committee, and the official souvenir was a wooden nickel that sold for five cents.)

Cold weather came early that year. After a bountiful midday dinner, most Knoxvillians spent Sunday afternoons reading the newspapers and listening to music on the radio. On Sunday, December 7, they tuned in to the first bulletins announcing the Japanese attack on Pearl Harbor.

The country was plunged into war. This time, there would be no parades in Knoxville, and no bands playing on the street corners— just Kate Smith on the radio, singing "God Bless America." Unsmiling young men went down to the Post Office to volunteer, and something happened to them that was like an echo of the past. John Sevier had drafted half his men to stay home from the Battle of King's Mountain; now Uncle Sam was drafting Knoxvillians to stay on in their peacetime jobs for the duration of World War II. Employees of Rohm & Haas, the Aluminum Company of America, and the Fulton Sylphon Plant were told that their work was as essential to winning the war as though they were actually fighting. Many smaller local industries were also classified as "defense plants," because their products were required by the armed forces. Each plant, large or small, strove to earn the coveted blue eagle

Achievement Banner awarded for meritorious service to the war effort, and to fly it from the rooftop for all to see.

The number one song on the Radio Hit Parade was "You're in the Army, Mr. Jones." Blue service stars appeared in the front windows of Knoxville homes; some would later be replaced by gold stars. Churches and private clubs prominently displayed rows of stars with the names of their members in the service; stores did the same for their employees. The University, whose masculine enrollment had dropped almost to the level of fifty years before, welcomed an Army Air Corps training squadron that marched to classes on The Hill as had UT cadets in the 1880's, and drilled in front of Tyson House on Temple Avenue, singing "Off we go, into the wild blue yonder...."

Events were taking place in Washington that would literally have world-shaking effects. On August 13, 1942, President Roosevelt created a special segment of the Corps of Army Engineers called the "Manhattan District." The name was intentionally misleading, for this group had nothing whatever to do with Manhattan Island or the City of New York. In accordance with previously made plans, the Engineers at once began a secret survey in East Tennessee's Anderson and Roane counties; on September 9, they reported that the tentatively selected site was ideal for their purpose. Immediately, the Army set about acquiring 92 square miles of land along the Clinch River, eighteen miles north of Knoxville.

This task was made easier by the proximity of Norris Dam, whose downstream neighbors were already familiar with the federal government's irresistible power of condemnation. Knowing the loss of their land to be inevitable, patriotic farmers took comfort in the thought that it was urgently needed for the war effort. "But when the government's through using it," they told the Army purchasing agents, "we'd like to buy it back." Some of these people had previously been forced out of their homes by the waters of Norris Lake, and at least one family was dispossessed three times: by the Great Smoky Mountains National Park, by TVA, and finally, by "the war."

Naturally, the farmers wanted to know what the Army planned to do with their land, and they were not alone in asking that question. From Washington, Congressman Albert Gore made an "official announcement" that the government had purchased the property for a demolition range.

Early in 1943, the land acquisition was complete, and bulldozers moved into the Clinch River Valley, rearranging its contours overnight into a "temporary" U.S. Army Reservation called "Oak Ridge." Trees were ruthlessly uprooted, roads built, and the whole area surrounded by an impregnable fence. The reservation could be entered at four checkpoints, from existing highways, but only authorized personnel could pass the armed guards who manned the gates. Behind the fence, 47,000 carefully screened laborers toiled around the clock, constructing huge underground plants in which 40,000 security-cleared persons were to be employed. Secrecy was the watchword. Each person hired was told the name of the employer who would sign his paycheck, the identifying number of the plant where he would work, and the duties his own job would entail— *but nothing more.*

These stringent precautions paid off. For more than two years, only President Roosevelt, a few high-level advisers, and the top echelon of Army Engineers knew that the Oak Ridge plants were engaged in a race to split the atom. The contest was won on November 4, 1943, when the first atomic chain reactor was placed in operation by the E.I. Dupont de Nemours Company, using the gaseous diffusion process. On January 12, 1944, U235 was successfully produced by the electromagnetic process at the Tennessee Eastman Corporation plant. There was no public announcement of either triumph.

In the meantime, Knoxville was coping with an invasion of Oak Ridge employees. Not since the closing days of the Civil War had so many people descended on the city in search of food and shelter.

East Tennessee's defense plants were off limits to the Army recruiters seeking employees for Oak Ridge, and only one of three persons interviewed could meet the strict security requirements. After exhausting the local labor market, the recruiters searched elsewhere for qualified applicants. Those who were hired poured into Knoxville by jam-packed train, by overcrowded bus, by overloaded car, and there was absolutely no place to put them. (Lucky early arrivers had rented every available hotel room and tourist cottage, by the month.) Trailer parks and tent cities sprang up along the highways and on vacant city lots, and still the people came.

Knoxvillians employed at Oak Ridge appealed to the patriotism of their fellow citizens. "You really ought to rent that empty guestroom to a war-worker" . . . "Your son's in the service, and his bedroom's vacant. Why don't you put it to good use?". . . "Couldn't you double up with your next-door neighbors, and let a family with children have your house?". . . "Like the Bible says, 'Be ye not unmindful to entertain strangers'."

Amazing shortages developed. Not only the people who had poured into Knoxville to live, but all the others housed in the surrounding towns had to be fed by means of Knoxville's wholesale markets. For reasons of security, the number of workers at Oak Ridge could not be told, or even hinted, so Knoxville's wholesale allotments were not measurably increased and no other provision was made to ensure adequate supplies. Some of the shortages were trivial, to be sure— candy bars, cigarettes, and nylon stockings had gone to war all over the country— but many necessities were in very short supply. Poultry, eggs, potatoes, and green vegetables virtually disappeared: they had formerly been provided by the now-vanished farms in Anderson and Roane counties. Tomato plants replaced geraniums in ornamental concrete urns; rosebushes and daffodil bulbs were dug up to make way for Victory Gardens.

Prices zoomed. Knoxville was number one on the list of American cities experiencing a tremendous rise in the cost of living.

Rationing was intended to ensure equitable supplies of scarce commodities to all parts of the country, but Oak Ridge was not on any map when the master distribution plan was drawn up. Hopeful Knoxville housewives presented their ration books at grocery stores, only to be told there was no meat, no sugar, no butter, and no coffee. Worst of all, canned baby food and evaporated milk were missing from the shelves for weeks at a time. Knoxvillians received "care packages" from friends and relatives who lived in areas where rationing was working. Servicemen coming home on leave brought whatever was available at the Post Exchange.

There was a nationwide soap shortage, and the government instructed every housewife to strain all cooking fats into a tin can which, when filled, was to be handed in at the nearest meat market. Fat-recycling was just one more messy extra chore— until the day when a local radio announcer interrupted a program of recorded music with the exhortation: "Ladies! Get your fat cans down to the grocery store!"

Suddenly housing, which had seemed to be in a hopeless muddle, began to straighten out. The government was not only building plants at Oak Ridge, but a complete city, which by 1945 had 75,000 inhabitants and was (temporarily) Tennessee's fifth largest metropolis. The feat of providing living quarters for all those people could never have been accomplished without the newly developed prefabricated houses— plywood, or cemesto— and house-trailers. Whatever type of housing the newcomers were assigned, they found it surrounded by a sea of the thick red clay mud that was for several years the trademark of Oak Ridge. The town constructed in such frantic haste was, frankly, hideous; yet there were remarkably few complaints from its residents. To live with shortages and with mud was a far smaller sacrifice than Americans in the armed services were being called upon to make.

Knoxville's housing shortage eased, but the food scarcity remained acute. Tempers frayed. What did the government *want* with all those people, anyway? What were they making out there at Oak Ridge that was so all-fired important? Rumors ranged from poison gas to synthetic rubber tires.

There was a sense of mounting tension in Oak Ridge and in Knoxville. Sooner or later, everyone felt, the lid was going to blow off.

August 6, 1945 was the day it happened. With the news that the first atomic bomb had been dropped on Hiroshima came a further announcement: the radioactive heart of the bomb had begun to beat at Oak Ridge, Tennessee.

The nation— and the people living at Oak Ridge— received this information through the newspapers and radio stations in Knoxville, where the news-releases had been ready and waiting for days. Editors and station managers were summoned to a conference, sworn to secrecy, and told the purpose of the Oak Ridge project; on the morning of August 6, they got the go-ahead signal from the Oak Ridge Information Office. In Knoxville and in Oak Ridge, it was a strange and frightening moment of truth.

As the days passed, more and more details of the Hiroshima devastation were published; Americans were warned that, in retaliation, the continental United States might be attacked by enemy bombers. Knoxvillians had an uneasy feeling. If that happened, their city (in the center of a triangle with Oak Ridge, Norris Dam, and the gigantic Alcoa aluminum plant as its points) might very well be number one on the enemy's hit parade.

In the same way that the breaking of the Hindenburg Line had hastened Germany's surrender in World War I, the use of the atomic bomb at Hiroshima and Nagasaki was the beginning of the end of World War II. "*Now* what will they do with Oak Ridge?" Knoxvillians wondered. "All that money spent, and all those people working all this time— just to make tiny little pieces of two bombs that were about the size of gallon jugs...."

Experiments in the peacetime uses of atomic energy had already begun at Oak Ridge, and at The University of Tennessee. Scientists had said all along, from the moment the news of the atomic bomb was released, that nuclear energy would serve humanity far better in peacetime pursuits than as an agent of destruction. In the months that followed, it seemed obvious that the men of science who were stressing the positive side of nuclear energy should be allowed to direct its future destiny. So, on August 1, 1946, President Harry Truman signed a bill establishing the civilian Atomic Energy Commission to take over the entire atomic project from the War Department.

Nuclear reactors offered a completely new method of generating electricity that was hailed as a safe, clean, and inexpensive source of power for the national economy, and other uses for atomic energy emerged. Medicine and agriculture advanced by giant strides as radioactive isotopes proved invaluable diagnostic tools and "tracer atoms" produced improved strains of staple crops.

Not until 1949 did Oak Ridge cease to be a closely guarded Army reservation. Gates that had barred the access highways were then unlocked, and for the first time, Knoxvillians without security clearance were allowed inside. Billboards welcomed them to OAK RIDGE— THE ATOMIC CITY, and signs directed them to "The World's Only Museum of Atomic Energy" that explained in layman's terms just how the atom's splitting was accomplished, and what marvels could be wrought by nuclear power. A popular apparatus demonstrated the effect of static electricity by making the visitor's hair stand on end; it was fascinating to watch the huge mechanical hands perform their delicate tasks with such dexterity, and there were miniature models of the full-size reactors to be scrutinized. The favorite memento was obtained by dropping a dime into a machine that returned the same dime, made harmlessly radioactive and sealed in a plastic casing labelled "Souvenir of Oak Ridge, Tennessee."

The coin contained considerably less radioactivity than do some types of natural rock, or some brands of pottery dinnerware.

THE PRESENCE OF THE PAST

During World War II, a Blue Eagle Banner for outstanding service to the war effort was flown from the roof of the Fulton Sylphon Plant, the nation's largest manufacturer of thermostatic controls. The company was founded in 1904 by Weston M. Fulton, who resigned as head of the Knoxville weather bureau to become a full-time inventor of such devices as the "sylphon," a seamless corrugated metal bellows extremely sensitive to changes in temperature; he was granted so many patents that his inventions were housed in a special section of the U. S. Patent Office. The former "defense plant" (bounded by Kingston Pike, the Southern Railroad tracks, the UT Agriculture Campus, and the Alcoa Expressway) is now the Fulton Sylphon Division of Robertshaw Controls.

Especially equipped to take advantage of the proximity of Oak Ridge in pursuing the uses of radioactive isotopes in medicine, The University of Tennessee Memorial Research Center and Hospital opened on Alcoa Highway in 1956. It was equally funded by the State of Tennessee, Knox County, and the City of Knoxville, to replace old Knoxville General Hospital, and was turned over to The University as the agency best qualified to administer it. The University of Tennessee Medical Center at Knoxville has grown from a single building to a spreading complex of exemplary patient facilities, laboratories, and doctors' offices; it is the region's premier teaching hospital, and the Knoxville area's Level 1 Trauma Center.

CHAPTER FOURTEEN

 # CHALLENGES AND CHANGES

Peace, it's wonderful! Especially in Knoxville, where four years of "Use it up, wear it out; make it do, or do without" had left a threadbare community whose citizens were exhausted to the point of apathy.

In the autumn of 1945, every day was a day of thanksgiving for blessings large and small. More and more servicemen were returning—older and wiser, and eager to exchange their uniform jackets for civilian suitcoats with "ruptured duck" honorable discharge buttons on the lapels. And there was fresh-brewed coffee to welcome them home!

All over town, radios were tuned at lunchtime to Station WNOX, where toe-tapping "Country Music" was first introduced on Lowell Blanchard's Midday Merry-go-round. The daily show and the Saturday night Tennessee Barn Dance were broadcast live from the roomy WNOX Auditorium on Gay Street; admission was free, and fans flocked to see and hear such homegrown favorites as Roy Acuff, Chet Atkins, and "Grandpappy" Archie Campbell.

That year, there were plenty of traditional cedar Christmas trees for sale, but no new strings of lights or glittering ornaments. As in grandmother's day, a few carefully hoarded, tarnished trimmings were eked out with homemade cookies, popcorn chains, and polished winesap apples. In the spring, the public golf course reopened at Whittle Springs with weed-infested greens and bumpy fairways, but the tennis courts at Tyson Park were in surprisingly good shape. Come summer, there was paint for downtown's peeling storefronts, and asphalt to fill the chugholes in the city streets. Before autumn ended, new automobile tires and derationed gasoline brought the mountains and the lakes within reach ....

This gradual easing back into normality was rudely interrupted in 1947, when John Gunther's best-selling new book *Inside U.S.A.* named Knoxville the ugliest city in America, "with an intense, concentrated, degrading ugliness." Those harsh words made headlines in the local newspapers, and were widely quoted on radio broadcasts.

Former servicemen dismissed the insult as "one man's opinion." Businessmen joked about it. ("Who *is* John Gunther, anyhow?" "Oh, he's some fellow who passed through Knoxville on a rainy day in January, and never got off the train.") Like every other American city, Knoxville had a disillusioned group of post-war pessimists, and they accepted the assessment at face value. Pointing to the pall of soft-coal smoke that hovered over factories and homes, they declared: "The man's right. This town's as ugly as homemade sin!"

Believing that the best defense is a good offense, a few citizens went out of their way to stress Knoxville's strong points. They called attention to the city's natural assets that its natives took for granted: the wooded hills; the shining lakes and rivers; the horizon filled with mountains shading from deep purple to sky blue. They praised the climate season by changing season, and noted that the abundant rainfall and the richness of the red clay soil made the native dogwood trees grow large, and gave them a profusion of snowy blossoms.

Surrounding the central business district, like the points of a compass, were charming residential areas where each well-kept lawn donned a lacy mantle of white bloom at dogwood time. For contrast, masses of azaleas added vibrant color; rock gardens glowed in the sun; and wildflowers carpeted the shady slopes. The most breathtaking streets were far off the beaten path and very hard to find, SO, in 1949 it was suggested to the Chamber of Commerce that a dogwood trail be marked to and from those streets, beginning at the nearest major highway.

The first of Knoxville's famous Dogwood Trails opened in Sequoyah Hills in 1955. Soon there were six: east of downtown, in Holston Hills; north, in Fountain City; south, on Chapman Highway and in Lakemoor Hills; and west, in Sequoyah and Westmoreland. Trail markers painted directly on the pavement guided cars and buses over more than fifty miles of residential streets where dogwoods and azaleas grew in great abundance. Beginning experimentally with one short Sequoyah street in 1957, public-spirited homeowners lighted their lawn trees for night viewing, and the dogwoods' trunks and branches blended with the surrounding darkness, while their blossoms seemed to float unsupported in mid-air.

The Dogwood Trails clearly demonstrated that the way to foster civic pride was to begin with an existing asset and build upon it. Knoxville had a surprising number of cultural attractions for a city its size, and plans were soon underway to combine the fine and lively arts in a yearly festival timed to coincide with the peak of the spring blooming season. In 1960, under the joint sponsorship of the Chamber of Commerce and the Junior League of Knoxville, the annual Dogwood Arts Festival began offering local, regional, and national art shows; concerts ranging from symphony to rock; bluegrass and marching-band competitions; opera, ballet, and dramatic productions; expositions of traditional and contemporary crafts; sports and watersports events— plus flower shows, public and private open gardens, and of course, the Dogwood Trails that started it all. Community-wide cooperation, and hundreds of hard-working volunteers, made the first Festival an instant success: even congenital critics admitted that capsule-culture was very easy to swallow. As the Festival grew, short Garden By-Ways were added, along with free bus tours of the Trails, and the annual extravaganza began to attract national and international attention.

All across the country, suburban subdivisions had sprung up like weeds in the post-war decade, and outlying shopping centers had drained dollar volume from downtown stores. Use of public transportation declined— in a nation of two-car families, nobody rode the bus. America's cities were suffering from congestive heart failure, complicated by traffic arteriosclerosis, and Knoxville was no exception. Civic leaders cast a seeing eye on downtown buildings begrimed by coal soot, and on deteriorating inner city neighborhoods, and conceded that John Gunther might have had a point.

In 1957, property owners and merchants jointed forces in the Downtown Knoxville Association that completed a series of locally-financed palliative projects aimed at improving the business district. Knoxville's antiquated Market House failed to meet the fire codes, and its primitive plumbing was a definite health hazard, but when DKA suggested replacing it with a pedestrian mall, traditionalists rose up in righteous indignation. "Do away with downtown's biggest drawing card? Ridiculous! Where else can anybody buy chow-chow, or homemade cottage cheese, or sulphured apples?"

In the middle of the argument, the Market House settled its own fate by burning down.

Market Square Mall was completed just in time to be the center of activities for the first Dogwood Arts Festival. "A patch of giant toadstools," diehards dubbed the umbrella-shaped concrete sections that formed the sidewalk canopies and the small marketing facility built to satisfy the reversionary clause in Market Square's deed of gift.

Meanwhile, City Council had not been idle. Under the Urban

Renewal Act, federal funds were available to clear a large "blighted area" east of the downtown plateau. Bulldozers razed the buildings, rearranged the streets, and regraded the steep hills into a single mound of raw red clay from which prospective developers stayed away in droves; but government rushed in where private investors feared to tread. In 1961, the fine $5,000,000 James White Memorial Auditorium/Coliseum opened in the Mountain View Renewal Area, and the Chamber of Commerce announced that Knoxville was now ready to compete for major regional and national conventions.

"You've got to be kidding," scoffed the city's hotelkeepers and restaurant owners. "Who's going to schedule a convention in a *dry community*?"

Nullifying a city ordinance in effect since 1907, Knoxville's voters turned out in record numbers, and marked their ballots FOR the sale of alcoholic beverages in package stores.

The red clay in Mountain View had hardly had time to erode before bulldozers moved into a second renewal area— west, this time, of Downtown Knoxville. Until the 1920's, the entire campus of the University of Tennessee had been The Hill to which Blount College moved from Gay Street in 1828. Extensive structural repairs required by the Civil War bombardments had enabled historic Old College to survive another 60 years, but in 1922, the University's beloved but crumbling main building was replaced with handsome and dignified Ayres Hall. Then the University began to spill over onto neighboring tree-lined streets. A plan for gradual expansion was formulated and a style of architecture approved, with Ayres Hall as its prototype. The main library was located across the street from the entrance to the main campus. New self-contained colleges were built. New men's and women's dormitories were constructed; before they were completed, more were needed: in the 1960's The Hill was *still* covered with dozens of flat-tops, brought in from Oak Ridge at the end of World War II as emergency housing for veterans attending college on the G.I. Bill.

Step-by-step expansion had been woefully inadequate, so, in a mammoth urban renewal program, the University acquired 135 acres of land between The Hill and the College of Agriculture. The end result of this tremendous campus extension was desirable, but not the means to it. In order to qualify for federal renewal funds, a neighborhood built up in the palmy days of the late 19th and early 20th centuries was declared a "potential slum," and the substantial citizens who lived there were justifiably angered by the unjust designation. While their cherished homes were being leveled and the familiar green hills flattened into a red clay plain, they railed against high-handed seizure by eminent domain. The tree-shaded residential area took on the appearance of a bombed city. Fires smoldered in cellars open to the sky; concrete steps led up to nothing. Students referred to the new campus as "Hiroshima West."

Growing civic pride had suffered a set-back when the 1960 census figures were released. Comparable cities recorded phenomenal gains but Knoxville, whose city limits had not been extended in more than forty years, was barely holding her own. The solution seemed obvious: annex the heavily populated suburbs; give city services; and collect city taxes. Turning a deaf ear to the protests of suburbanites about to be touched in the wallet, Knoxville increased her area and her population in one fell swoop. Downtown revitalization, urban renewal, cultural emphasis, legal liquor, and territorial expansion paid off in national recognition. In 1963, *Look Magazine* named Knoxville an All-American City! (One local newspaper headlined the front page story with a jubilant **JOHN GUNTHER, PLEASE TAKE NOTE.**)

In 1963, the Knoxville Zoo was a mere menagerie whose most impressive inmate was a talking crow, and the unexpected gift of a splendid African bull elephant from Ringling Brothers Circus was a liability rather than an asset. (Where do you put an animal thirteen feet tall? How much will it cost the taxpayers to feed a creature weighing close to 14,000 pounds?) A perennial City Councilman, Cas Walker, appointed himself the champion of the elephant. His "amateur hour" on Knoxville's first television station, WROL, devoted almost as much time to the Save Old Diamond campaign as to the Cas Walker Family of Grocery Stores. Donations poured in, and sentimental citizens started a Sapphire Fund to buy the lonely pachyderm a mate. City Council reluctantly rose to the occasion by building a shelter for Old Diamond, and by sprucing up the Zoo that was attracting so many of his fans.

Forty years after a scenic riverfront route was first proposed, four-lane Neyland Drive was completed in the 1960's from Kingston Pike to the mouth of First Creek. Beside it, a new three-step sewage treatment plant detracted considerably from the scenery, but complied with strict state and federal regulations to improve the water quality of Fort Loudoun Lake.

A nationwide network of interstate highways was under construction, and the nation's railroads suddenly and arbitrarily discontinued passenger service. In Knoxville, the L&N and Southern Stations stood empty and abandoned, but a new terminal was urgently needed at McGhee Tyson Airport to handle the sharp increase in airline passengers.

Three major interstates would ultimately intersect in Knoxville, and in preparation for their coming, historic First Creek was encased in a gigantic concrete culvert and buried beneath the Downtown Loop. East of the Loop, the Mountain View Renewal Area acquired a new Hyatt-Regency Hotel on the high bluff above Riverside Drive. That building's innovative design inspired the apocryphal story of a native who returned home after an absence of many years, and spotted the wedge-shaped structure on the skyline. "Look what TVA's gone and done!" he shouted. "Built a dam and missed the river!"

After forty years of occupying scattered rental office space, the Tennessee Valley Authority was about to move into a home of its own. Two blocks of Market Street had been closed to allow the fraternal twin TVA Towers to face the north end of Market Square Mall, and planners decreed that a new street was needed to provide better access to the Agency's headquarters. Its route would erase Commerce Avenue on both sides of Gay Street, as well as several small streets on Summit Hill. It would also remove all buildings in its path, from Central Avenue to Henley Street, including the Commerce Avenue Fire Hall, the adjunct buildings of the Church of the Immaculate Conception, and the Lawson McGhee Library, left vacant when the public library moved to a new location in 1970.

Hoping to halt present and future demolition of the city's landmarks, Margaret (Mrs. Ernest) Newton became the moving force behind the formation of Knoxville Heritage, Inc. Its members contended that although the marble Lawson McGhee Library might not be an architectural gem, it was attractive and structurally sound; having been built for the express purpose of holding heavy books, it would make an ideal repository for the archives of Knoxville and Knox County dating back to territorial days. City Council vacillated for months, but finally voted to go ahead with Summit Hill Drive. Wrecking equipment instantly rolled in to level the library.

While one preservation battle was being lost, another was being won. After serving for a century as the kitchen wing of a State Street residence, James White's 1786 log house had been dismantled by a Knoxville printer, Isaiah Ford, in 1906 and moved log by log to Woodlawn Pike south of the river, where it was re-erected; it had then been the residence of the Ford family for more than fifty years. At this point, Hettie (Mrs. Earl) Coulter rallied the City Association of Women's Clubs to purchase Knoxville's oldest house, and move it back downtown where it belonged. The original location of White's Fort was fully occupied by business buildings, so the member clubs selected a substitute site with two advantages: the triangular lot was across the street from the James White Memorial Auditorium/Coliseum, and it overlooked the town founded by James White, across the First Creek valley. However, the lot was in the Mountain View Urban Renewal Area, and its use was restricted to commercial development. It took a special act of Congress, sponsored by Senator Estes Kefauver, to free the property for historic purposes. In 1970, the peripatetic house was once again dismantled, and Isaiah Ford's 1906 numbers on the logs made them easy to reassemble in the new location.

I-40, I-75 and I-81 were finished at last, but all three interstates funneled into a single intersection so poorly designed that it became known nationwide as "Malfunction Junction." Through trucks and buses were inextricably snarled with tourists' and commuters' cars, and all too often, a minor fender-bender backed the traffic up for miles. Then the flow of interstate travel was slowed to a trickle by the gasoline shortage that presaged a worldwide energy crisis.

Long before that crisis arose, energy had been a household word in Knoxville. Thanks to TVA's reasonable rates, 90% of the new small homes constructed in the 1950's enjoyed the cleanliness and convenience of built-in electric heat. In the affluent 1960's, the stoker-fired coal furnaces in public buildings, commercial properties, and older homes were converted to oil or natural gas; as a result, the city was no longer blanketed with sooty smoke.

Here and throughout the Tennessee Valley, electricity-use increased enormously after World War II— just when TVA ran out of rivers suitable for damming. To supply the ever-escalating demand for power, the Authority began to augment hydroelectric generators with coal-fired steam plants. When, in the 1960's, "coal" became a dirty four-letter word, TVA announced that it was switching to nuclear energy: long-range plans called for the construction of 17 nuclear power plants in several states.

For three decades, the American public's fear of the dangers of radiation had prevented atomic energy from coming into widespread use, and the nation's economy ran on fossil fuels; air-polluting coal and volatile natural gas were plentiful, but petroleum reserves were rapidly being depleted. Statesmen and economists agreed that it was not only diplomatically dangerous but financially ruinous to rely too heavily on imported oil.

The raw materials for nuclear energy were rare and costly, and disposal of still-radioactive spent fuels was an unsolved problem, so researchers were happy to discover that plutonium could be recycled and would reproduce itself almost *ad infinitum* in a breeder reactor. This meant, experts announced, a new source of inexhaustible energy; they added that, since the reactor was a controversial project and unwelcome elsewhere, it should be located at Oak Ridge, Tennessee, where the residents were living proof that fissionable materials were safe if properly controlled.

But nuclear energy was not the only game in town. Alternative sources of power were being studied at the University of Tennessee, where emphasis was focused on solar energy, fusion, synthetic fuels, and coal gasification. UT, the federal government's Energy Research and Development Administration at Oak Ridge, and TVA were national power pioneers. With major research programs already underway, they consolidated their efforts by forming an energy consortium.

When an international oil embargo revealed that the United States was dependent on imports for 40% of its gasoline and fuel oil, the government scheduled a series of regional meetings to discuss more efficient use of petro-products, and more effective methods of energy conservation. President Gerald Ford attended the first White House Energy Conference, which was held in Knoxville in October of 1975. In his opening remarks, he explained the choice of the conference site by saying: "When you think of energy, think of Knoxville. This is where it is!"

The President's statement was prophetic.

THE PRESENCE OF THE PAST

Sharp's Ridge Park, which opened in 1953, commands a spectacular 180° view across the far flung city to the Smoky Mountains on the distant horizon. The Park was paid for by public subscription, and is a memorial to veterans of all wars. Nearby Sharp's Gap, a landmark since the days of earliest exploration, has always provided easy access to Knoxville from the north— first for a wagon road, then for railroad tracks, and now, for Interstate 75.

While the James White Memorial Auditorium/Coliseum was going up in the Mountain View Urban Renewal area in 1960, sidewalk superintendents dubbed it "the world's largest caterpillar" because of its humped roof. The Auditorium is the right size for plays and symphony concerts; the larger Coliseum converts with ease from a professional ice hockey rink or sawdust circus rings to the setting for the annual Nativity Pageant.

Lawson McGhee Library moved in 1970 from its marble building on Summit Hill to a functional brick fortress at the corner of Walnut and Church Streets. The Knox County Public Library System is headquartered here, and maintains 16 neighborhood branches throughout the county; the Library's McClung Historical Collection is in the Customs House, two blocks away.

When it opened in 1972, across East Hill Avenue from the Coliseum, the "ultra modern" Hyatt Regency Hotel was a tourist attraction for local residents: they came to ride the glass-walled elevators that ascend through the triangular five-floor lobby, and emerge above the roof to offer a panorama of the city.

On Summit Hill at the north end of Market Street, the fraternal-twin TVA Towers are separated by a brick plaza with islands of trees and flowers, and a symbolic fountain ornaments the flight of stairs leading up to the plaza from Wall Avenue: Water sheets over what appears to be a dam, and then descends in a series of steps representing the TVA lakes and locks on the Tennessee River.

CHAPTER FIFTEEN

 ## THIS WAY TO THE FAIR

In the early 1970's, Downtown Knoxville's TVA Towers and two new high-rise bank headquarters were models of contemporary office architecture, with hermetically sealed windows and year-round "indoor climate control." Traditional buildings were stigmatized as obsolete, and many store-fronts had been faced with black glass or metal sheathing in a misguided attempt to bring them up to date. This sort of spot-rehabilitation was making the area look worse instead of better, and a team of urban-design specialists was employed by the City to draft an overall rejuvenation plan.

Blaming the unhappy juxtaposition of old and new buildings for the central business district's failure to attract outside development, the planners advocated an orderly arrangement of brand-new office towers and hotels, connected by pedestrian malls— plus high-rise condominiums to keep people downtown around the clock instead of just from 9 to 5. (The out-of-town experts warned that Knoxville's chances of attracting good hotels and first class restaurants were nil unless the law was changed to permit the sale of liquor by the drink as well as by the bottle.)

As an inducement to developers, the consultants recommended tax-increment financing: this would enable the City to eliminate all low-tax-yield buildings by condemnation and start over, underwriting highly taxable new private projects with municipal bonds. ("You'll be paying Peter to rob Paul!" downtown taxpayers stormed at City Council.) But although Council was committed to the tax plan, outside developers evinced little interest in its offered opportunities. To start the ball rolling, the governments of Knoxville and Knox County agreed to build a joint headquarters at the opposite end of Market Street from the TVA Towers.

Downtown Knoxville was not the only area where development was slow. City-wide, a lack of venture-capital was hindering the establishment of new businesses and the expansion of existing enterprises. The major banks had come into being during the Depression, and the ultra-conservative lending policies they then adopted had remained unchanged for almost forty years. It was frequently said that anybody who could get a loan from a Knoxville bank didn't need one— and this is where the "Butcher boys" came in.

They were the sons of Cecil H. Butcher, the owner of the Union County Bank in Maynardville (pop. 675), and C.H., Jr. had learned the banking business at the grass-roots level as his father's assistant. Politically ambitious Jake Butcher was the American Oil Company's distributor for several rural counties, and had been known to drive the tanker-truck himself. The brothers joined forces in 1968 to buy the little City & County Bank of Lake City. They borrowed the necessary money from the Union Planters Bank of Memphis, and formed a firm and lasting friendship with Jesse Barr, the charismatic loan officer who handled the transaction.

In 1971, (against their father's advice,) they decided to expand into the Knoxville area with a new state-chartered bank; once again, they obtained the required funding through Jesse Barr at Union Planters. The City & County Bank of Knox County opened in a trailer on a vacant lot at Powell, and lured customers away from older banks with a lenient loan policy. C&C expanded rapidly, branching out across Knox County and purchasing several small-town banks in Tennessee and Kentucky.

Jake Butcher sought the Democratic nomination for governor of Tennessee in 1974. He carried upper East Tennessee and Shelby County, where Jesse Barr was a member of his finance committee, but was defeated in the statewide primaries by Ray Blanton.

Since meeting the Butchers, Jesse Barr had risen like a rocket from loan officer to executive vice president of Union Planters Bank. In 1974, illegal activities resulting in heavy losses for Union Planters were traced to him; while charges of bank fraud were pending against him in Memphis, Barr took refuge with his friends in Knoxville. At this time, the Butcher brothers ostensibly separated their financial interests. C.H., Jr. retained the C&C Banks, while Jesse Barr helped put together the $16,000,000 loan package with which Jake bought a controlling interest in the solvent but stagnating Hamilton National Bank of Knoxville.

Exuding optimism and self-confidence, Jake Butcher took over as the Hamilton's chief executive officer, and proceeded to convert that staid institution into the state-chartered United American Bank. This change excused the UAB from the stringent liquidity and cash-reserve requirements of the Federal Reserve System, while allowing it to retain the protection of the Federal Deposit Insurance Corporation. Then, instead of waiting for loan applications, UAB aggressively pursued them. In its first year of operation, the new bank dramatically increased its loan portfolio and its profits— and jarred other local banks out of their complacent passivity. Jake Butcher was moving into "upstream banking" at the national and international levels, yet he continued to lend money on a handshake, as his father had always done.

In 1975, Jesse Barr was indicted by Memphis grand juries on 41 counts of bank fraud; in 1976, he was convicted in federal court there, and sentenced to five years' imprisonment. This felony conviction forever prohibited him from being employed by any financial institution, in any capacity. He was paroled after serving one year of his sentence, and returned to Knoxville where he evaded the letter of the law by becoming Jake Butcher's "personal financial consultant."

Meanwhile, a county-wide referendum had allowed hotels and restaurants to obtain liquor licenses, but this failed to spark a major development downtown. Business leaders were frank to say that the city's rehabilitation plan for the area would never get underway without some strong incentive— some deadline toward which momentum could build.

When Stewart Evans, the executive secretary of the Downtown Knoxville Association, reported the 1974 World Fair's revitalizing effect upon the city of Spokane, Washington, a delegation of DKA members went to see for themselves. After visiting Spokane and Seattle, the site of the 1962 World's Fair, they concluded that a "limited" international exposition centering around a single theme would not be an impossible undertaking for Knoxville, and that such an event well might provide the necessary spur to downtown redevelopment. Accordingly, in November 1974, the DKA proposed to Mayor Kyle Testerman that a World's Fair be held in Knoxville in 1980.

Public reaction to this bizarre proposal was predictably negative. "A World's Fair? That'll be the day!" ... "Why would we want a Fair? We've got the Dogwood Arts Festival." ... "This town couldn't handle an international flea circus— much less a World's Fair." ... "Sure, downtown's got a redevelopment problem, but *that's* not the solution."

To which DKA's answer was: "If not, then what?" But no one came up with a viable alternative.

Preliminary inquiries brought such encouraging response from municipal authorities in Spokane and Seattle that in August, 1975, the Mayor appointed a World's Fair Advisory Committee headed by Jim Haslam, the president of Pilot Oil Company, and Jake Butcher, the president of the United American Bank. (Jake was not the Mayor's first choice. He was recommended by someone who declined the honor, as being "more of a promoter than a banker, and that's what you really need.")

The choice of energy as the theme of the "limited" Fair was almost inevitable, since TVA, Oak Ridge, and the University of Tennessee already formed a nationally recognized isosceles triangle of energy research. The Fair Proposal prepared for the U.S. Department of Commerce included an unprecedented "extra:" leading scientists from around the world would be invited to participate in a preliminary series of symposia on "Increasing World Energy Production and Productivity."

Timing was of the essence. Presented in Washington during the worldwide oil embargo, the idea of an international energy exposition, enhanced by top-level seminars, instantly captured the attention and support of the Administration. So at the first White House Energy Conference in October of 1975, President Gerald Ford placed his seal of approval upon the Fair that was thereafter known as Energy Expo.

(Two energy-related events received national media coverage: Site preparation for the Clinch River Breeder Reactor began amid predictions of a rosy future for Oak Ridge; and TVA's rates escalated sharply as coal price-increases and construction cost-overruns at nuclear power plants were passed on to consumers.)

Knoxvillians began to realize that a World's Fair was a serious possibility, and football season brought specific doubts about the project's feasibility. The University had recently enlarged the seating capacity of Neyland Stadium by enclosing the field with a solid oval of stands, and at every home game, the Tennessee Volunteers played to a packed house of 90,000 loyal fans. All motel rooms for miles around were booked months in advance. Parking was at a premium, and the post-game traffic jam gave homegoing citizens plenty of time to think. "Look what happens when you get ninety thousand people in the same place at the same time. Six *million* people went to that World's Fair in Spokane."

Concern mounted when newspapers mentioned that almost ten million visitors had attended the 1962 World's Fair in Seattle. "There's no way a crowd like that could even get here. Malfunction Junction would back the cars up a hundred miles, on all three Interstates!"

Several possible Fair sites were considered and rejected before February, 1976, when the Advisory Committee settled on the economically (and geographically) depressed Second Creek valley that separated the campus of the University from the central business district. Here, where the empty L&N Station towered over neglected buildings and abandoned tracks obscured by rampant weeds, two birds were about to be killed with one stone. The Lower Second Creek Area was slated for urban renewal; the World's Fair would be an interim use of the cleared site.

The World's Fair Advisory Committee was reorganized as the Knoxville International Energy Exposition with S.H. (Bo) Roberts, formerly the University's Vice-President for Alumni Affairs and Development, as its president. Jake Butcher was named chairman of the policy-making board composed of business and civic leaders, bankers, lawyers, educators, and corporate executives.

In April of 1976, the Department of Commerce turned down Knoxville's original proposal to host a limited energy-themed World's Fair in 1980 with: "That's too soon. You haven't allowed enough time to get ready."

"In that case," shot back Expo's president Bo Roberts, "How about 1982?"

News of the rejection caused little stir among citizens caught up in the excitement of the nation's Bicentennial celebration. The first project approved by the joint Knoxville and Knox County Bicentennial Commission was the restoration of the Customs House vacated by TVA, as a repository for local archives dating back to 1791, when Knoxville was founded as America's first Territorial Capital. A second (under the sponsorship of Knoxville Heritage, Inc.) was the restoration of Gay Street's oldest building, the historic Lamar House built in 1816, and its adjunct Bijou Theater added in 1909. A third was the creation of Bicentennial Park on the riverfront at the mouth of First Creek, where the Treaty of Holston had been signed in 1791, and where a great chain stretched across the river had caught food-laden rafts during the Siege of Knoxville in 1863.

Another Bicentennial project, in Chilhowee Park, was the restoration of the marble bandstand that had been the music center for the National Conservation Exposition in 1913. The collective memory of Knoxville's first national exposition had long since run out, and retrospective articles about that long-ago success came at just the right time to encourage support for Energy Expo.

Something remarkable had happened to Chilhowee Park itself. In order to provide a proper home for his pet lion, Joshua, Guy L. Smith, III had become the dollar-a-year director of the Knoxville Zoo. Under his determined and progressive leadership, the small menagerie was expanding into a model zoological park where hundreds of exotic animals (including Old Diamond) were housed in environmental enclosures rather than in cages, and where all the buildings were solar-heated. (In 1978, Old Diamond became a proud father and the Knoxville Zoo became internationally famous as the birthplace of Little Diamond, the first African elephant born in this hemisphere.)

In August, 1976, Knoxville received a Bicentennial remembrance from the U.S. government: the approval of a limited World's Fair in 1982. The Department of Commerce also announced that it had submitted a recommendation on the Fair's behalf to the Bureau of International Expositions in Paris.

The review team that arrived from B.I.E. was the first of many international visitations. This group, composed of representatives from France, Denmark, and the Soviet Union, spent several days inspecting the site and evaluating each and every Energy Expo plan before recommending B.I.E. approval of a license for Knoxville's Fair.

Seeming defeats for the Fair in the local and national 1976 elections were victories in disguise. Opposition to Energy Expo worked against the reelection of Mayor Testerman, who was seen as its chief proponent. Expo dissenters received an unpleasant surprise when the successful candidate, Randy Tyree, adopted the Fair as his principal project. In January, 1977, upon Mayor Tyree's recommendation, City Council appropriated a whopping $11,600,000 to purchase the Second Creek site.

On the national scene, President Gerald Ford, under whose administration Energy Expo had received federal approval and support, was defeated by Jimmy Carter— who happened to be Jake Butcher's friendly fellow Democrat. In April, 1977, President Carter formally requested B.I.E. approval of the Knoxville Fair, and recommended that Congress allocate funds for a United States Pavilion.

A few days later, B.I.E. gave its official sanction to an energy-themed World's Fair in Knoxville, and set its dates as May 1 to October 31, 1982.

The vast majority of the Fair's early opponents were people genuinely convinced that Knoxville's streets could not handle any increase in the existing traffic, and that there would be no place for thousands of daily out-of-town visitors to park their cars or lay their weary heads. Their doubts persisted after the B.I.E.'s official sanction, but now that the decision was firm they accepted it— with the devout hope that they, and the city, would survive the summer of 1982.

There was, however, a small but vociferous group who violently opposed the Fair, for no good reason. Told that it was officially on the way, they demanded a referendum to stop it. But once an international exposition had been approved for Knoxville by the U.S. government and sanctioned by the B.I.E., it was too late for a local election to call it off. Denied the opportunity to vote Energy Expo down, the "anti-bodies" set out to undermine it.

When, in October of 1978, President Carter announced federal redevelopment grants of $12,450,000 for the Second Creek area, they belittled the amount as "a drop in the bucket." When, in December of 1978, the Secretary of State issued formal invitations to foreign governments to participate in the Fair, they predicted that not a single country would sign up.

Russia was the first nation to reply: The U.S.S.R. was tremendously interested in an energy-themed international exposition, and expected to participate. In the meantime, a Soviet Sports Exhibit would be sent to three American cities— including Knoxville— to promote the upcoming Olympic Games in Moscow. In the summer of 1979, the entire main floor of the barely-completed City/County Building was filled with an impressive array of Soviet sports photographs, banners, murals, sculptures, and memorabilia. Slide shows and movies offered Russian scenery along with athletic events, and a souvenir shop was stocked with Misha bears, amber jewelry, dolls, and handcrafts. Soviet authorities were gratified by the friendliness shown to their exhibitors, and by the fact that attendance in Knoxville was far larger than in New Orleans or San Francisco.

No doubt other considerations influenced the Kremlin's decision, but after the 1980 Moscow Olympics were boycotted by the United States, Russia withdrew from the 1982 World's Fair.

Jake Butcher, the chairman of Energy Expo's board, was defeated in the 1978 race for governor of Tennessee by Lamar Alexander, a native of Maryville. (Tennessee's voters had not been pleased by C. H. Butcher, Jr.'s announcement that he would personally supplement his brother's gubernatorial salary of $70,000, which would represent a punitive pay cut.)

"Jake can forget about state participation in his Fair," exulted the anti-bodies. But since Maryville is only sixteen miles from Knoxville, Governor Alexander was all too familiar with East Tennessee's Interstate bottleneck. Immediately after the election, he announced that the elimination of Malfunction Junction would be the first priority of the Tennessee Department of Transportation, and that the work would be completed in time for Expo '82.

The Department of Transportation warned that Knoxville's traffic situation would have to get worse before it could get better. As section after section of Interstate highway was closed for widening or rerouting, through trucks and out-of-town cars were shunted onto already overcrowded city streets, and everyday traffic jams were like football Saturdays'. "If you think this is bad," forewarned the anti-bodies, "just wait till the Fair comes."

Before the Interstate construction was completed, work began on the streets themselves. Local traffic was detoured around the Second Creek valley while nearby access-arteries to downtown were being rearranged. An east/west viaduct that spanned the Fair Site was closed; a railroad overpass was doubled in width for a pedestrian walkway. Downtown job-holders were often late to work as a result. "After the Fair opens," the anti-bodies ominously— and erroneously— foretold, "you won't be able to get to work at all."

In August, 1979, the 1000-day countdown to Expo's opening began. Basing their opinion on marketing surveys, experts associated with previous World Fairs announced an estimated total attendance for the six month period of 11,000,000.

From the beginning, the press in major metropolitan areas had taken a dim view of an international exposition in what they chose to think of as the wilds of Appalachia. Now, the *Wall Street Journal* gave front page placement to Kathleen Harrigan's story that began: "Suppose you gave a World's Fair, and nobody came?"

City and federal renewal funds could be used only to buy the site and clear it for ultimate redevelopment; the interim-use Knoxville International Energy Exposition (KIEE) provided its own financing. In October, 1979, a $30,000,000 line of credit was obtained from a consortium of 43 local, regional, and New York banks, and the package was the more easily put together since Jake Butcher, himself an up-scale banker, had friends in high-financial places.

Bulldozers began turning the Second Creek valley into a sea of mud. In clearing the site, Expo's local architects took into account

Knoxville's propensity for hanging onto the past with one hand while reaching for the future with the other, meanwhile keeping both feet firmly on the ground. They decided to retain any structurally sound buildings that could be converted for temporary use during the Fair, and might also play a part in the eventual site-redevelopment. These included the L&N Station, a multi-story warehouse that had begun life as a candy factory, and a huge post-Civil War foundry somewhat damaged by a recent fire.

The orphaned Station was befriended by a local construction company with the expertise— and the determination— to re-do it right. Its unique stained glass windows had been sold when passenger service was discontinued; now their replacement was the first consideration. A few could be bought back. Some incorporated into other buildings were photographed, and so expertly copied from the color transparencies by local stained-glass artisans that it was impossible to tell re-installed originals from reproductions. Careful cleaning brought back the pristine splendor of the intricately patterned tile floors hidden under a thick encrustation of ground-in grime. The soot-blackened exterior returned to its original rose-pink brick with quoins and window surrounds of white stone. Black paint replaced orange rust on the elaborate ironwork of the concourse overlooking the entire Fair Site, and on the gigantic stairway leading down to Expo's principal pedestrian thoroughfare.

Seeing the Station restored to life before their very eyes, doubting citizens began to suspect that anything was possible.

Hoped-for developments were happening downtown, where the United American Bank had moved into its new 27-story skyscraper sheathed with blue-sky glass. (C.H. Butcher, Jr. had announced plans for a 31-floor C&C Bank Building in the next block.) Jake Butcher's presidential office was furnished with handsome antiques and oriental carpets, and the UAB's board room suite contained a dining room where luncheon was served daily to "insiders" and to visiting corporate executives being wooed by Fair officials. The view from the building's top-floor Club LeConte was a breathtaking 360° panorama of the undulating cityscape, with the sun-silvered lake and misty mountains toward the south, and Sharp's Gap interrupting the northern sky-line. Toward the west, the Second Creek valley was a gash of raw red clay amid the tree-green hills; just east of the First Creek valley was the foreshortened triangle of the Hyatt-Regency, Knoxville's excellent but only hotel.

However, three major hotel chains had agreed with the Downtown Knoxville Association that a World's Fair deserved first-class accommodations within walking distance. First to open would be the Quality Inn, across Summit Hill Drive from the TVA Towers. The Hilton was going up one block from the Fair's eastern entrance gate, to which it would be linked by an elevated covered walkway. Beside the East Gate, a Holiday Inn was rising on the edge of the site itself, on top of a tremendous exhibition hall that was designed to be a post-Fair convention center.

Because of the popularity of the Great Smoky Mountains National Park, the Knoxville/Gatlinburg area had an unusually large number of good motels, campgrounds, and overnight parking lots for recreational vehicles, and Knoxville was about to be blessed with four first-class hotels. Still, many people were convinced that housing would prove inadequate in '82. In responding to this often-expressed concern, the management of KIEE made a serious mistake. On the advice of expert consultants, an official housing agency was set up to handle all bookings for hotels, motels, campgrounds, rental properties, and rooms in private homes. Establishing a reservations system instead of a referral service was an error of judgement rather than intent, but the results would be disastrous.

Fair officials began to breathe easier in December, 1979, when Italy became the first foreign nation to make a formal announcement of participation. At the ground-breaking ceremonies for Italy's pavilion in May of 1980, they were cautiously optimistic. Although no other country had made a definite commitment, they felt reasonably certain that the Spokane Fair's total of 10 participating nations would be equalled, if not surpassed. In July, 1980, Italy was joined by France. August brought Great Britain, West Germany, and the European Community that added Belgium, Denmark, Greece, Ireland, Luxembourg, and the Netherlands for a sub-total of 10. With almost two years still to go, Fair officials raised their sights to 20 and Jake Butcher joined the jet-set, touting the 1982 World's Fair in Central and South America, the Orient, and the Middle East.

In 1981, Ronald Reagan became the 39th President of the United States, and promptly accepted an invitation to open Energy Expo. Spectators at his Inaugural Parade on January 20, and television viewers nationwide, were invited to the 1982 World's Fair in Knoxville by the State of Tennessee's eye-catching float featuring a gigantic globe, covered with the colorful flags of many nations, that slowly revolved above the motto "Energy Turns The World."

1981 brought a succession of announcing nations: Japan in January; Australia in February; Mexico and Saudi Arabia in March; Canada and Korea in June; Hungary, the only representative of the Soviet bloc, in September. In October came the exciting news that the People's Republic of China would participate. For the first time since the St. Louis Exposition of 1904, mainland China would take part in a World's Fair.

In the summer of 1981, construction moved into high gear behind the see-through fence around the Fair Site. Small prefabricated information booths, food service areas, and souvenir shops began to dot the scene. In the early stages, before their colorful rigid-plastic coverings were added, the metal-pipe frameworks looked like jungle-gyms. Centering the site was the unfinished theme structure, apparently put together with a supersize Erector Set. The anti-bodies were all betting that the Fair would not be ready to open on time, and on rainy autumn days when no construction work was possible, even faithful Expo '82 supporters were inclined to agree.

These were discouraging days for the promoters of an energy-themed Fair. When the oil imbargo ended, know-it-alls had denounced the whole "energy crisis" as a scam devised by the international oil cartel to drive up prices at the gas pump. There was *plenty* of petroleum, they insisted. The Alaska Pipeline would see to that. In the wake of Three Mile Island, it did no good for scientists to point out that the reactor had "failed safe." To millions of increasingly vocal Americans, nuclear power was now anathema. Early in 1982, TVA bowed to the inevitable by mothballing four unfinished nuclear power plants, and canceling four more. (The fate of the Clinch River Breeder Reactor would hang in the balance for one more year, while environmental and political controversy raged, before the project was scrapped.)

However, since the Great Smoky Mountains National Park drew a majority of its visitors from the Midwest, New England, and the South, the Fair's advance publicity had been primarily directed to those areas, and well received. Travel agencies were offering special package tours to the 1982 World's Fair, with the Smokies thrown in as a bonus, and by the hundreds of busloads, prospective visitors were signing up.

Final preparations for the Fair were going on apace. A large amusement area had begun to fill the land between Fort Loudoun Lake and the University's football stadium, where the seating had been upped to 95,000 by top-decking the stands. Funland's centerpiece, a colossal ferris wheel, was being shipped in sections from the Netherlands when a storm at sea washed several of its huge steel braces overboard. Hastily cast replacements arrived in the nick of time on the largest *passenger* plane that had ever landed at McGhee Tyson Airport, from which all the cabin seats had been removed.

Until the very last minute, countries continued to sign in. Panama and the Philippines were announced in February; in March came Egypt and Peru. Six weeks before opening day, the number of participating foreign nations stood at 22. Counting the host country, the United States, *the grand total was 23!*

The Fair's most important residual benefit arrived in advance, when the reconstructed Interstates opened exactly on time. New by-passes made it possible for through traffic to change Interstates with ease, and for local residents to drive from one outlying section of the city to another without passing through downtown. Malfunction Junction no longer existed, and its demise was marked by a mock funeral with jazz bands.

In a last-ditch offensive, anti-bodies declared that the improved Interstates were making it easy for the nation's muggers, prostitutes, and pickpockets to converge on Knoxville; they falsely prophesied that crime would be uncontrollable on the Fair Site. Local law enforcement agencies already had that situation well in hand, and their immediate concern was for the safety of the President of the United States. Fully recovered from an attempted assassination, Ronald Reagan was keeping his promise to open the Fair.

In the seven years since an international exposition was first proposed, the local attitude toward Energy Expo had progressed from incredulity to apprehension, to uneasy acceptance, to qualified enthusiasm. Community reaction to persistent criticism-from-within changed from annoyance to disgust. The condescension of the national media was a continuing irritation, and the *Wall Street Journal* summed up the attitude of the press in the flat statement that the "scruffy little city" could never bring off a World's Fair. This gratuitous insult was a dare!

"The Fair" suddenly became OUR FAIR.

Knoxvillians paid in advance for season tickets, by the tens of thousands. As opening day approached, they donned the Knoxville Beautification Board's outsize lapel buttons that expressed their sentiments exactly:

CONGRATULATIONS!
The Scruffy Little City
DID IT!

THE PRESENCE OF THE PAST

Two blocks of Market Street, from Neyland Drive to West Main Avenue, disappeared forever beneath the City/County Building into which both local governments moved in 1980. In addition to court rooms and offices, the glass and concrete structure contained a high-ceilinged main level concourse and a semi-circular auditorium, multi-level parking, and the County Jail. At the time it was built, urban planning leaned heavily toward pedestrian malls, and Market Street was envisioned as a landscaped walkway between the City/County Building and the TVA Towers; to this end, low fountains were installed beside the Customs House, and trees were planted along the sidewalks.

The innovative blue-glass United American Bank Building on Gay Street between Main and Cumberland was destined to change its name to Plaza Tower in 1983. The helicopter-landing on the flat roof of Knoxville tallest structure was in daily use before and during the 1982 World's Fair.

Without the impetus of an imminent world-class tourist attraction, it would have been impossible for Knoxville to obtain three new first-class hotels in a single year. And without the Knoxville Hilton, the Holiday Inn/World's Fair, and the former Quality Inn that has become the Radisson Hotel, it would not now be possible for Knoxville to attract the regional and national conventions that are a boon to the city's economy.

A major attraction for tourists *and* residents is the outstanding Knoxville Zoo that has expanded far beyond its original hillside location in Chilhowee Park to become an exemplary 100-acre zoological park, dedicated to the principles of Conservation: As a member of the international organization of breeding zoos, it helps to ensure the survival of endangered animal species; in its shady woodlands, endangered native plants have found a happy home; and in the best sense of adaptive use, the African Plains Exhibit is located on the reclaimed Cherry Street City Dump, alongside I-40 E.

CHAPTER SIXTEEN

 ## TWENTY-THREE FLAGS OVER KNOXVILLE

HALLELUJAH!

The 1982 World's Fair opened on May 1 with construction complete, exhibits in place, and all flags flying!

The weather was perfect— crisp and clear, with just enough breeze to snap bright banners against their poles and set Alcoa's flame-shaped mobile spinning in the center of the man-made lake. The immediate impact was one of color: of light blue international pavilions, yellow shops, red information booths, and conical white food service shelters set against the new-leaf green of myriad trees. Establishing the theme of energy was the Sunsphere, a blazing gold-glass ball balanced on Eiffel-Tower underpinnings.

Air Force One had landed at McGhee Tyson Air Base, and President Ronald Reagan was on his way to open the Fair and dedicate the United States Pavilion. Security precautions were intensified for this, his first public appearance since the attempted assassination. Every nook and cranny of the U.S. Pavilion had been searched repeatedly, with the aid of trained police dogs. Armed guards ringed the ramps and balconies overlooking the ground floor, where President and Mrs. Reagan would be in the midst of invited guests who entered through a battery of sensing devices. The open-air Court of Flags, where the Fair's opening ceremonies would take place, was under the protective custody of the Secret Service, and uniformed contingents from the various armed services were much in evidence. On the stage, a bullet-proof glass shield surrounded the lectern; the audience was seated on the opposite side of the narrow "Waters of the World."

Bands played. Dignitaries introduced each other. One by one, the flags of the 23 participating nations fluttered to the tops of tall flagpoles. A fanfare of trumpets and a 21-gun salute welcomed the President of the United States. The balloons went up.

Released from formalities, the crowd scattered. All the

international exhibits were invitingly open, except Panama's which was expected momentarily, and tourists with just one or two days to "do" the Fair headed like homing pigeons for China, Mexico, and Japan. (Lines at these pavilions continued to be the longest in days to come.) With six months stretching out before them, area residents could afford to be leisurely. They made this a day to soak up atmosphere, to spot old landmarks in disguise, to take inventory of what lay in store for future visits. And even die-hard doubters were impressed by what they saw.

The huge wedge shape of the U.S. Pavilion looked oddly familiar, and someone jokingly identified it as "the crate the Hyatt-Regency came in." Tennessee had made a contribution to be proud of: a fine amphitheater with 1400 seats, where a talented cast from Nashville's Opryland was putting on a review of the state's history called "Sing Tennessee." (History would be made in the Amphitheater two weeks later, when the Tennessee Legislature met once again in the state's first capital.)

The Tennessee Valley Authority was celebrating 50 years of utility with a retrospective display, built by retired employees on river barges, that included a working model of the Tennessee River's system of lakes and locks. It was fitting and proper that the Siamese-twin floats were moored on the shore of Fort Loudoun Lake, at the headwaters of TVA's 9-foot shipping channel to the sea.

At the reincarnated L&N Station, the welcoming-arms stairway led up to two fine restaurants. Beyond the purling fountain that filled the 3-acre Waters of the World with potable city water, the L&N Freight Depot's upper level held the Fine Arts Pavilion (where a questionable Rembrandt would attract more attention than verified Old Masters.) The brassy music of a German band was pouring from the former foundry, now the Strohaus. (This large and lively restaurant would be the rendezvous for young and old; the favorite dance was not the polka, but "the chicken.") Outside the Candy Factory, a sign proclaimed "We're playing with a full deck," and went on to list five restaurants and a nightclub, a whole floor-full of crafts booths, and— shades of the building's past— a shop where fine candies were made and sold.

The architects' thoughtful site planning had preserved not only usable buildings but natural features. High on a hillside, the spreading branches of a majestic elm tree shaded a small amphitheater fitted into the contours of the slope. Down at the bottom of the valley, Second Creek meandered through a quiet park. Great trees overshadowed the wooden bridges and the walkways lined with benches; a paved terrace centered with modern sculpture looked back across the stream to a Victorian gazebo in a shady garden.

Above the site's main thoroughfare, Sky Transpo's swinging seats offered a moment's rest, and a view from aloft. Natives were astounded to find themselves looking down upon the erstwhile railroad overpass, now a walkway crowded with pedestrians who, in turn, were looking down at the moving traffic on familiar Cumberland Avenue. Behind Australia's grove of whirling silvery windmills rose the steep hill of the University campus, shaded by oaks, and green with ivy. Straight ahead, outlined against the blue sky of East Tennessee, was the anomaly of a tall Chinese pagoda.

At nightfall, the scene underwent a startling transformation. Every structure was dramatically illuminated, and the lake-mirror doubled the number of trees whose branches had blossomed out in tiny lights. At the eastern edge of the site, a colorful neon-sculpture filled the blank wall of a building, and across the huge screen outside the Federal Express Pavilion moved an ever-changing laser light show. In floodlighted Funland, the giant ferris wheel was a whorled kaleidoscope of jewel colors.

Two eye-catching displays were not part of the plan. Unable to remove a large electrical sub-station from the site, the Knoxville Utilities Board had made a virtue of necessity: at the tops and sides of the transformer towers, sparks of white light flashed intermittently. And, rising from UT's hilltop toward the west, the tower of Ayres Hall was a softly luminous landmark.

At closing time, the first of the Fair's nightly fireworks extravaganzas showered the dark sky with blazing color, and green laser beams imprinted the lingering smoke with the Fair's flame symbol.

With the Fair officially open (and the President safely back on Air Force One) Expo officials realized that none of the opening day's anticipated crowd and car problems had arisen. The attendance of 80,000 was much smaller than expected: Most Knoxvillians were at home, watching the ceremonies on TV, because an apprehensive but misguided spokesman for KIEE had urged residents to stay away and leave room for out-of-town visitors. Downtown streets were less congested than on ordinary working days, and parking lots within walking distance of the entrance gates remained half-empty. Most of the people on the site had arrived by bus— chartered-tour, private-shuttle, or public-transit.

Under cloudless skies, attendance climbed to 85,000...90,000... and the Fair welcomed its one-millionth visitor on May 16 before the first drop of rain fell on the site. Flower beds and recently transplanted shrubs were wilting in the unseasonable drought. Fair-goers were wilting, too. (KIEE hastily installed more drinking fountains, and added more benches. Prefabricated restrooms were set up at strategic spots.)

In October, 1980 and November, 1981, outstanding energy experts from Europe, Africa, the Far East, and the Americas had gathered in Knoxville for the first and second International Energy Symposia; in May, 1982, they returned for a third and final meeting-of-the-minds. By hosting high-level conferences on the technical aspects of global energy problems, the 1982 World's Fair had made a significant contribution to international understanding; but by the time the Fair opened, energy no longer was a burning issue. (In fact, 1982 would go down in history as a year of oil-glut.)

Habitual fault-finders complained that the international and corporate pavilions told them more about energy than they cared to know, but under the rules of the Bureau of International Expositions, countries participating in a "limited" World's Fair are required to build their exhibits around its central theme. Twenty-two nations had come together at Energy Expo '82, and each was contributing a share of knowledge to the common fund. No one nation emerged as the energy-technology leader of the world.

The United States summed up the uses and abuses of energy in a thrilling 3-D movie on the Imax Theatre's concave screen. Members of the European Community jointly presented the definitive exhibit on solar power: A computer-portrait of the fiery sun's variable heat was reproduced with red, yellow, and black tiles on a tall flame-shaped sculpture, and the random pattern of intense color was repeated on the facade of their row of buildings. Most visitors admired this collective effort as Art, but missed its scientific significance entirely. However, everybody got the message when Australia dramatized fuel-economy with a series of animated cartoons and a catchy jingle. People strolled around the Fair Site humming "Let's all get together— this one's for AusTRYlia. There's at least a dozen ways to save our petrol!"

Most international pavilions displayed their scientific prowess against a backdrop of alluring scenery, and worked in the lifestyles of their people with great ingenuity. Experienced travellers happily revisited Italy, Canada, France, and Japan. For the vast majority of Fair-goers, who never expected to see mainland China, Saudi Arabia, or

Peru, this was the opportunity of a lifetime to find out how the other side of the world lives.

Visitors compared notes while they stood in line. Hungary had the world's largest Rubik's Cube...Peru had $43,000,000 worth of pre-Columbian gold, and two Inca mummies!...The Philippines' gaudy Jeepneys ran on charcoal...Australia's 40-foot color murals of Sydney Harbor and the arid Outback were "painted" by computer on the wool-carpeted walls...Korea's huge pagoda-shaped golden crown was covered with dangling drops of pale green jade that looked exactly like little gherkin pickles!...Saudi Arabia's miniature mosque show was a must, because it traced Arab genealogy back to Abraham's son Ishmael, and explained Mohammed's influence on the Middle East today...Seeing Egypt's 5,000-year succession of art and artifacts was much better than looking at King Tut's tomb furnishings....

Every visitor was determined to see the Chinese Pavilion, and the slow-moving China line sometimes stretched halfway across the Fair Site. Inside (contrary to B.I.E. rules) the "national culture" exhibits changed from day to day because everything in the pavilion was for sale! Price tags in Chinese characters were on all the delicately carved ivory, jade, and cinnabar, the porcelains and statuary, the hand woven rugs, the delicate embroidery, and the inlaid furniture— even on the seismograph guaranteed to drop a pearl into a dragon's open mouth in case of earthquake. Pavilion employees demonstrated and sold crafts, and operated a large souvenir shop, a restaurant, and a cafeteria.

All that commercialism was not everyone's cup of tea, but one room made the hours-long wait worth while. Here was an actual section of the Great Wall of China. Here, too, were lifesize statues (of two men and one horse) from the Xi'an tomb where, 2000 years ago, a Chinese emperor was buried with an entire army reproduced in clay.

The two-millionth visitor appeared before the end of May, although Panama's pavilion did not. KIEE officials were confident, in June, that attendance would far surpass the predicted 11,000,000 and that unlike its predecessors, the 1982 World's Fair would end up with a substantial profit.

Each week, one of the participating countries was singled out for recognition, and the honored nation responded with a special event that typified its culture. Japan's Grand Kabuki Theatre was delightful; so were the Korean Dancers. Great Britain's can-you-top-this event was unscheduled. In the middle of Britain Week, on the very day the Lord

Mayor of London visited the Fair, a hastily hand-lettered sign appeared on the door of the pavilion: **IT'S A BOY!** The crowd outside reacted with three cheers for the new heir to England's throne, and a spontaneous celebration swept across the site.

Official delegations from the featured nations were headed by ambassadors, prime ministers, or presidents who expected to be entertained in a manner befitting their exalted station. Jake Butcher took over as the Fair's official host, and "Whirlwind," his palatial lakeside home near Clinton, was the scene of a series of glamorous dinner parties planned by the caterer who was a full-time employee of UAB.

On the Fair Site, live entertainment was everywhere, at every hour— at Stokely-VanCamp's Folklife Festival where banjoes and dulcimers, cloggers and craftsmen represented Appalachia; at the Baptist Ministries Pavilion, where "The Word is Energy" came alive; and at the Electric Energy Pavilion, where the good word was "Up With People." Three times a day, the Tennessee Amphitheater echoed to a standing ovation for "Sing Tennessee." The Elm Tree Theatre was a showcase for singers, dancers, and combos. Clowns, mimes, and jugglers entertained the crowds that stood in long pavilion lines; Bluegrass, Dixieland, Country, and Mexican Folk music swirled around food service areas. DuPont's marching band led the daily 5 o'clock parade, followed by the incomparable Budweiser Clydesdales and Eastman Kodak's photogenic animal characters. Every night, the Energy Express trundled its way around the grounds to the strains of a calliope while its four energy-source floats flashed light and emitted bursts of steam.

On rainy days, the huge Technology and Lifestyle Center came into its own. At this fair within the Fair, NASA's exhibit symbolized America's triumphant ventures into space with actual moon rocks; African America's exhibit stressed human energies; the State of West Virginia led visitors through a simulated coal mine; the Power of the Spirit was manifested through holograph technology. Children of all ages played with Union Carbide's battery of battery-operated toys, and marvelled at the miniature circus wherein every colorful delight of the Big Top was faithfully reproduced to scale.

Expensive off-site events could not compete with what was going on at the Fair where, except for Funland's rides and games, all the entertainment came free with the price of admission, but the Fourth of July Spectacular at nearby Neyland Stadium was an unqualified success. Country music stars were outshone by the set pieces: All in fireworks, horse-drawn sulkies raced across one end of the stadium; Star Wars were fought in the sky above; a flying saucer attempted a landing on the field; a rippling American flag dangled from a moving helicopter.

On July 12, the five-millionth visitor passed through the turnstile. (Panama's promised exhibit still had not materialized.) On the surface, everything was going smoothly and the Fair was living up to its promoters' fondest expectations; but there was big trouble in Our Fair City.

KIEE's reservations system was not working. Tourists who had paid in advance for first class accommodations found themselves assigned to non-existent campgrounds, converted warehouse dormitories, and sub-standard motels. Complaints were ignored, and refunds were not forthcoming. "A computer foul-up" was conveniently blamed. Fair officials undertook to correct the situation by placing the housing agency under new management, but problems continued to surface. Months after Energy Expo ended, some refund problems would still be unresolved.

Meanwhile, KIEE faced a financial dilemma of its own, the direct result of timing. The Fair had been built during a period of double-digit inflation when construction costs enormously exceeded estimates, and no one could have foreseen that the variable interest rate would reach an incredible 20-plus percent. The uncertain economy was now causing many middle-income families to curtail or cancel their vacation plans, and early Expo visitors' housing horror stories were keeping their relatives and friends away.

Attendance declined sharply during July and August. Ticket sales were off, and so were concessionaires' profits. Publicly, Fair officials expressed confidence that the crowds would return in September and October with the cooler weather. Privately, they were doubtful of reaching their goal of 11,000,000 visits, and were no longer sure that Expo '82 could break even— much less show a profit.

There were other problems— minor by comparison, but nonetheless distressing. On several hot and humid days, air conditioning failures caused the temporary closing of some pavilions. One of the two paddlewheel excursion steamers sank like a stone. (Fortunately, this happened at the dock, in the wee hours of the morning when no one was aboard.) Next, there was the afternoon when an escaped aluminum-coated balloon lodged against a transformer, and shorted out the University of Tennessee's entire electrical system. Then, the site was drenched by a torrential August rain that caused what TVA referred to as "the kind of flooding that occurs once in 500 years." The placid waters of Second Creek boiled up, scooping out the foundations of the terraces and bridges along the Quiet Walk, and pouring through the pedestrian tunnel to the TVA barges as though it were a mill race.

The crowds were not only smaller during July and August, but different. There were fewer senior citizens, and many more families with school-age children; anyone not wearing a World's Fair T-Shirt was out of uniform. Sit-down-and-be-served restaurants were by-passed, while customers congregated at Buddy's Barbecue and Belgian Waffle stands. Everyone wanted to try a Petro, the taco-in-a-bag that had been invented for Energy Expo.

Watching the huge river carp fight for tidbits at the mouth of Second Creek was the favorite family pastime. Funland took preference over staid pavilions. Long lines waited for the sound and laser light show at Federal Express; the Gas Industries' animated dinosaur died to resounding cheers. Japan's Painting Robot, whose pre-programmed brush designs made such splendid souvenirs, was exceeded in popularity only by the walking/talking Heinz Catsup Bottle that handed out free pickle pins.

Suddenly, there was a new foreign pavilion: KIEE had assigned Panama's space adjoining Hungary to six Eastern Caribbean Islands. The islands were not all independent, and could not be counted as "participating nations," but when their steel band coaxed pipe-organ tones from recycled oil drums in the Hallelujah Chorus, Fair-goers were more than happy to accept the bright-green-parrot Caribbean banner in lieu of the Panamanian flag.

Daily attendance began to pick up in September, and reached its all-time high on the October Saturday when former President Jimmy Carter was one of the 102,000 persons on the site.

Fortunately for the Fair and for the city, not all early out-of-town visitors had been involved in the housing hassle. Those who were spared went home with very favorable impressions. They wrote back to both Knoxville newspapers, praising the cordiality and genuine friendliness of every citizen they met.

The most enthusiastic comments came from visitors who had attended previous World Fairs. They said that each such event reflected the personality of its host city. This one was filled with trees and flowers, and places to sit down! (They noticed that even the retaining walls were at seat height.) They liked the battery-powered "wheelies" that made the whole site accessible to the handicapped, the elderly, or the merely weary. If help was needed, a golf-cart ambulance was instantly on its way. The Fair's guests responded to the cheerfulness of its employees by being good natured. There was no shoving, and no voices were raised in anger. In short, Knoxville's Fair was a happy place, where they felt safe.

Those experienced Fair-goers were right. Instead of escalating, Knoxville's crime rate actually declined during Energy Expo, and any untoward on-site incident was summarily dealt with by the watchful security guards.

After Labor Day, the composition of the crowds changed back. Once again, people were waiting for tables at the Mexican, Hungarian, and Korean pavilions' exotic restaurants. Fine imported and locally handcrafted gifts were selling well, and an elaborate system of barter grew up around the colorful pins and buttons made especially for the 1982 World's Fair. Corporation presidents and teenagers traded avidly, and on equal terms, for employees' insignia and VIP gift pins from the international and corporate pavilions, and for the buttons of commercial exhibitors. It was against the rules of the game for money to change hands. Instead, the collectors established their own standard of currency, based on scarcity and demand. Coca-Cola pins bearing the flame symbol had the highest trading value; the ubiquitous souvenir pins from the Chinese Pavilion counted as small change.

October 15 was a doubly joyful day. Attendance reached 10,000,000, and KIEE paid off its $30,000,000 debt! At a sundown ceremony in the Court of Flags the note, marked PAID IN FULL, was ceremonially burned.

The success streak continued on October 16, when the Tennessee Vols defeated Alabama's Crimson Tide. While Fair visitors jammed the pedestrian bridge across Neyland Drive to watch the fans arriving for the game by boat, Knoxvillians lined the ramp outside Neyland Stadium to photograph the "Vol Navy's" cabin cruisers tied up alongside the TVA barge exhibits and the Fair's paddlewheel excursion steamer. Attendance was 90,000 at the Fair, and 96,000 at the game, but chartered buses kept the traffic problems minimal.

October is the month when tourists come from near and far to see the Smokies dressed in brilliant autumn hues; this year, the "color crowd" was stopping off to see the Fair. With only 15 days remaining, season ticket holders were hurrying to revisit their favorite pavilions, and to look around for interesting exhibits they might have missed. Providing the daily crowds continued large, there was an outside chance that attendance might reach 11,000,000.

With the goal almost in sight, the media began to question the accuracy of the attendance figures. The turnstiles clicked automatically each time a person entered the gates, whether that person was a first-time visitor, a season ticket holder, or a Fair employee on the way to work. KIEE should not, the press insisted, be allowed to include repeaters in the totals.

It was a question of semantics. Reporters were calling for a head-count of visitors; Expo '82 was counting visits.

The method of counting had long since been established by the Bureau of International Expositions, and was the same one used at the Spokane and Osaka (Japan) Fairs. A special turnstile at each gate admitted only employees, non-paying VIP guests, and season ticket holders. Every time an employee showed his pass, the turnstile guard pressed the button on a hand-counter; when the gates closed, the number of entering employees was deducted from the day's attendance. The total of paid admissions for the day was determined by subtracting all visits recorded by the special turnstiles.

The official attendance totals actually erred by being too low rather than too high. No charge was made for children under three, nor did any turnstile click them through. Yet the 1982 World's Fair was a family experience, and on any given day, the crowd contained a liberal sprinkling of young couples pushing strollers and/or carrying babes in arms. Uncounted thousands of Expo '82's youngest visitors may not remember the experience, but they were there.

The final days of the Fair were blessed with "October's bright blue weather," and marked by special events. Participating nations' commissioners and employees had been surprised by the warmth of their welcome in Knoxville, where UT's international students sought out their compatriots and local residents of Italian, French, or German descent "claimed kin" with the appropriate pavilion. Citizens entertained their new-found friends at home, or took them to the mountains and the lakes. In an unusual gesture of appreciation, the International Pavilions collaborated on a THANK YOU, KNOXVILLE party at the Court of Flags, enclosed for the occasion with colorful tents where the invited honorees were treated to foods and entertainment from around the world.

At ten minutes past noon on October 30, an ecstatic salvo of cannonfire signalled that the race to reach 11,000,000 visits had been won! (All summer long, members of the media had dialed a special telephone number and listened to a recording of the day's attendance and the total visits to date. That night, they heard a jubilant announcement: "Two years ago, Kathleen Harrigan said in the *Wall Street Journal*: 'Suppose you gave a World's Fair, and nobody came?' *Today, the eleven millionth Nobody came to the 1982 World's Fair!*")

On October 31, every person passing through the gates received a souvenir button saying *I WAS THERE ON CLOSING DAY.* These words also applied to the 89 corporate participants; to the states of Georgia, Kentucky, North Carolina, Oklahoma, South Carolina, Tennessee, and West Virginia; to the United States of America and to 21 participating foreign nations— but not to Panama, although that country never did officially withdraw.

The final day's attendance brought the total number of visits to 11,127,786. Knoxvillians had turned out in force to bid their temporary fellow-citizens goodbye, and to say "Hurry back!"

The 1982 World's Fair was ending on a high note, with its goals achieved. It was time to ring the curtain down on an unforgettable summer, and lower the flags. Bands played as the warm and cloudless evening turned to night. The Energy Express flashed and steamed and tootled its way across the Court of Flags. The lake reflected a procession of flickering candles, and a grand finale of fireworks lit the sky.

Impressive though they were, the closing ceremonies seemed an anticlimax after what had happened just at dusk, with a full moon rising behind the downtown skyline. The lights flicked on for the last time across the site, and at that very moment, from the Tennessee Amphitheater came the soft strains of a familiar Spiritual:

Till that great gettin' up mornin'—
Fare thee well, fare thee well...

CHAPTER SEVENTEEN

 THE AFTERSHOCK

On November 1, the 1982 World's Fair was history.

That mammoth six-month celebration had taken place in an enduring community that did not close down for the duration. All summer long, across a broad and busy intersection from the revitalized L&N Station, expert restoration was turning the clock back to 1848 for beautiful Old City Hall. On the UT campus (fifteen feet away from Funland) spring quarter ended; the summer session ran its course; fall quarter began, and so did football season. The annual Tennessee Valley Fair was well attended at Chilhowee Park in September, and in October, Saturday Night on the Town drew an estimated 100,000 people to a downtown street party.

While Energy Expo was still in full swing, a foundation was formed to develop the Tennessee Technology Corridor linking Knoxville and Oak Ridge; a 25,000 seat basketball arena, to be built on the parking lot at Funland's entrance, was in the planning and fund-raising stages. These benefits might conceivably have occurred in the natural course of events, but Knoxvillians were sure that nothing short of a World's Fair could have brought in three new hotels and straightened out the Interstates!

On Expo's closing day, KIEE's coffers contained a surplus of $1,003,801, but that figure was by no means final: a $3,000,000 phase-out loan from UAB remained to be repaid from the sale of on-site properties. A series of auctions disposed of everything from gates and turnstiles to the Energy Express, and representatives from the 1984 World's Fair in New Orleans were among the interested bidders. The international and corporate pavilions were sold "as is, where is" by their owners, and most of the structures were taken apart for reassembly out of state as doctors' offices, corporate headquarters, or warehouses. The amazing 3-D movie at the Imax Theatre was on loan from the Alabama Space and Rocket Center, and would go home to Huntsville. To the University went the southwestern portion of the site, where the park along Second Creek would be kept intact.

The theme-structure Sunsphere was slated to remain and be incorporated into the site-redevelopment plan, along with the Tennessee Amphitheater, the Court of Flags, the fountain-fed lake, the L&N

Station, the Foundry, and the Candy Factory. As soon as the last exhibits in the Technology and Lifestyle Center were dismantled, workmen began turning the building into the city's new Convention Center.

The U.S. Pavilion was now government-surplus property and, like Muscle Shoals in the 1920's, a white elephant. The 6-story wedge shaped design that won a national architectural competition had been perfect for its purpose during the Fair. It was entered from the top, by means of outside escalators, and the displays were arranged on a series of balconies that overlooked the ground floor atrium; visitors descended from level to level on ramps, facing a towering glass wall that framed the entire Fair Site. But the sprightly showcase had no heating system, and there was only one small bank of elevators; ramps and balconies did not lend themselves to standard office or research-laboratory use, and the cost of retro-fitting the structure for any such pedestrian purposes would be prohibitive.

While the Second Creek Valley was still cluttered with Expo's leftovers, it began to fit into the community's pattern of events. Plans for Christmas in the City were expanded in 1982 to include the new downtown hotels and the restaurants in the L&N Station; the lighted Sunsphere sparkled like a colossal Christmas ball. A preview of the new Convention Center was offered in February by the House and Garden Fair, a preliminary event of the 1983 Dogwood Arts Festival.

That same month, the city was shaken to its very foundations by a financial earthquake.

On February 14— after a "saturation" weekend media blitz that stressed stability and promised an infusion of new capital— the United American Bank was declared insolvent by Tennessee's commissioner of banking. Stepping in to take immediate control, the Federal Deposit Insurance Corporation announced that more than 80% of the bank's $485,000,000 loan portfolio was "questionable," and that its stock was "valueless." Nevertheless, UAB's purchase by First Tennessee Bank, already a corporate citizen of Knoxville, provided a safety net for depositors: even those accounts that far exceeded the FDIC-insured maximum of $100,000 were fully guaranteed by the new owner.

As early as 1977, according to a spokesman for the FDIC, government auditors had found cause for complaint in the UAB's excessive top-management salaries and "insider loans." In May of 1982, FDIC representatives had attended the bank's board meeting and warned the directors that "unless substantial improvements were evident by the year's end, a formal enforcement action would be forthcoming." But, when UAB reported heavy losses for the final quarter of 1982, rumors of the bank's insolvency had been hotly denied by management.

United American was the flagship of a fleet of 21 banks controlled

by the Butcher brothers, and federal examiners were convinced that
"doubtful" loans were being sold back and forth; to prove that this was
true, it had been necessary to conduct a simultaneous audit of UAB and
eleven major affiliates. This audit was delayed until November 1,
1982— not out of concern for Energy Expo, but because there were no
hotel rooms available in Knoxville until after the Fair closed. On that
day, the FDIC assigned 10% of its total manpower (180 agents) to
conduct the in-depth investigation.

The FDIC was not alone in monitoring the Butchers'
machinations. Beginning in the late 1970's, the U.S. Attorney's Office
for the Eastern District of Tennessee had received reports of their
legally questionable banking practices. Even before the bank examiners
began the sweeping audit, a task force comprised of FBI and IRS agents
was investigating those complaints.

The national media indulged in a Roman holiday! Along with
Energy Expo's tireless anti-bodies, the press in distant cities blamed the
World's Fair for the bank's demise. However, UAB was only one of the
43 banks that provided working capital for KIEE in the form of a
$30,000,000 line of credit, and this loan had been repaid in full two
weeks before the Fair ended. The $3,000,000 phase-out debt to UAB
was secured by the on-site properties, and was settled after their sale.
Moreover, in March of 1983, FDIC Chairman William Isaac testified
before a congressional investigating committee that UAB loans to high-
risk ventures contingent on the 1982 World's Fair totalled $11,800,000
— a small proportion of the $211,300,000 loaned to "Butcher family
members, close friends, and business associates of insiders."

In the weeks that followed the UAB crash, Knoxville was
embroiled in a financial soap-opera, and each daily episode brought
appalling new disclosures: Many high-risk investments had been
"parachute loans" that floated down from on high to branch managers
and the presidents of small-town affiliates....Advance notice of bank
examiners' visits had enabled top-management to shift unsecured loans
back and forth within the Butcher network, by computer....

On May 1, 1983, there was a welcome interruption, when 45,000
people gathered on the former Fair Site to celebrate the first
anniversary of Energy Expo's opening. Once again, cloggers were
dancing at the Court of Flags. Once more, the valley echoed to the
(recorded) sounds of the Energy Express. Mimes, clowns, and costumed
characters reappeared beside the lake.

Expo's ambience had so impressed professional entrepreneurs that
the 1983 Miss USA Pageant was being held in Knoxville. This year's
contestants for the crown took part in the Fair's anniversary parade, and
the pageant finals were telecast live from the Civic Auditorium. As the
program opened, the nationwide audience saw the reigning Miss USA

perched atop the Sunsphere; during the pageant's on-stage intermission, television coverage continued with helicopter panoramas of the city, serene and beautiful in spring green, ringed by shimmering lakes and soaring mountains.

The respite was brief. C.H. Butcher, Jr.'s City & County Bank of Knox County was one of five Tennessee banks that failed on May 27; it was purchased and immediately reopened by the Bank of Knoxville. C&C's fall, like United American's, was cushioned by an established local bank: although its stock was worthless, depositors' funds were protected by the FDIC.

Customers of the Southern Industrial Banking Corporation were far less fortunate. SIBC was not a bank, but a misleadingly named loan/thrift company founded by Cecil H. Butcher, Sr. in 1929; it continued to accept deposits, at temptingly high interest rates, until the very day it was declared bankrupt. Then depositors learned to their sorrow that their savings could not be returned to them until the company's outstanding loans had been collected. But worse was yet to come. Auditors discovered that SIBC had been used by the C&C banks as a dumping ground for worthless loans, and that most of the "assets" on its books were uncollectible. In order to repay any part of the savings accounts, the trustee in bankruptcy obtained a court order: Everyone who had, for whatever reason, cashed a certificate of deposit less than 90 days before SIBC's collapse was required to give the money back.

Who, what, when, where...With each installment, the serial's plot thickened and its cast of characters grew longer. The deepening probe unearthed evidence of dummy corporations, forged signatures on loans, and stock manipulations master-minded by computer experts. There were Federal Grand Jury subpoenas, preliminary hearings stymied by the Fifth Amendment, involuntary bankruptcies, and suicide.

The meteoric growth of the Butcher banking empire had been a conjurer's trick— done not with wires and mirrors, but with computers.

Before the end of 1983, all 21 of the Butcher-controlled institutions had either been closed or sold by the regulators. The total combined loss of more than one billion dollars made this the most costly bank failure in United States history. (It was soon surpassed.)

Who, or what, was ultimately responsible for the UAB's collapse? When that question was put to Jake Butcher's cronies, they replied: "C.H. was the banker. Jake was too busy running for governor and hosting a World's Fair." Associates in a position to know said: "Jake trusted everybody. A lot of people took advantage of him." A few lawyers placed the blame equally upon Jesse Barr who had served time in prison for defrauding the Union Planters Bank, and on the Butchers, who had involved a convicted felon in UAB's affairs. "They set a fox to guard the henhouse."

Conservative bankers gave the correct and truthful answer: "Greed is one of the Seven Deadly Sins."

Quite a few people had distrusted Jake Butcher from the outset. In their opinion, "he looked and acted like a riverboat gambler." With 20/20 hindsight, Expo '82 officials saw Jake's flamboyant enthusiasm and incorrigible optimism as having been vital to the World's Fair; but they were devoutly thankful that his financial exuberance had been held in check by KIEE's practical governing board. Old timers pointed out that the entire lifespan of the United American Bank was only seven years, and said of the debacle that followed its crash: "This, too, shall pass." But first, the courts would have their say.

Federal prosecutors worked carefully, but with remarkable speed, to unravel the snarl of evidence. On November 13, 1984, Jake Butcher and two primary aides, Jesse Barr and Jack H. Patrick, were indicted on multiple counts of bank fraud and embezzlement involving several Butcher-controlled institutions. On the eve of his April 22, 1985 trial, Jake Butcher pled guilty to four of the most significant indictments against him, involving fraudulent loans and misapplications of funds for his own benefit. Under the terms of his plea-bargain, he was subject to a 20-year sentence. Federal Judge William Thomas of Cleveland, Ohio, who had no ties to East Tennessee, was designated to hear the case. On June 3, 1985, he sentenced Jake Butcher to the full 20 years' imprisonment, and further decreed that one-third of that sentence must be served before the defendant would become eligible for parole. In handing down one of the heaviest sentences ever meted out in this country for white-collar crime, Judge Thomas' opinion made it clear that Jake Butcher had enriched himself at the expense of his banks' depositors, and that his actions had substantially contributed to the failure of the banks.

The investigators' full attention then centered on C.H. Butcher, Jr., and in February of 1986, he was charged with massive bankruptcy fraud for concealing millions of dollars siphoned from banks under his control. In a highly unusual legal manoeuvre, he was immediately arrested and held in jail without bond: U.S. Attorneys had convinced the court that he undoubtedly had substantial assets stashed outside the United States, and that there was good reason to believe he was on the point of fleeing the country. In the course of the next year, along with associates and members of his family, C. H. Butcher, Jr. was additionally charged with tax fraud, securities fraud, bank fraud, and money laundering. Butcher's first trial, for falsely representing SIBC certificates of deposit as being federally insured, resulted in a surprising verdict of not guilty. However, on April 27, 1987, he pled guilty to state charges of the same securities fraud. At that time, he also pled guilty to multiple federal indictments of bankruptcy, tax, and bank fraud, and money laundering. He, too, received the maximum 20-year penitentiary sentence, but without parole restriction.

More than 30 persons have been convicted in the Butcher bank fraud trials, but thousands of people have been penalized, although they were guilty of nothing more than misplaced confidence.

As a result of unrelenting national press and media coverage of the Butcher scandal, the city's image was seriously tarnished, and while the banking furor was at its height, Knoxville was subjected to a different sort of adverse national publicity. Promoters of the upcoming 1984 World's Fair branded Energy Expo as "six months of boredom in Dullsville," claiming that every day of *their* international exposition would be Carnival in New Orleans, "the city that care forgot." New Orleans was not the first city to capitalize on one of Knoxville's good ideas: Nashville made off with the Country Music that began here in 1936; and Atlanta's Dogwood Festival was copied from Knoxville's spectacular spring celebration. This time, however, no amount of hype could overcome the fact that it was simply too soon for another World's Fair in the Southeast. Plagued by lax management and poor attendance, the 1984 World's Fair was a financial disaster.

On the other hand, the much-maligned 1982 World's Fair had exceeded its predicted attendance of 11,000,000 and was about to end up in the black. KIEE's books were finally closed in 1985. With all assets sold, all debts paid, and all claims settled, Knoxville's International Energy Exposition showed a net profit— of $57!

Hallelujah!

THE PRESENCE OF THE PAST

History repeats itself. Like the next-door Andrew Johnson Hotel, C. H. Butcher, Jr.'s C&C Bank Building stood unfinished for two years after the bankruptcy of its owner. Minus several of its planned 31 floors, and renamed "Riverview Terrace," it was completed— only to remain vacant until 1987, when it became the headquarters of the Bank of East Tennessee.

CHAPTER EIGHTEEN

 ## "THE PAST IS PROLOGUE. . . ."

Fashions change— in urban design as well as in furniture or clothing.

The Bicentennial of the United States focused attention on the nation's history, and as never before, Americans became interested in the visible evidence of their heritage. What would New York be without the Statue of Liberty? Or New Orleans without the French Quarter? Preservationists pointed out that keeping the best of the old while adding the necessary new gave a city its distinctive character. Whether they did so deliberately by urban renewal, or inadvertently by rampant growth, communities that erased the past and rebuilt in the mode-of-the-moment ended up looking like Anyplace, U.S.A..

Knoxville's cost-conscious downtown property owners discovered that it was cheaper to renovate a structurally sound building, and bring it up to code, than to demolish and replace it. Repolished gems of 19th and early-20th century architecture were so attractive that new office buildings on Main and Gay streets copied their traditional combination of red brick and white stone. As an offshoot of this reemphasis on the past, a portion of the warehouse district at Jackson and Central avenues was rejuvenated and turned into a lively restaurant and retail enclave christened the Old City.

The persistent reports of Downtown Knoxville's death had been (like Mark Twain's) greatly exaggerated. While losing out as the region's retail shopping center, the area was gaining strength as the center of governmental, legal, and financial activity where more than 20,000 people converged each day. Open space was at a premium, and a splendid new amenity was added in 1984 when the east side of Market Street, between Market Square and the Customs House, became Krutch Park. This green oasis was made possible by a $1,500,000 bequest to the City of Knoxville from a native son, Charles E. Krutch. (He was TVA's chief photographer in the agency's early days, and compiled a visual record of the Depression years that is preserved in the Authority's K-File.)

While the park was under construction, a simultaneous renovation of Market Square installed the large fountain spilling into a gentle stream that disappears beneath Union Avenue— only to emerge as a cascading rivulet in Krutch Park. Property owners returned the buildings alongside the Square to their late-Victorian appearance, and bright awnings replaced the concrete-mushroom sidewalk shelters that had typified the Mall for 25 years. A new marketing facility/entertainment center was topped with a tower containing the city's historic fire-bell.

Knoxville was striving to erase the stigma of the Butcher banking scandal, and help came unexpectedly from geographer Robert Pierce of New York State University. In his nationwide 1984 study, Knoxville tied with Greensboro, North Carolina for the title of "America's Most Livable City."

Attention centered on Gay Street in 1985, when Knoxville was chosen to participate in the Main Street Program of the National Trust for Historic Preservation. The exodus of retail stores had left empty buildings, cut off at the knees by the shed-like sidewalk canopies installed in 1962 to shelter shoppers from rain and sun. Removal of the Gay/Way canopies was the first step in Main Street, Knoxville's revitalization effort. Dignified buildings could then be seen in their entirety, and between them, the street itself was lightened and visually widened. The next step, which was not completed until 1989, involved the public infrastructure: locating and upgrading a mystic maze of underground utilities dating back to the 1890's; rebuilding the street and repaving the sidewalks with brick; removal of unsightly overhead wires, and replacement of dim street lights with copies of the original 19th century clusters of white globes.

Consequently, Knoxville had a head start on Tennessee Homecoming '86, during which each of the state's communities was asked to search out its heritage, examine its present condition, and plan for future improvement.

Governor Lamar Alexander, who originated the yearlong Homecoming, observed Statehood Day on June 1 in Tennessee's first capital. Descendants of Knoxville's founding families gathered on the grounds of Blount Mansion for the unveiling of a mammoth commemorative quilt, on which each of the state's 95 counties was represented by an intricately appliquéd square. Knoxville looked to the future by inaugurating the free trolleys that connect the University and downtown areas, provide transportation for office workers from peripheral parking facilities, and make it easy for conference delegates to move from one hotel to another or to the Convention Center. The grand finale of Tennessee Homecoming '86 was First Night Fest, a family New Year's Eve gala featuring entertainment at various downtown sites and culminating in a flashlight parade to the Fair Site for the midnight fireworks, but one special event proved such a success that it became an annual tradition. From Thanksgiving weekend through the Christmas holidays, Market Square is transformed into an open-air ice skating rink.

Three major public buildings were erected in the late 1980's, and each was an architectural law unto itself. The 25,000 seat Thompson-Boling Arena on Neyland Drive resembled a million-times-magnified hatbox made of corrugated cardboard. Downtown, the John J. Duncan Federal Office Building was faced with brown glazed tiles; upper floors extending out above a recessed corner were supported on what appeared to be a gigantic fossilized tree-trunk. On the UT Campus, the original John C. Hodges Library became the South's most technologically advanced repository for printed and recorded materials when it was encapsulated within an enormous red brick ziggurat.

Chris Whittle, who with two friends had founded the 13/30 Corporation while he was a UT student, headed the influential Downtown Organization and was president of far-reaching Whittle Communications. When the company elected to keep its headquarters in Downtown Knoxville, building a contemporary office tower was ruled out. Instead, one more block of Market Street was permanently closed to vehicular traffic (but not to pedestrians) to allow construction of a "campus quadrangle" of brick buildings designed to tie in visually with their historic neighbor, the Old Knox County Court House. With the exception of the Lamar House/Bijou Theatre and the Sevier/Park House, all buildings in the area bounded by Main, Gay, Cumberland, and Walnut streets were superseded by the multi-cupola complex scheduled for completion in 1991.

Three blocks away, the former Fair Site had by now determined its own destiny. Two outside development firms had tried, and failed, to come up with an acceptable plan for the Second Creek valley's future: In each case, the suggested mix of condominiums, offices, and festive retailing left too little breathing room to suit the citizenry.

The 1982 World's Fair left an invaluable legacy of open space in the heart of the city, where thousands of people can and do congregate for outdoor events. Where else would it be possible for ArtFest to hold its autumn Riverfeast? Where else could tremendous throngs gather for "Boomsday," the annual Labor Day fireworks spectacular mirrored by Fort Loudoun Lake? In addition, the Second Creek valley's trees, flowers, and flowing water create a welcome green belt between the congested downtown and University areas. To recognize the former Fair Site's dual attributes, its name was changed in 1988 to World's Fair Park and Festival Center.

A brand new attraction opened in the Park in 1989, beside the one-time Elm Tree Theatre. For 20 years, through the generosity of Mrs. Clifford Folger, the Dulin Gallery of Art had occupied the beautiful V-shaped Kingston Pike residence of Mr. and Mrs. H.L. Dulin; its permanent collection included 9 of the famous miniature period rooms created by Mrs. James Ward Thorne of Chicago. After Expo '82, the Gallery changed its name to the Knoxville Museum of Art. In 1988, it took up temporary quarters in the Candy Factory during construction of its sumptuously simple Clayton Building, designed by a specialist in museum architecture, Edward Larrabee Barnes. (In an uncharacteristic burst of generosity, the City of Knoxville not only contributed $1,000,000 to the Museum, but provided an on-going income for it with a 50-year lease on the rentable next-door Candy Factory, at $1 a year.)

Moving from Chilhowee Park to this central location is the East Tennessee Discovery Center (formerly the Students' Museum). Its first exhibit in the Candy Factory, the Knoxville Academy of Medicine Auxiliary's Health Discovery Center, was made possible by a remarkable outpouring of interest and cooperation from all six Knoxville hospitals. Among the coming attractions are a planetarium and a large aquarium.

Down on the floor of the valley, the U.S. Pavilion had remained untenanted since the Fair's closing day. When the government's General Services Administration tried to dispose of this $12,000,000 surplus-property at public auction in 1983, there were no bidders. Attempts to obtain the structure at nominal cost, for educational or scientific purposes, met with curt refusals. Eventually, the City of Knoxville paid $1,400,000 for the deteriorating building, in order to control the land on which it stood.

Abandoning hope of finding an appropriate use for the building, City Council voted to raze it. Then came a proposal to utilize the Pavilion as a Columbus Celebration Center during the 500th anniversary of America's discovery, but financing the project proved to be an insuperable stumbling block. In December of 1990, the Pavilion's demolition contract was signed. The fate of the Fair's centerpiece structure had been sealed by the faltering economy, and the threat of war.

Like the militia in the 18th century, today's National Guard and armed services reserve units are composed of volunteers who may be summoned to active duty in emergencies, and military units from the Volunteer State were among the first U.S. troops sent to the Persian Gulf. Knoxville proudly blossomed out in flags and yellow ribbons as hundreds of local reservists and Tennessee National Guard members were called to take part in Operations Desert Shield and Desert Storm.

The city's 200th birthday was inexorably approaching. Long before a crisis arose in the Middle East, Mayor Victor Ashe had appointed a Bicentennial Commission to direct the twelve-month celebration in which schools, churches, neighborhoods, civic clubs, and individuals were urged to participate. On New Year's Eve, a spectacular Countdown '91 would usher in a year of special events, including art exhibits, concerts, operas, ballets, and musical revues of history. A Religious Heritage

Celebration was scheduled for April, the season of rebirth, and Knoxville would be on the itinerary of the Bicentennial Exhibit of the Bill of Rights. The Fourth of July would have unique significance as a day to honor local volunteers, returned victorious from the Middle East. The origin of Country Music would be remembered with a revival of the Tennessee Barn Dance. Festivities would culminate with parades and ceremonies on the official birthday, October 3, and would end on December 31 with a gala Bicentennial Finale.

The 1913 National Conservation Exposition, the 1976 Bicentennial of the United States, the 1982 World's Fair, and Tennessee Homecoming '86 had all left residual benefits for the city. Knoxville's own Bicentennial should surely do no less! Fort Kid, a playground built by adult volunteers to the specifications of local school children, will be a lasting reminder in the World's Fair Park, and the new Museum of East Tennessee History, begun on the first floor of the Customs House, will continue to commemorate this historic occasion.

Finally, what better way to emphasize Knoxville's heritage than by beginning to revitalize the river that was responsible for the city's founding? The first step in the resuscitation process is the obvious one of overcoming pollution in the main stream and its large tributary creeks. Experts representing the City of Knoxville and Knox County, TVA, UT, the State of Tennessee, and the United States government comprise the Water Quality Task Force that is already hard at work. Long range plans call for widening Neyland Drive into a scenic boulevard, and creating better pedestrian access to the riverfront from the downtown plateau, the World's Fair Park, and the Coliseum complex. Historic-emphasis areas have been designated at the mouths of First, Second, and Third Creeks, and near the Alcoa Highway Bridge. As the first visible evidence of river reemphasis, the dramatic lighting of the Henley Street Bridge was completed in the Bicentennial year.

Any city that has survived for two centuries is entitled to deck its streets with banners and set off fireworks, but Knoxville has more to celebrate than the mere passage of time. In its 200 year continuum, America's first Territorial Capital has grown from a sixteen-block town surrounded by primeval forest to a spreading city whose history bridges the gap between the Amerinds and advanced technology— a city small enough to have retained its individuality, but large enough to offer the advantages of a metropolitan area. Along the way, there have been stirring events and day-to-day drudgery, periods of prosperity and times of hardship, but succeeding generations have found this a good place to live, and a hard place to leave.

The long-vanished lifestyles of earlier days are preserved in 10 widely differing house museums. The words "wilderness outpost" acquire real meaning for visitors to James White's Fort built in 1786 by

Knoxville's first settler. In 1792, the Governor of the Southwest Territory managed to construct and furnish elegant Blount Mansion in a frontier area where rivers were the only roads. (On the Mansion's grounds, 1818 Craighead-Jackson House is the sole survivor of the commodious brick townhouses that lined the city's streets in the early 19th century.) Ramsey House represents the height of suburban affluence in 1797, when Knoxville was Tennessee's first capital. Tennessee's first governor, John Sevier, built "Marble Springs" at the same time, not far away, but the two houses are in startling contrast: "Marble Springs" typifies rural East Tennessee's isolated, self-sufficient "plantations." The dignity and charm of antebellum days still linger in riverside "Crescent Bend," built in 1832, and in countryside "Middlebrook," dating from the 1840's. The Civil War seems to have happened only yesterday at Confederate Memorial Hall and Mabry-Hazen House, both built in 1854. The 20th century is represented by 1922 "Hopecote," which is the guesthouse for the UT, Knoxville campus.

This remains a community where home ownership is important— in inner-city neighborhoods as well as in high-priced subdivisions and high-rise condominiums. Knoxville is still blessed with a diversified economy, in which homegrown high-tech industries have replaced the former textile mills, and this is still a city of churches. In recent years, the city has become a nationally recognized focal point for medical research and treatment. The University of Tennessee Medical Center at Knoxville is an outstanding teaching hospital and the region's Level I Trauma Center; the presence of UT, Knoxville, and the proximity of the Oak Ridge National Laboratory have made it possible for break-through research in nuclear medicine to be achieved here. Furthermore, all types of specialized patient care are collectively provided by Fort Sanders Regional Medical Center and its Patricia Neal Rehabilitation Center; East Tennessee Children's Hospital; St. Mary's Medical Center; East Tennessee Baptist Health Care System; and the Thompson Cancer Survival Center.

The capital city established by William Blount has never ceased to be a center of education and culture. Blount College and its lineal descendants have enjoyed a synergistic relationship with Knoxville since 1794. Today, the University of Tennessee is a city within the city, where upwards of 40,000 persons— faculty and administrators, undergraduate and graduate students, office and support staff— rub elbows daily. It is the flagship of the state's higher education system, the regions's premier research institution, and the city's largest employer. Since 1843, the Tennessee School for the Deaf has provided quality education for young people with impaired hearing. Knoxville College, a four-year liberal arts institution with a host of distinguished graduates, was founded in 1875. A relative newcomer, Pellissippi State Technical

Community College, offers two years of applied study in many fields, plus a special curriculum for students planning to transfer to the University for advanced courses leading to a bachelor's degree. Continuing education is fostered by the excellent libraries open to the public: the University's main John C. Hodges Library and its Special Collections; and Knox County's main Lawson McGhee Library with sixteen neighborhood branches and the specialized McClung Historical Collection.

East Tennessee's rich heritage of Indian culture is on view at the University's Frank H. McClung Museum. The Beck Cultural Exchange Center is a mecca for students of Black History; the collection is memorable for the likenesses of individuals, and the details of important events, captured by Knoxville's outstanding black photographer, Boyd Browder. The East Tennessee Discovery Center electronically interprets astronomy and the health sciences for area pupils, and the Knoxville Museum of Art exhibits paintings and sculpture on loan from the collections of major museums, corporations, and individuals.

Music is in the air. The Knoxville Symphony Orchestra, founded in 1934, is the oldest professional symphony in the Southeast. Two ballet companies interpret music in graceful motion. The Knoxville Opera Company and the University's Opera Workshop combine music with drama, while locally cast musical and dramatic productions are offered at the Clarence Brown and Carousel theatres on campus, and at the downtown Bijou.

Local sportswriters and sportscasters allow no one to forget that this is Big Orange Country, and fans of the Tennessee Vols take pride in the fact that Neyland Stadium is the second largest college football stadium in the nation, and is one of only two that are accessible by boat. Spectator sports also include men's and women's intercollegiate basketball, tennis, softball, soccer, swimming, and track— plus minor league baseball and professional ice hockey. All cities offer public and private golf courses, tennis courts, and swimming pools to devotees of active sports, but Knoxville augments these with watersports and fishing on six encircling TVA lakes, and with hiking and camping in the nearby Great Smoky Mountains National Park.

Man-made amenities are important, but a city's quality of life is shaped and colored by its natural environment.

Looking across the broad and shining ribbon of the river to the undulating green hills and the tiered blue mountains, James White well might have said with the Psalmist: *Behold, the lines are fallen unto me in pleasant places;* ...

After two centuries, a citizen of Knoxville can echo the sentiments of the city's first settler, and complete his quotation: ... *yea, I have a goodly heritage* .

SELECTED BIBLIOGRAPHY

Brownlow, William G. *Parson Brownlow's Book*. Philadelphia:
        George W. Childs, 1862.

"Civil War Monuments and Memorials in Tennessee." Nashville:
        Civil War Centennial Commission, 1963.

Creekmore, Betsey Beeler. *Knox County Tennessee*, a History in
        Pictures. Norfolk, the Donning Company, 1988.

_____*Knoxville*. Knoxville: The University of Tennessee Press,
        1958, 1967, 1976.

_____*Knoxville, Our Fair City*. Knoxville: Greater Knoxville
        Chamber of Commerce, 1984.

Deaderick, Lucille, (Ed.) *Heart of the Valley*. Knoxville: East
        Tennessee Historical Society, 1976.

"50th Anniversary, The Great Smoky Mountains National Park."
        National Park Service, 1985.

The First Exhibition of Conservation and its Builders. Knoxville:
        1914.

"The Future of Our Past." (Historic Sites Survey). Knoxville:
        Knoxville/Knox County Metropolitan Planning Commission,
        1987.

Folmsbee, Stanley J. and Deaderick, Lucille. "The Founding of
        Knoxville." Knoxville: East Tennessee Historical Society's
        Publications, 1941.

_____and Dillon, Susan. "The Blount Mansion, Tennessee's
        Territorial Capitol." Knoxville: reprint from *Tennessee
        Historical Quarterly*. No. 22, 1963.

Gilchrist, Annie S. *Some Representative Women of Tennessee*.
        Nashville, 1902.

Hicks, Nannie Lee. "The John Adair Section of Knox County,
        Tennessee." Knoxville, 1968.

History of Homes and Gardens of Tennessee. Nashville: Parthenon
        Press, 1936.

History of Tennessee. (East Tennessee Edition). Nashville:
        Goodspeed Publishing Company, 1887.

Humes, T.W. *The Loyal Mountaineers of East Tennessee*. Knoxville:
        1888.

Kelley, Paul. "Historic Fort Loudon." Fort Loudoun Association,
        1958.

Knox County in the World War. Knoxville: Knoxville Lithographing
        Company, 1919.

Lilienthal, David E. *TVA: Democracy on the March*. New York: Harper & Bros., 1944.

Luttrell, Laura E. "One Hundred Years of a Female Academy." Knoxville: East Tennessee Historical Society, 1945.

Masterson, William H. *William Blount*. Baton Rouge: Louisiana State University Press, 1954.

Memoirs of General W.T. Sherman. New York: Charles L. Webster & Co., 1891.

Morse, Charles R. (Ed.) *The University of Tennessee Magazine, Historical Edition*. Knoxville, 1920.

Personal Memoirs of P.H. Sheridan. New York: Charles L. Webster & Co., 1888.

Poe, Orlando M. "Occupation of East Tennessee and the Defense of Knoxville." Reprint, Knoxville: East Tennessee Historical Society, 1963.

Ramsey, J.G.M. *The Annals of Tennessee to the End of the Eighteenth Century*. Charleston: Walker and James, 1853.

_____ "History of Lebanon Presbyterian Church," 1875. Reprint, Knoxville: Hubert Hodge Printing Company, 1973.

Rothrock, Mary U. (Ed.) *The French Broad-Holston Country*. Knoxville: East Tennessee Historical Society, 1946.

Rule, William. (Ed.) *Standard History of Knoxville, Tennessee*. Chicago: Lewis Publishing Company, 1900.

Scott, Nancy N. *A Memoir of Hugh Lawson White*. Philadelphia: J.B. Lipincott & Co., 1856.

Thornborough, Laura. *The Great Smoky Mountains*. Knoxville: The University of Tennessee Press, 1956.

Timberlake, Henry. *Memoirs, 1756-1765*. Watauga Press, 1927.

Williams, Samuel Cole. *Tennessee During the Revolutionary War*. Nashville: Tennessee Historical Commission, 1944.

The Knoxville Times
Brownlow's Knoxville Whig
The Knoxville Journal
The Knoxville News-Sentinel

PHOTOGRAPHIC SOURCES

Ernest B. Robertson, Jr.: Color cover. Indian mound; Art Museum.

Paul Moore: Fort Loudoun Dam; Oak Ridge housing.

Carlos Campbell: Sightseeing in the Smokies.

George B. Fritts: Customs House.

Jack Kirkland: 1863 Anchor.

Bill Tracy: Blount Mansion in 1976.

McClung Historical Collection: Sequoyah; Hugh Lawson White; Dr.
    Thomas W. Humes; Lawson McGhee; John Sevier statue; Old City
    Hall; Lamar House; Knoxville Iron Foundry; Elkmont cottage.

Greater Knoxville Convention and Visitors Bureau: Marble Springs; First
    Presbyterian Church; L&N Station; Candy Factory; Sunsphere,
    Amphitheatre; Technology & Lifestyle/Convention Center; Plaza
    Tower; "Little Diamond."

UT Special Collections Library: James Kennedy house; James White's
    house — as kitchen wing, and on Woodlawn Pike; Henry Knox;
    Lawrence D. Tyson.

Knoxville News-Sentinel: James White's house in 1970; Brownlow portrait
    removal; Dogwood.

Beck Cultural Exchange Center: James Mason; Cal Johnson Park.

Blount Mansion Association: William Blount.

UDC, Chapter 89: Confederate Memorial Hall.

UT Photographic Center: Pencil portraits in the tower.

Knoxville Committee, Tennessee Homecoming '86: Market Square.

50th Anniversary Publication, Great Smoky Mountains National Park:
    Mrs. W. P. Davis; Col. David Chapman.

History of Homes and Gardens of Tennessee: Island Home.

Some Representative Women of Tennessee: Bettie Tyson.

Author's collection: 1897 Courthouse plate; Flag pendant; Tyson House;
    Marble bandstand; 1937 Souvenir plate.

A NOTE FROM THE AUTHOR

In the final analysis, "history" is the story of people, and what happened to them.

As a primary part of my research for the first edition of *Knoxville*, which was published in 1958, I consulted with the families of Hugh Lawson White, Perez Dickinson, William G. Brownlow, Abner Baker, and Lawrence D. Tyson. Those kind friends graciously supplied me with previously unpublished facts and with some very surprising sidelights. I am deeply indebted to Mrs. J. Earnest Briscoe (Isabelle White) for details of the private life of Hugh Lawson White; to Mrs. John Hudson (Lucie Dickinson Givin) for much of the information in the chapter on Perez Dickinson; to Mr. John Fouché Brownlow for interesting events in the life of Parson Brownlow and in the life of Knoxville during the Civil War; to Mr. James M. Meek for the story of his uncle, Abner Baker, and for a strange coincidence reported in the Tyson chapter; to Mrs. William C. Ross (Lida McClung) for many incidents in the chapter on the Tysons; and to Mrs. Kenneth Gilpin (Isabella Tyson) who more recently regaled me with anecdotes about her parents that appear for the first time in these pages.

As *Knoxville!* approaches completion, I am exceedingly grateful to Mayor Victor Ashe for writing its timely Foreword, and to the East Tennessee Historical Society for undertaking its publication.

Many eye-witnesses have contributed their recollections to this book's final chapters, and I am devoutly thankful to Mr. John Gill, the United States Attorney for the Eastern District of Tennessee, for clarifying the chronology and legal proceedings of the Butcher trials.

Obtaining the 51 illustrations was made easy by the kind cooperation of Ernest B. Robertson, Jr. of the UT Center for Educational Video and Photography; Steve Cotham and Sally Ripatti of the McClung Historical Collection; Jim Lloyd and John Dobson of the UT Library's Special Collections; Robert Booker of the Beck Cultural Exchange Center; Al Treadaway and Virginia Schriver of the Knoxville Convention and Visitors Bureau; and Kent Whitworth of Blount Mansion Association.

The camera-ready manuscript was prepared with exemplary patience by Donna M. Cord.

INDEX

Abingdon, Virginia, *18, 19, 28, 33*
Adair, John, *29, 41, 55*
Adams, Pres. John, *21, 22, 23*
Adams, Pres. John Quincy, *57*
Alabama, *50, 58, 73, 103, 111, 117, 203*
Alcoa Highway/Bridge, *51, 150, 172, 216*
Alcoholic beverage control, *65, 130, 159, 176, 179, 182, 184*
Alderman, *55, 57, 69, 79, 99, 112, 114, 147*
Alexander, Charles, *107, 108*
Alexander, Gov. Lamar, *188, 189, 213*
"All-American City", *177*
Aluminum Company of America, *166, 170, 195*
American Legion, *135, 136, 137*
"America's Most Livable City", *213*
"America's Ugliest City", *173-174*
Amherst College, *104, 106*
Andrew Johnson Hotel, *159, 164*
Anderson County, *167, 169*
"Angel of the Hospitals", *74*
"Antibodies", *188, 189, 192, 193, 208*
Appalachian Exposition(s), *130-131, 139*
APTA, *39*
Appalachian Club, *142, 149*
Armstrong, Drury P., *59, 63*
Armstrong, Jenny, *34, 35*
Armstrong, Robert H., *77, 86*
Armstrong, "Trooper" James, *7, 34*
Army Air Corps, *167*
ArtFest, *214*
Ashe, Mayor Victor, *215*
Asylum Hospital, *69, 74, 82*
Atlanta, Georgia, *66, 211*
Attakullakulla, Chief, *5*

Audigier, Eleanor Deane, *132*
Austin, Emily L., *110-111*
Australia, *192, 197, 198, 199*
Ayres Hall, *176, 197*

Baker, Abner, *95*
Baker, Dr. Harvey, *75, 95*
Baker, Josephine Knaffl, *132*
Baker-Peters House, *75, 101, 102*
Bandstand, Chilhowee Park, *131, 133, 139, 186*
Bank of East Tennessee, *211*
Bank of Knoxville, *209*
Bank of the State of Tennessee, *54, 55, 57, 58*
Baptist Ministries Pavilion, *200*
"Barbara Hill", *19, 65*
Barr, Jesse, *183, 184, 209, 210*
Battle of Campbell's Station, *64, 77*
Battle of Fort Sanders, *80-82, 87, 93, 118*
Battle of King's Mountain, *42, 45, 48, 134, 166*
Battle of Lookout Mountain, *80, 83*
Battle of Mobile Bay, *84*
Baxter, Col. George, *124*
Bearden, Marcus deLafayette, *66*
Bearden, Mayor Marcus D., *67*
Beck Cultural Exchange Center, *218*
Belgium, *191*
Bell, John, *89*
Benjamin, Judah P., *92*
Benjamin, Lt. Samuel N., *81*
Berry, Ellen McClung, *38-39, 63*
Bicentennial of Knoxville, *102, 215-216*
Bicentennial of the United States, *63, 102, 139, 186, 212, 216*

Bicentennial Park, *186*
Bijou Theatre, *63, 186, 214, 218*
Blacks, *33, 69, 93-94, 99, 101, 104, 108-112, 121, 132, 147-148, 159, 218*
Blanchard, Lowell, *173*
Blanton, Gov. Ray, *183*
"Bleak House", *77, 86*
Blockhouse Fort, *9, 31-32, 37, 46, 55, 116*
Blount, Barbara, *19, 34*
Blount, Mary Grainger, *17-18, 20, 25, 34, 54*
Blount, Gov. William, *7-9, 14-27, 29-30, 31, 32, 33, 34, 37, 46, 47, 48, 53, 54, 66, 71, 76*
Blount, Willie, *15, 22, 25, 50, 54-55*
Blount College, *21, 34, 52, 65, 152*
Blount County, *25*
Blount family, *15, 20, 25-26, 34*
Blount Mansion, *18-20, 23, 25, 26-27, 31, 34, 38, 74, 146, 217*
Board of Trade, *115*
Bonny Kate Chapter, DAR, *130, 146, 147*
"Boomsday", *214*
Boston, *84, 90, 105, 106, 110, 113*
Bowman's Ferry, *78*
Boyd, Belle, *74-75*
Boyd, Sue, *74*
Boyd family, *26, 74, 146*
Boyd's Ferry, *76, 78*
Bragg, Gen. Braxton, *76, 80, 83*
Branner, Mayor H. Bryan, *118*
Branner, Magnolia Bryan, *118*
Branson, Lloyd, *115, 116, 126, 132*
Bristol, *18, 71*
British Army, *3-5, 40, 41-42, 50*
Broadway, *70, 138, 149*
Browder, Boyd, *218*
Brown, David, *99*
Brownlow, Sue, *90*
Brownlow, William G., *70, 88-101*
Brownlow, Mrs. William G., *90, 93, 101*
Buckner, Gen. Simon B., *75*

Budwiser Clydesdales, *200*
Bullett, Alfred Bult, *100*
Bullock, Marylyn, *102*
Bureau of International Expositions, *187, 188, 198, 204*
Burlington, *131, 148*
Burnett, Frances Hodgson, *121*
Burnside, Gen. Ambrose, *75, 76, 77, 78, 83, 95*
Burwell Building, *152*
Butcher, Cecil H., *183, 209*
Butcher, C.H., Jr., *183, 188, 190, 208, 209, 210-211, 213*
Butcher, Jake, *183, 184, 185, 187, 188-189, 190, 191, 200, 208, 209-210, 213*

Cades Cove, *144, 149, 150-151*
Cal Johnson Park, *148*
Campbell, Carlos, *143*
Campbell's Station, *36, 59, 64, 66*
Canada, *192, 198*
Candy Factory, *190, 196, 207, 215*
Cansler, Laura Scott, *110*
Carrick, Elizabeth, *46*
Carrick, Rev. Samuel, *31, 34, 46, 52, 61*
Carter, Pres. Jimmy, *187, 188, 202*
Cavett's Station massacre, *9, 32, 46*
Central Avenue, *48, 148, 212*
Chamber of Commerce, *120, 143, 158, 174, 175, 176*
Chamberlain, Col. Hiram S., *95*
Champion Fibre Co., *148*
Chapman, Col. David, *144, 148, 150*
Chapman Highway, *51, 121, 164, 174*
Chattanooga, *71, 77, 80, 83, 84, 163, 164*
Chattanooga Fire Dept., *120*
Chattanooga Times, *126*
Cherokee Boulevard, *13*
Cherokee Country Club, *152*

Cherokee Dam/Lake, *162*

Cherokee Heights, *77-78, 107*

Cherokee Indians, *2-13, 14, 16-17, 28, 29-30, 32, 37, 40-41, 43, 46, 60, 166*

Cherokee, N.C., *11*

Cherokee towns, *2, 3, 7, 9, 11, 17, 29, 32, 43, 46-47*

Cherokee War, *9, 17, 20, 31-32, 46-47*

Chilhowee Park, *131-133, 139, 186-187, 194*

China, Peoples' Republic of, *192, 196, 197, 198, 199*

Chisholm's Tavern, *31, 34, 36, 38*

"Christmas in the City", *207*

Church of the Immaculate Conception, *68, 116, 122, 178*

Church Street, *30, 32, 38, 67, 86, 181*

Church Street Methodist Church, *67, 82, 164*

Churchwell, William, *68*

Cincinnati, *92*

City Association of Women's Clubs, *39, 179*

City & County Bank(s), *183, 190, 209, 211*

City Council, *136, 145, 175, 178, 182, 187, 215*

City/County Building, *70, 182, 188, 194*

City Hall(s), *70, 87, 98, 117*

Civil War, *67, 69, 71-87, 103, 108, 118, 123, 127, 166, 168*

Civil War Centennial, *86, 87*

Clark, Bertha Walburn, *158*

Clayton Building, *215*

Claxton, Dr. Philander P., *128-129, 158*

Clinch River, *157, 162, 167*

Clinch River Breeder Reactor, *180, 185, 192*

Clinch Street, *34, 37, 38, 75, 100, 113-114, 118, 154, 157*

Club LeConte, *190*

Cobb, William, *16*

Coliseum, *39, 176, 179, 180-181, 216*

Commerce Avenue Firehall, *178*

Concord, *66*

Confederate Army, *72-73, 75, 76-79, 90, 91-92, 93, 95, 107, 123, 125*

Confederate Cemetery, *74, 83, 86*

Confederate Memorial Hall, *86, 87, 217*

Confederate States of America, *72, 73, 90, 92, 108*

Conservation movement, *130-131, 143, 144, 148, 150-151, 194*

Constitution(s) of Tennessee, *21, 26-27, 32, 33, 37, 47, 99*

Continental Congress, *14, 17*

Convention Center, *191, 207, 213*

Coolidge, Pres. Calvin, *136, 148*

Coulter, Hettie, *179*

"Country Music", *173, 211, 216*

Court of Flags, *195, 203, 204, 205, 206, 208*

Cowan, James and James H., *104*

Cowan, James D., *118*

Cowan, Lucy (Alexander), *107, 108*

Cowan, Mary, *107, 108*

Craighead-Jackson House, *27, 38, 217*

Creek Indians, *1, 32, 46, 47*

Creek War, *50, 56*

"Crescent Bend", *59, 63, 217*

Cumberland Avenue, *38, 49, 51, 55, 68, 90, 101, 109, 111, 112, 138, 148, 149, 165, 197, 214*

Cuming, Sir Alexander, *3*

Cunningham, Paul, *55*

Currey, Dr. Richard O., *74*

Customs House, *100, 102, 136, 157, 181, 186, 194, 212, 216*

Dale Avenue Settlement House, *134*

Dandridge, *162*

Dartmouth College, *52, 65*

Davis, Annie L., *143, 145, 150*

Davis, Willis P., *143, 144, 150*

Deaf and Dumb Asylum, See

Tennessee School for the Deaf
Denmark, *187, 191*
Depression years, *154-166, 183, 212*
Desert Shield/Storm, *215*
de Soto, Hernando, *1, 2*
Dickinson, Emily, *107*
Dickinson, Col. Perez, *103-121*
Dickinson, Susan P., *106, 112, 121*
Dickinson Light Guard, *114, 119*
Dogwood Trails/Arts Festival, *174-175, 184, 207*
Doublehead, Chief, *9*
Douglas Dam/Lake, *162*
Downtown Knoxville, *13, 30, 38, 107, 122, 162, 163-164, 182, 212*
Downtown Knoxville Association, *175, 184, 191*
Downtown Organization, The, *214*
Dugout canoes, *2, 13, 29, 46*
Dulin Gallery of Art, *214*
Dunlap, Hugh, *65*
Dupont Corporation/Marching Band, *168, 200*

East Tennessee, *1, 2, 4, 5-6, 7, 8, 40, 43, 66, 71, 72, 73-74, 84, 98, 99, 106, 129, 159, 162-163, 164, 168, 210*
East Tennessee Baptist Health Care System, *217*
East Tennessee Children's Hospital, *217*
East Tennessee College/University, *59, 62, 65, 66, 73-74, 76, 78, 84, 85, 94, 97-98, 104, 106, 115*
East Tennessee Discovery Center, *215, 218*
East Tennessee Historical Center, *102, 216*
East Tennessee Historical Society, *146*
East Tennessee National Bank, *154, 155*
Eastern Caribbean Pavilion, *202*
Egypt, *193, 199*

Electric Energy Pavilion, *200*
Elkmont, *141-142, 144*
Elm Tree Theatre, *196, 200, 214*
Emancipation/Day, *84, 85, 99, 108-109, 159*
Emmerson, Mayor Thomas, *55*
Emory Road, *29, 38*
Energy Expo, See World's Fair, 1982
Energy Express, *200, 205, 206, 208*
England, *3, 22, 40, 191, 199-200*
Estabrook, Joseph, *104, 115*
Etowah, *9, 46-47, 53, 60*
European Community, *191, 198*
Evans, Stewart, *184*

Farragut, Adm. David G., *84, 131, 139, 162*
Fair Site, *186, 187, 189-190, 192, 193, 200, 207, 208, 214*
FBI, *208*
FDIC, *207-208, 209*
Federal Express Pavilion, *197, 202*
Ferguson, Col. Patrick, *41, 42*
Fine Arts Pavilion(s), *132, 196*
Fire engine(s), *57, 69, 98, 117*
First Baptist Church, *68, 82, 106, 151-152*
First Creek, *7, 28, 30, 37, 38, 39, 53, 54, 57, 60, 62, 76, 85, 114, 148, 177, 179, 186, 190, 216*
First National Bank, *108*
First Presbyterian Church, *31, 38, 52, 62, 67, 82, 94, 98*
First Tennessee Bank, *207*
Flag Pond, *30, 54, 60, 68, 76, 85*
Flint Hill, *62, 76*
Flood Control, *155-156, 161, 163-164*
Florida, *24, 44, 57, 58*
Folger, Mary K. Dulin, *214*
Foothills Parkway, *144*
Ford, Pres. Gerald, *180, 185, 187*
Ford, Isaiah, *39, 178-179*
Forks-of-the-River, *28, 35, 58, 78, 79, 100*

Fort Adair, *29, 38*
Fort Dickerson, *76, 87*
"Fort Kid", *216*
"Fort Loudon", *77, 78*
Fort Loudoun, *3-5, 9, 13*
Fort Loudoun Dam/Lake, *13, 162, 163, 164, 177, 192, 196, 214*
Fort Sanders, *78, 80-82, 93, 118*
Fort Sanders Regional Medical Center, *87, 217*
Fouché Block, *102, 113*
Fouché, Dr. John, *75-76, 102*
Foundry, The, *101, 190, 196, 207*
Fountain City, *29, 125, 138, 174*
Franklin, State of, *6, 28, 42-44, 47, 50*
Freedmen's Bureau, *94, 98*
French & Indian War, *3-5*
French Broad River, *5, 18, 28, 35, 77, 78, 79, 84, 87, 162*
Fulton, Weston M., *171-172*
Fulton Sylphon Plant, *166, 171*
Funland, *192-193, 197, 200*

Gaines, Gen. Edmund Pendleton, *34*
Gas Industries Pavilion, *202*
Gas lighting, *68*
Gatlinburg, *149, 191*
Gay Street, *32, 34, 38, 54, 55, 57, 67, 68, 69, 75, 85, 102, 103, 104, 112, 113, 114, 115, 120, 121, 135, 138, 152, 154, 164, 178, 186, 212, 213, 214*
Gay Street Bridge(s), *86, 114, 115-116, 119, 122, 164*
General Building, *152*
Georgia, *44, 95, 103, 111, 205*
Gibbs, Nicholas, *38*
Gore, Rep. Albert, *167*
Governor Blount's Office, *18, 19, 26, 32*
Grainger County, *25*
Grant, Gen. Ulysses S., *63, 76, 83, 106*
Great Iron Chain, *77, 79, 86-87, 186*

"Great Lakes of the South", *156, 162, 163-164, 218*
Great Seal of Tennessee, *33*
Great Smoky Mountains, *3, 5, 10, 11, 15, 28, 56, 133, 137, 140-145, 148-151, 203, 218*
Great Smoky Mountains Conservation Association, *143*
Great Smoky Mountains National Park, *136, 137, 143, 145, 148-151, 167, 191, 192, 218*
Greece, *191*
Greene County, *45*
Greeneville, *5, 6, 16, 33, 43, 72, 137*
"Greystone", *138*
Gulf of Mexico, *5, 163*
Gunther, John, *173-174, 177*

Hall, William, *95*
Hall of Fame, *11, 40*
Hamilton National Bank, *154, 183*
Hampden-Sydney Academy, *56, 62, 65, 104*
Haslam, James, *185*
Hayes, Pres. Rutherford B., *63, 106*
Hazen, Evelyn, *85*
Hazen, Gideon Morgan, *67, 70*
Heiskell, Frederick S., *39, 56*
Henley, David, *23, 26, 32, 36*
Henley Street/Bridge, *36, 122, 154, 164, 216*
Hicks, Judge Xenophon, *161*
Highland Memorial Cemetery, *137*
Hill Street, *19, 38, 39, 115, 164*
Hilton Hotel, *191, 194*
Hindenburg Line, *134, 135, 170*
Hiroshima, *170, 177*
Hit Parade, *167, 170*
Holbrook College, *125*
Holiday Inn/World's Fair, *191, 194*
Holston, Stephen, *5*
Holston Hills/Country Club, *152, 174*

Holston River, *5, 18, 29, 35, 40, 46, 77, 78, 79, 100, 162*
Holston-Union National Bank, *154*
Hope, Emma Fanz, *132, 152*
Hope, Thomas, *27, 35-37, 38, 39*
"Hopecote", *152, 217*
Hoskins, Dr. James D., *166*
Hoskins Library, *87, 176*
House & Garden Fair, *207*
House museums, *26-27, 39, 63, 70, 85, 86, 216-217*
Houston, Robert, *63*
Hoxie, J.B., *81*
Humes, Thomas, *55, 104*
Humes, Dr. Thomas W., *65, 68, 85, 98, 104, 106, 109, 115*
Hungary, *192, 199, 202, 203*
Hyatt-Regency, *178, 181, 190*
Hydroelectric power, *155-156, 163, 179*

Ijams Park, *121*
Imax Theatre, *198, 206*
Indian Gap, *3, 149*
Indian Territory, *5, 6, 10, 12, 29, 43*
Inside USA, *173*
International Energy Symposia, *185, 198*
Interstate highways, *177-178, 179, 180, 186, 189, 193, 194, 206*
Ireland, *191*
IRS, *208*
Isaac, William, *208*
Island Airport, *121*
"Island Home", *112-113, 114, 119, 120-121*
Italy, *191, 198*

Jackson, Pres. Andrew, *10, 49, 56, 58, 59, 63, 155*
Jackson Avenue, *103, 212*
Japan, *166, 192, 196, 198, 199, 202, 204*
Jefferson, Pres. Thomas, *21, 22, 23*
Jeffersonian Ordinances, *6, 42*

John C. Hodges Library, *214, 218*
John J. Duncan Federal Building, *214*
John Sevier Highway, *38, 51*
John Watts, Chief, *9*
Johnson, Pres. Andrew, *63, 84, 93-94, 95, 96, 97, 99*
Johnson, Cal F., *112, 147-148*
Jonesborough, *33, 43*
Junior League of Knoxville, *134, 158, 175*
"Junto, The", *105*

Kain, Kittie, *34*
Kain, Mattie, *34*
Kain family, *34, 36*
Kefauver, Sen. Estes, *179*
Kennedy, James, Jr., *37, 39*
Kentucky, *59, 72, 99, 103, 183, 205*
Kern, Peter, *95, 114*
Kern's Bakery, *95, 114, 121*
Kern's Ice Cream Parlor, *114-115, 121*
King, James, *18*
King Fisher, Chief, *9, 53, 60*
King's Iron Works, *18-19*
Kingsport, *33*
Kingston, *36, 53*
Kingston Pike, *36, 59, 64, 69, 76, 77, 86, 137, 172, 177*
Knaffl, Joseph/Madonna, *132*
Knox, Gen. Henry, *8, 9, 17*
Knox County, *28, 32, 33, 36, 55, 66, 67, 71-72, 76, 84, 100, 108, 139, 172, 182, 216*
Knox County Court, *33, 36, 55, 114, 119*
Knox County Court House, *31, 50, 51, 74, 82, 94, 95, 116, 117, 126, 127, 214*
Knoxville:
  Founding, *1, 8, 17, 28, 30, 186*
  Original streets, *30, 38*
  City government, *55, 70, 91-92, 145, 182,*

City services, *57, 67, 69, 116-118, 177, 213*

Industries, *53-54, 56, 60, 111, 127, 166-167, 171-172, 217*

Shops and stores, *33, 55, 73, 108, 112, 120, 145-146, 169*

Wholesale Firms, *103-104, 114, 121*

Population, *33, 69, 127, 145, 177*

City Flag, *126*

Amenities, *30-31, 33-34, 56, 58-59, 63, 65-66, 67, 68, 114-115, 116, 119-120, 158-159, 174, 212, 217-218*

Knoxville College, *101, 111, 121, 124, 217*

Knoxville Cookbook, *127-128*

Knoxville Dragoons, *66, 69*

Knoxville Female Academy, *59, 65, 66, 82, 94, 104, 164*

Knoxville Garden Club, *26, 158*

Knoxville Gazette, *30, 31*

Knoxville General Hospital, *117, 172*

Knoxville Heritage, Inc., *63, 178, 186*

Knoxville High School, *135, 139*

Knoxville International Energy Exposition, *101, 186, 198, 199, 201, 203, 204, 206, 210, 211*

Knoxville Iron Co., *95, 101, 143*

Knoxville Museum of Art, *215, 218*

Knoxville Opera Co., *218*

Knoxville Register, *39, 56, 105*

Knoxville Sentinel, *136*

Knoxville Symphony Orchestra, *158, 218*

Knoxville Times, *105*

Knoxville Utilities Board, *197*

Knoxville Zoo, *159, 177, 194*

Korea, *192, 199, 203*

Krutch, Charles Christopher, *132, 142*

Krutch, Charles E., *212*

Krutch Park, *212*

Ku Klux Klan, *98, 108*

Ladies' Memorial Association, *86*

Lake Ottosee, *117, 118, 131*

Lamar House, *55-56, 63, 78, 82, 186, 214*

"Land Grab Act", *5, 15, 16*

Land Grant College, *97, 124*

Land warrants, *5, 15, 16*

L&N Railroad Station, *138-139, 178, 190, 196, 206-207*

Lawson McGhee Library, *62, 106, 133, 135, 136, 178, 181, 218*

Lebanon-in-the-Forks, *46, 52*

Lee, Gen. Robert E., *85*

Lenoir City, *75, 77*

Liberator, The, *104, 105*

Libraries, *56, 102, 115, 181, 214, 218*

Lilienthal, David E., *156*

Lincoln, Pres. Abraham, *39, 85, 89, 93, 94, 95, 99*

Lindbergh, Charles A., *136*

Little River, *6, 141, 142, 150*

Little River Lumber Co., *141-142, 144-145*

Little Tennessee River, *2, 3, 6, 7, 29, 163*

Locust Street, *68, 125, 137, 152*

Logan A.M.E. Zion Church, *109, 110*

Long, Col. Stephen H., *155*

Longstreet, Gen. James, *69, 76, 77-78, 79, 80-82, 83, 86, 118*

"Lost State of Franklin", see Franklin

Lottery (Oct. 3, 1791), *30, 31, 55*

Loudon, *76*

Loudoun, Earl of, *4*

Louis Philippe, *34*

Louisiana, *22, 24, 44*

Lowe's Ferry, *84, 131*

Loyston, *161, 162*

Luttrell, Mayor James C., *79-80*

Lutz, Adelia Armstrong, *132*

Luxembourg, *191*

Lyon's View, *116, 122, 152*

Mabry, Joseph A., Jr., *67, 72, 74, 76, 83, 85-86*

Mabry-Hazen House, *85, 217*

Main Street, *38, 54, 67, 104, 114, 116, 119, 126, 151, 164, 194, 212, 214*

"Malfunction Junction", *179, 185, 189, 193*

Maloney, Gen. Frank, *144, 150*

Manefee, John, *43, 47*

Manhattan District, *167*

Mann, George, *47*

Marble, *35, 36, 38, 51, 100, 131, 138, 165*

"Marble Springs", *47-48, 51, 217*

Market House, *67, 79-80, 94, 119-120, 175*

Market Square, *67, 68, 72, 98, 114, 116, 212, 175, 178, 212, 213-214*

Market Street, *38, 67, 86, 100, 181, 182, 194, 212*

Maryville, *25, 59, 83, 84, 150, 188, 189*

Mason, James, *109, 111, 117, 120*

Massachusetts, *104, 105, 106*

Mathers, James, *23-24*

Maynard, Benjamin, *109, 119*

Maynard, Horace, *97, 100, 106, 109*

Maynardville, *106, 183*

McAdoo, William Gibbs, *38, 117-118*

McClung, Annie McGhee, *125-126, 135-136*

McClung, Barbara Adair, *136*

McClung, Calvin M., *135-136*

McClung, Charles, *30, 32-33, 34, 36, 38, 39, 48, 59, 66*

McClung, Margaret White, *30, 34*

McClung, Col. Pleasant M., *75*

McClung, Polly, *34*

McClung Historical Collection, *102, 121, 136, 181, 218*

McClung Museum, *12-13, 218*

McCulloch, Dr. J.S., *111*

McDowell, Col. Charles, *42, 45*

McGhee, Col. Charles, *111, 124, 125, 133, 136, 137-138*

McGhee, Cornelia White, *124, 125*

McGhee, Lawson (Williams), *62, 125*

McGhee family, *124, 125-126, 133, 135-136*

McGhee Tyson Airport, *136, 137, 178, 193, 195*

McIntire, Dr. Walter H., *147*

McLaw, Gen., *77, 78*

McNutt, George, *55*

Mechanicsville, *111*

"Mecklenburg", *79, 100*

Medical Arts Building, *152*

Meek, James M., *135*

Meek, Mary Fleming, *126*

Meeman, Edward J., *143*

Melrose Art Center, *158*

Melton Hill Dam/Lake, *162*

Memphis, *183, 184*

Men's Cotillion Club, *158*

Mero District, *44*

Methodist Campgrounds, *138*

Mexican War, *66, 69*

Mexico, *192, 196, 203*

Midday Merry-Go-Round, *173*

"Middlebrook", *70, 217*

Middle Tennessee, *25, 29, 44, 55, 56, 93, 98*

Military Brass Band, *66, 68*

Militia, *8-9, 29, 32, 41-42, 43, 215*

"Million Dollar Fire", *120, 121*

Miro, Don Estevan, *44*

Miss U.S.A. Pageant, *208-209*

Mississippi River, *5, 10, 22, 44, 56, 129, 155*

Mississippian Indians, *1, 2*

Monroe, Pres. James, *50, 57*

Monuments, *51, 86, 118, 127, 135*

Morgan, Arthur E., *156*

Morgan, Calvin, *70*

Morgan, Dr. Harcourt A., *156*

Morris, John, *20*

Morton, Mayor Ben A., *145*

Moses, James C., *105, 106*
Moses, John L., *106, 111, 120*
Mount Le Conte, *144, 149-150*
Mount Rest Home, *63-64*
Mount Zion Baptist Church, *109*
Mountain View Renewal Area, *176, 178, 181*
Museum of Atomic Energy, *171*
Murfreesboro, *56*
Muscle Shoals, *29, 58, 60, 155*

Nashville, *33, 53, 54, 55, 57, 59, 61, 66, 93, 124, 196, 211*
National Conservation Exposition, *131-133, 139, 143, 186, 216*
National Federation of Women's Clubs, *146, 158*
National Park Service, *149, 151*
National Trust, *213*
Netherlands, The, *191, 193*
New Orleans, *22, 44, 50, 139, 163, 188, 206, 211, 212*
New York, *17, 90, 106, 138, 147, 167, 212*
Newfound Gap, *149, 150*
Newton, Margaret Albers, *178*
Neyland Drive, *38, 177, 194, 203, 214, 216*
Neyland Stadium, *185, 192, 200, 203, 218*
Nicholson Art League, *132*
Nolichucky River, *5, 40*
Norris, Sen. George, *155*
Norris Act, *156, 162*
Norris Dam/Lake, *157, 159-161, 162, 167, 170*
Norris, town of, *159-160*
North Carolina, *3, 5-7, 11, 14, 15, 16, 18, 19, 21, 28, 29, 32, 40, 41, 43, 44-45, 50, 103, 106, 123, 144, 148, 205*
Nuclear Energy, *170-171, 179-180, 192*

Oak Ridge, *168-171, 176, 180, 185, 206, 217*

O'Brien, Lt. James, *93*
Ochs, Adolph, *126*
Oconostota, Chief, *4*
Ohio River, *5, 29, 155*
Oklahoma, *10, 11, 12, 205*
Old Abraham, Chief, *41*
Old City, The, *212*
Old City Hall, *70, 87, 206*
"Old College", *65, 176*
"Old Diamond", *177, 187*
Old Gray Cemetery, *68, 70, 82, 101, 120, 135, 137*
Old Masonic Temple, *138*
Ossoli Circle, *125, 130, 146, 158*

Panama, *193, 196, 199, 201, 202, 205*
Papermill, *67, 70, 82*
Parades, *85, 113-114, 131, 135, 147*
Park Family, *35, 51, 68*
Park National Bank, *155*
Patrick, Jack H., *210*
Peale, Charles Willson, *45*
Peay, Gov. Austin, *145, 150*
Pelissippi State Technical Community College, *217-218*
Pershing, Gen. John J., *147*
Peru, *193, 199*
Philadelphia, *8, 17, 20, 22, 23, 45, 53, 84, 89, 105, 110, 113, 137*
Philharmonic Society, *74, 112*
Phillippines, *193, 199*
Phillips Petroleum, *101-102*
Pinchot, Gifford, *130, 132, 133*
Plaza Tower, *190, 194*
"Plum Grove", *40, 47*
Poe, Gen. Orlando M., *76-77, 81, 83*
"Poet-priest of the Confederacy", *85*
Polk, Pres. James K., *59, 63, 66, 69*
Pontoon bridge, *76-77, 87, 95-96, 114*
Post Office, *100, 102, 157, 165*
Powell, Columbus, *75*
Powell community, *43, 76*

Prince Street, *67*
Public schools, *110, 111, 139*
Puerto Rico, *127*

Quality Inn, *191, 194*
Qualla Reservation, *11, 166*

Racetrack(s), *59, 131, 148*
Radisson Hotel, *194*
Railroads, *66-67, 68-69, 73, 75, 76, 92, 99, 103, 106, 108, 132, 134, 138-139, 177-178*
Ramsey, Francis Alexander, *28, 35, 36, 38, 43, 104*
Ramsey, Dr. F.A. Jr., *74*
Ramsey, Dr. J.G.M., *27, 37, 66, 79*
Ramsey, Margaret (Russell) Cowan Humes, *56, 104*
Ramsey House, *35-36, 38-39, 217*
Rayl, Jesse A., *110*
Reagan, Pres. Ronald, *191, 193, 195, 197*
Reconstruction Era, *93, 95, 123*
Red Cross, *134*
Retail shopping center, *33, 120, 145-146*
Revolutionary War, *5, 6, 14, 15, 17, 41-42, 50, 134*
Reynolds, Robert (house), *69, 77*
Richmond, Virginia, *73, 76, 92*
Rickard, Captain, *31*
Riverfeast, *214*
Riverview Terrace, *211*
Roane, Gov. Archibald, *48, 52-53*
Roane County, *167, 169*
Roberts, S.H. (Bo), *186*
Rockefeller, John D., Jr., *148*
Rockefeller, Memorial, *150*
"Rocky Mount", *16, 18, 19*
Rogersville, *30*
Rohm & Haas Co., *166*
Roosevelt, Eleanor, *159*
Roosevelt, Pres. Franklin D., *150, 167, 168*
Roosevelt, Pres. Theodore, *129,*
130, 131, 150
Roulstone, George, *30, 31*
Rural Electrification Program, *161-162*
Russell, Avery, *77*
Russell house, *64, 77*
Rutledge, *33*
Ryan, Father Abram Joseph, *85*

Salisbury, N.C., *19, 28, 106, 123*
Sanders, Gen. William P., *75, 78, 86, 98*
Sanford, Justice Edward T., *136*
"Saturday Night On The Town", *206*
Saudi Arabia, *192, 198, 199*
Savannah, Georgia, *59, 66*
Scenic Loop, *149-150*
Scott, Col. Joseph, *63*
Scott, Gen. Winfield, *10-11*
Seattle, Washington, *184, 185*
Second Creek, *53, 60, 66, 76, 85, 95, 196, 202, 206, 216*
Second Creek valley, *186, 187, 190, 207, 214*
Second Presbyterian Church, *67, 78, 79, 82, 86, 113, 119*
Semi-centennial of Knoxville, *65*
Sequoyah, *11-12, 40*
Sequoyah Hills, *13, 174*
Sesquicentennial of Knoxville, *166*
Sevier, Catherine Sherrill, (Bonny Kate), *41, 48, 50, 51, 147*
Sevier, Gov. John, *6, 8-9, 21, 22, 27, 40-51, 53, 55, 68, 71, 117, 147, 166*
Sevier, Sarah Hawkins, *40, 41, 51*
Sevier County, *91*
Sevier-Park House, *49, 51, 68, 214*
Sevierville, *91*
Sharp's Gap, *180, 190*
Sharp's Ridge Park, *180*
Shelby, Col. Evan, *29*
Shelby, Col. Isaac, *41-42*
Sheridan, Gen. Phillip, *84*

Sherman, Gen. William T., 83-84
Shields, Judge John K., 160-161
Shields-Watkins Field, 166
Shiloh Presbyterian Church, 109
Siege of Knoxville, 77-83, 84, 86, 87, 93, 98, 100, 186
Sky Transpo, 197
Smith, Guy L. III, 187
Snail-darter, 163
South Carolina, 3, 4, 5, 89, 103, 111, 205
Southern Industrial Banking Corp., 209, 210
Southern Railway Station, 102, 138, 178
Southwest Territory, 7, 8, 13, 14, 15, 16, 17, 18, 19, 28, 29, 32, 217
Soviet Sports Exhibit, 188
Soviet Union, 187, 188
Spain, 22, 24, 44, 57
Spanish-American War, 126-127
Spokane, Washington, 184, 185, 191, 204
State Street, 19, 37, 38, 178
"Statesview", 34, 36, 39, 59
Statehood Day, 213
Staub, John Fanz, 152
Staub's Opera House, 74, 112
Steamboats, 58, 60, 67, 69, 96, 106
Stewart, Gen. A.P., 80-81
Stokely Bros. cannery, 163
Stokely-VanCamp Folklife Festival, 200
St. John's Episcopal Church, 68, 79, 98, 106, 109-110, 125, 138
St. Louis Exposition, 130, 192
St. Mary's Medical Center, 217
Streetcars, 114, 117-118, 119, 131, 132, 213
Summer School of the South, 128-129
Summit Hill, 75, 76, 116, 178, 181
Summit Hill Drive, 122, 178
Sunsphere, 195, 206, 207, 209
Swan, James, 109

Swan, William G., 67, 68, 75
Syracuse, N.Y., 108

Taft, Pres. William Howard, 131
Technology and Lifestyle Center, 200, 207
Telephone companies, 116
Tellico Dam/Lake, 163
Temple, Mary Boyce, 26, 146-147
Tennessee:
    Constitutional Convention, 1796, 21, 47
    admission to the Union, 21-22, 47, 71
    capital(s), 23, 33, 35, 37, 53, 55, 56, 117, 196, 213
    legislature, 24, 25, 50, 53, 55, 59, 60-61, 65, 96-97, 99, 129-130, 145, 155, 196
    "Volunteer State", 42, 50, 66, 69, 127, 215
    secession, 71-72, 90, 97, 107
    readmission to Union, 96-97
    Constitution of 1870, 99
    Centennial, 51, 126
Tennessee Amphitheatre, 196, 200, 205, 206
Tennessee Barn Dance, 173, 216
Tennessee Eastman Corp., 168, 200
Tennessee Homecoming '86, 213-214, 216
Tennessee River, 5, 7, 12, 19, 28, 29, 30, 53, 58, 60, 66, 76-77, 83, 97, 152, 162, 164, 181, 216, 218
Tennessee School for the Deaf, 63, 66, 70, 74, 82, 87, 94, 106, 111, 120-121, 217
Tennessee Technology Corridor, 206
Tennessee Theatre, 34, 152-153, 158-159
Tennessee-Tombigbee Waterway, 163
Tennessee Valley, 1, 155, 156, 157, 159, 179

Tennessee Valley Authority, *12, 70, 102, 156, 163-164, 167, 178, 179, 180, 181, 185, 186, 192, 196, 202, 212, 216*

Tennessee Valley Fair, *139, 159, 206*

Territorial capital, *1, 8, 13, 17, 28, 30, 31, 35, 53, 66, 186, 216*

Territorial legislature, *21, 25, 52*

Territory South of the River, Ohio, see Southwest Territory

Testerman, Mayor Kyle, *184, 185, 187*

Third Creek, *70, 82, 97, 136, 216*

Thomas, Abishai, *32*

Thomas, Judge William, *210*

Thompson, James E., *143*

Thompson-Boling Arena, *206, 214*

Thompson Cancer Survival Center, *217*

Three Mile Island, *192*

Toms, William Perry, *63*

Townsend, *141, 150*

"Trafalgar", *34, 36*

"Trail of Tears", *11*

Treaty of Dumplin Creek, *6, 28, 43*

Treaty of Holston, *7-8, 16-17, 30, 46, 53, 166, 186*

Treaty of Hopewell, *6, 14, 16, 43, 46*

Truman, Pres. Harry, *171*

Tsali, Chief, *10*

Tuesday Morning Musical Club, *126, 130*

TVA Towers, *102, 178, 181, 182, 194*

Tyree, Mayor Randy, *187*

Tyson, Bettie McGhee, *123-124, 125, 126, 127, 129, 130, 134, 135, 136-137*

Tyson, Isabella (Gilpin), *126, 134, 137*

Tyson, Lawrence D., *70, 123-137*

Tyson, McGhee, *124, 135, 136, 137*

Tyson House, *126, 130, 137, 167*

Tyson Park, *136-137, 173*

Unaka Mountains, *40, 155-156*

UDC, (Chapter 89), *86, 130*

Underground cisterns, *69, 79*

Underground Railroad, *107*

Union Avenue, *37, 114, 120, 121, 212*

Union Planters Bank, *183, 209*

Unionists, *71, 72, 73, 75, 76, 78, 79, 85, 87, 89, 90, 91, 99, 100, 106, 107*

United American Bank, *184, 185, 190, 200, 206, 207-210*

United States Government, *5-7, 8, 10, 14, 20, 43, 45, 216*

U.S. Army, *9, 10-11, 17, 23, 46, 50, 75, 78-80, 83-84, 92, 95-96, 123-124, 133-134*

U.S. Army Engineers, *76, 78, 83, 87, 143-144, 155, 157, 167, 168*

U.S. Congress, *12, 24, 40, 45, 62, 96, 187*

U.S. Constitution, *14, 17, 21, 24, 45*

U.S. District Attorney, *208, 210*

U.S. House of Representatives, *24, 45, 50, 99-100, 106*

U.S. Pavilion, *187, 195, 207, 215*

U.S. Senate, *22-25, 48, 57, 58, 60, 61, 100, 136, 137*

University of Tennessee, *12, 35, 52, 69, 87, 106, 115, 119, 124-125, 126, 127, 128-129, 137, 154, 158, 167, 176-177, 180, 185, 186, 201, 204, 206, 213, 214, 216, 217-218*

UT Hospital, *172, 217*

UT Vols, *158, 185, 203, 218*

Urban Renewal, *175-177, 186, 189*

Van Buren, Pres. Martin, *10, 59, 60*

Van Gilder, Ella Bolli, *132*

Victory gardens, *169*

Vine Street, *122, 148*

Virginia, *3, 4, 28, 33, 40, 42, 54, 72, 73, 74, 95, 103*

"Vol Navy", *203*

Wall Street Journal, 189, 193, 205
Walker, Cas, 177
Walnut Street, 30, 38, 49, 51, 67, 68,
  86, 138, 181, 214
War Between the States, see
  Civil War
War of 1812, 50, 56
Warriors' Path, 3, 4
Washington, Pres. George, 8, 14,
  41, 45
Washington, D.C., 12, 40, 50, 58, 60,
  100, 106, 138, 167
Washington District, 9, 41, 42, 43,
  45
Watauga Association, 40, 41
Watauga Settlement, 5, 16, 40, 41
WATE, 138
"Waters of the World", 195, 196,
  206
West Germany, 191
West Tennessee, 56, 93, 98
West Virginia, 72, 200, 205
Whig, The, 88-91, 92, 93, 100
"Whirlwind", 200
White, Ann Peyton, 62
White, Elizabeth Carrick, 61-62
White, James, 7, 28-29, 31, 37, 39, 43,
  46, 52, 56, 67, 178, 218
White, Hugh Lawson, 52-62, 67,
  125
White, May Lawson, 28, 52, 62
White, Melinda (Williams), 56-57,
  63, 111
White House Energy
  Conference, 180, 185
White's Fort, 7, 16, 17, 29, 37, 39, 52,
  53, 179, 216
Whittle, Chris, 214
Whittle Communications, 214
Whittle Springs, 173
Wholesale distribution center,
  103, 120
Willard, Frances, 147
Williams, John, 56-57, 63
Williams, Tennessee, 63
Wilson, Pres. Woodrow, 38, 118,

  133
Winstead, Mamie, 86
WNOX, 159, 173
Woman's Building, 126, 130
Women's Building, 131, 132
Women's Lyceum, 130, 164-165
Wonderland Hotel, 142, 149
Woodland Indians, 1, 2, 79
Woodruff, Capt. W.W., 95
Woodruff's, 95, 116, 121
World War I, 121, 133-135, 155
World War II, 121, 166-170, 179
World's Fair, 1982, 139, 184-186,
  187-194, 195-205, 206-207, 208, 209,
  211, 214, 215, 216
World's Fair, 1984, 206, 211
World's Fair Park and Festival
  Center, 101, 139, 214-215, 216
WROL, 177
Wylie, Catherine, 132
Wylie, Eleanor, 132
Wyoming Territory, 123-124

Yardley, William F., 101
YMCA, 164
YWCA, 152

Zollicoffer, Gen. Felix, 72, 73